Enjoy reading the enclosed!

Love Jan

December 2005.

# KAZAKHSTAN

## POWER AND THE ELITE

SALLY N. CUMMINGS

I.B. TAURIS

LONDON · NEW YORK

Published in 2005 by I.B.Tauris & Co Ltd
6 Salem Road, London W2 4BU
175 Fifth Avenue, New York NY 10010
www.ibtauris.com

In the United States of America and in Canada distributed by
Palgrave Macmillan, a division of St Martin's Press
175 Fifth Avenue, New York NY 10010

ISBN 1 86064 854 1
EAN 978 1 86064 854 0

A full CIP record for this book is available from the British Library
A full CIP record for this book is available from the Library of Congress

Library of Congress catalog card: available

Typeset in Palatino Linotype by Steve Tribe, Andover
Printed and bound in Great Britain by MPG Books Ltd, Bodmin

# CONTENTS

*For Ann*

# ACKNOWLEDGEMENTS

I am greatly indebted to the many local and international residents in Kazakhstan who shared with me their time, insights and warm hospitality in Almaty, Pavlodar, Shymkent and Uralsk. My thanks also to all my panel of experts, those who agreed to be interviewed and to their assistants and support staff who helped arrange often difficult access to the central and regional elites.

The fieldwork for this study was generously funded by the Leverhulme Trust to whom I am extremely grateful. Jean Cater of the Trust was a stellar support throughout the eighteen months. My indebtedness extends also to the Economic and Social Research Council, University of London Central Research Fund and the Ford Foundation Subgrant through the British Academy of Slavic and East European Studies.

Numerous colleagues have offered suggestions and advice during the course of this research. I also very much appreciated the comments from Shirin Akiner, Gregory Andrusz, William Fierman, John Higley, David Lane, Martha Brill Olcott and Stephen White on an earlier draft of the typescript. My thanks go also to Lester Crook who encouraged me throughout the publication process. I am particularly indebted to Dominic (Chai) Lieven whose scholarship, wisdom and guidance remain a constant inspiration. Any errors in fact or judgement are, of course, my own.

I would also like to mention the friendship and hospitality of Graeme Loten during my time in Almaty and the logistical support and friendship of Aleksei and Lydia. I am grateful to Steve Tribe for his assistance in the production process. My thanks also to Mark Cummings for his editorial assistance, my mother and Susie for their patience and encouragement and my husband, Rick, for his unrelenting support. The memory of my father, who died in 2000, is always with me. This book was undertaken during an extended period of family loss, but completed after the joyous safe arrival of Ashley Caitlin.

I would, above all, like to thank my sister Ann who has travelled this journey with me and it is to her that I dedicate this book.

# INTRODUCTION

Kazakhstan was born by default. The republic's independence from the Soviet Union in 1991 was neither the result of secessionist demands by its leadership, nor a national liberation movement; it resulted from the decision by Moscow to withdraw its maintenance of the Soviet edifice. The withdrawal of central support, or the refusal by an external power to continue to prop up the existing regime, constitutes one of several definitions of elite and regime crises.[1] This book examines Kazakhstan's national political elite during the country's first ten years of independence and this introduction explains its rationale, approach and structure.

Kazakhstan sprawls across a territory of approximately 2.7 million square kilometres (eleven times the size of the United Kingdom, or more than ten times the size of Texas), encompasses three time zones with vastly varying topographies and climate and houses substantial metals and mineral wealth. Geopolitics is crucial: the republic is landlocked and borders the two great powers of Russia and China, and its major pipelines continue to run through Russia. The republic is home to over one hundred nationalities, the most influential of which remain the Russians.

The post-independence Kazakhstani elite was not only initially reluctant to assume power but also highly insecure in its new-found role. The elite was reluctant to renounce either the benefits its republic had accrued during the Soviet era or its reliance on Russia. The nascent elite's feelings of insecurity in 1991 sprang partly from the reality that the titular nationality, the Kazakhs, were in a minority. According to the final Soviet census, taken in 1989, Kazakhs constituted 40.1 per cent of the population, while Russians were 37.4 per cent. Combined with the Ukrainians (5.4 per cent) and the Belorussians (1.1 per cent), the Slavs constituted 44.2 per cent of the population. When added to the largely Russified Germans (5.8 per cent), non-Kazakhs formed a bare but absolute majority of the republic.[2] Moreover, many of these were, and are, settled in nearly homogeneous communities in the republic's north, hard against Russia's southern and Siberian cities. Faced with these ethnic and demographic cleavages, the republic's only post-independence president, Nursultan Abisevich Nazarbaev, has celebrated his country's maintenance of interethnic peace. By virtue of this multiethnicity, however, the elite was deprived of an immediate source of legitimacy: monoethnic nationalism.

Despite their new status, Kazakhs were thus still faced with this substantial Russian minority from the era of nineteenth-century Russian colonization and twentieth-century Sovietization, a constant reminder to the political elite of its continued vulnerability to external political and cultural influence. This legacy is such that one commentator contends that the Kazakh steppe cannot even be considered a part of Central Asia proper but 'should be viewed as a Eurasian territory with a longtime – and enduring – subjugation to or dependence on Russia'.[3] As a landlocked and buffer state with enduring historical, political, economic and social ties with Russia, one of the main challenges for the political elite has been to create a new foreign policy which is at once respectful of but less dependent on Russia. In the first ten years of Kazakhstan's independence, Russia remained the existential 'other' to the political elite – relations with Moscow were still viewed as *primus inter pares*, and developments in Russia were watched closely. But, simultaneously, the Kazakhstani leadership has forged its own directions in foreign relations which it has explicitly called a 'multivector foreign policy'.[4] China and the USA have emerged as two key players in this diversification. Politically, China and Kazakhstan have cooperated on dealing with nationalist separatism in China (including Kazakhstan's support for China's position on Taiwan); economically they have gradually developed a strategy on energy cooperation and in security issues China has been the other Great Power (with Russia) in the Shanghai Cooperation Organization, dealing primarily with terrorism and new security threats.[5] Some contend, however, that Chinese-Central Asian relations remain hampered by the 'legacy of mutual suspicion and fear'.[6] As part of the multivector policy, and to reduce dependence on the two Great Powers of Russia and China, the regime has also encouraged US, European and Japanese influence.[7] While, in the early years of independence, the USA focused its strategic attention on Kazakhstan, in the late 1990s, it began to focus on Uzbekistan. In the wake of September 11, Uzbekistan, geographically closer to Afghanistan and, with Tajikistan, on the 'front line' of the war on terror, had unequivocally supplanted Kazakhstan as the USA's key strategic partner in the region.[8] By the spring of 2001, Kazakhstan had already responded to changing American concerns in Central Asia by modifications to its foreign policy concept. Although remaining multivector, it was now prioritizing relations with immediate neighbours, such as Russia, Central Asia and China.[9]

One of the key reasons behind the Kazakhstani elite's promotion of its explicitly multivector foreign policy has been its goal of multiplying its pipeline routes and of attracting a diversity of economic investors. In particular, Kazakhstan aimed to reduce its dependence on Russia, as all existing pipeline routes continued to run through Russia. In 2001, a new pipeline that bypassed Russia (Baku-Tbilisi-Ceyhan) had been agreed and other routes were under discussion. By 1997, Kazakhstan had attracted the single highest per capita of foreign direct investment in the former Soviet Union (FSU).[10] This was in part a function of its more liberal foreign investment law, and in part of some economic advantages that Kazakhstan enjoyed upon independence in 1991. While all boasted some industrialization and urbanization, Kazakhstan alone emerged as a successor nuclear power, housing 1, 360 nuclear warheads, and home to the world's largest satellite-launching centre, Baikonur. The republic inherited a sometimes obsolete but nevertheless significant manufacturing and processing industrial sector (including phosphate fertilizers, rolled metal, train bearings, tractors and bulldozers).[11] With independence, Kazakhstan gained direct control of the substantial wealth beneath its soil. According to Nazarbaev, Kazakhstan holds 30 per cent of the world's proven reserves of chromium, 25 per cent of manganese, 19 per cent of lead, 13 per cent of zinc, 10 per cent of copper and 10 per cent of iron.[12] Kazakhstan possesses the longest border of the Caspian Sea and thus stands to benefit considerably more once its oil reserves are tapped.[13] In 1992, the Kazakhstani government signed two flagship oil/energy deals: with Chevron over the western Tengiz oilfield and with British Gas and Agip for the western Karachaganak gas-field. The offshore oilfield of Kashagan in the Caspian, considered one of the largest world discoveries of the last decade, alone is set to produce more oil than is produced by the entire US.[14] Oil reserves estimated for the Caucasus and Central Asia as a whole vary greatly but range from 30bn to 200bn barrels. These estimates include proven and possible reserves.[15]

The first decade of independence is significant because the nature of the regime has not been static, as we shall see in the next chapter. By various accounts, independence in 1991 constituted a 'critical juncture', [16] 'crisis'[17] or a 'critical institutional event.'[18] While the republic's first constitution was promulgated in 1992, Kazakhstan's second constitution was introduced in 1995, during a period in which several key issues affecting interethnic relations, notably the laws defining the national language and dual citizenship, were placed on the statute book. Non-titular emigration peaked in 1994–1995.[19] 1995 was also the year that saw the political space close, with the dissolution of parliament and the emasculation of legislative and judicial powers in favour of the executive. The 1995 referendum to adopt the second constitution and to prolong the rule of the president heightened the authoritarianism that began to differentiate the republic's earlier liberal political development after independence. The stabilization of interethnic relations and the increasingly authoritarian nature of the regime was accompanied, however, by rapid economic growth; GDP growth rates in 2000 and 2001 were among the highest in the world at 9.6 and 13.2 per cent respectively. With the calling in 1998 of early presidential elections for 1999 (originally scheduled for 2000) and the holding of a census in 1999 which confirmed ethnic Kazakhs as having at last reached a titular majority in their republic, authoritarianism seemed consolidated. The formation of a new political movement in November 2001 revealed the first serious fissure in the political debate, and elite conflict became visible and open. If 1995 marked primarily an institutional juncture, then 2001 marked an elite one. These differences in degree of authoritarianism prompt questions about the relationship between regime type and the elite system.

## AIMS AND SCOPE

In determining the relationship between the elite and the broader institutional and historical environment, this book has three principal approaches. First, it seeks to understand the formation of the political elite, who comprise that elite and the processes by which its incumbents have been recruited. Second, it analyses the functioning of the elite, how the core elite has managed to stay in power and how it has built authority and legitimacy. Third, it examines the axes along which elite functions conflict or cooperate and the factors that explain such elite behaviour.[20] This focus on the political elite as part of a system emphasizes both the group and the environment. The elite cannot be divorced from the broad historical and institutional environment in which it operates. Institutions, identities and interests have all kept the elite in power and provided it with the means to influence, for example, key processes and outcomes.

This is *not*, however, a book which treats elite policies as the dependent variable; a book on public policy would have concentrated on the policies themselves and been firmly rooted in public policy literature. Neither is it a *Who's Who* of political leaders in Kazakhstan. Nor does the book focus on the idiosyncratic, the political psychology or biographies of leadership. The bulk of our evidence for Kazakhstan is circumstantial; rarely do we encounter a direct and reliable attestation of political *relationship* or why a particular individual was recruited. One particular individual might have all sorts of credentials for having been chosen for a top job: social background criteria, beliefs, personality, ability to lead, relations with the gatekeepers of recruitment, purchase of office, the functional needs of the system, or symbolic representations of the nation. This is a record, not primarily of the people or their personalities, but of the parts they played, of their roles. The destiny of a group is not identical to that of the individuals within it.[21]

## CHAPTER BREAKDOWN

The immense resource, ethnic and geopolitical challenges are, after a brief summary of pre-independence history, explored in Chapter One. Five main policy challenges are identified in this chapter as having emerged in independent rule and have shaped the environment in which elites act: the consolidation of a new political post-communist regime; economic reform; the management of the centre's relations with the regions; the domestic-international nexus; and the promotion and management of identity. This last policy area is crucial because it provides the cultural and ideological context in which actors perform.

Most newly independent nations legitimate their rule in the name of the nation; Kazakhstani policies, by contrast, have been characterized by often reluctant and inconsistent nationalization. This ambivalence results both from the multiethnicity of the state and a reluctance to commit to full-scale nationalization in practice. We cannot say that the state has either succeeded in nationalizing the broader cultural space or that it has promulgated an inclusive, civic, multiethnic identity (see below and Chapter Four).

These inconsistent messages in the five policy spheres have therefore also shaped the environment. This heterogeneity, as we shall see in the coming pages, is the product of both agency and choice. Various opposites, fragmentations or cleavages have spun and are rooted in elite policies. The state is pulled in various directions and causes and consequences in the regime's politics are thus often complex and contradictory. Bargaining by forces within and outside the state has demanded balance, negotiation and measure in ideology, practice and policy. The elite is situated within this broader historical and institutional context.

In a society undergoing rapid social change where formal institutions lack force, [22] with a strong social hierarchy and with considerable economic resources that need to be managed and distributed, the role of the elite group as an instigator of reform is crucial.[23] In theory, such conditions should provide the elite with greater manoeuvrability and greater ability to shape events; in Alan Knight's terms: 'The greater relative elite autonomy, the more important elite decision-making is, and the more we are justified in focusing on elite activities: pacts, negotiations, settlements.'[24] In principle also, the identity and attitudes of the political elite should be found somewhere between the decision and policy stage. The political elite is the object of this study instead of the economic or cultural elite; members of the cultural elite who have played an important part in the first decade of independence are directly or indirectly linked to the political elite, while prominent economic players tend to be either part of, or closely allied to, key members of the political elite.

The degree to which a national elite can be said to be integrated may be assessed by examining key 'dimensions of integration' including social homogeneity, recruitment patterns (which also helps us to look at the permeability or ease of entrance into the elite), and – where possible – attitudinal consensus.[25] Chapters Two and Three look at the relationship of the elite to institutions and to their social background and, where possible, at the degree to which the elite agrees on the system of governance, the rules of the game. Chapter Two's focus on the relationship between institutions and elites assesses the nature of power in post-Soviet Kazakhstan, who counts as the elite, and what relationship that elite has career-wise with institutions.[26] John Higley, Jan Pakulski and Wlodzimierz Wesolowksi pay particular attention to the possible emergence of national elites that share a consensus on rules of the game and that are unified in defence of democratic institutions.[27] With such elite consensus and unity, they argue, stable demo-cracies are feasible, though perhaps not inevitable. Other conditions, such as economic growth, the absence of deep regionally based cultural conflicts, and a relatively benign international environment may also be necessary for stable democracy. But without elite consensus and unity, Higley et al. argue, these other conditions do not appear to be reliably related to it; if elites become deeply disunited, regimes that oscillate between pseudo-democratic and authoritarian forms, probably accompanied by much violence, are a virtual certainty.[28] They associate therefore different national elite configurations with different regime types: consolidated democracies where there is both strong unity and wide differentiation (consolidated elite); authoritarian or sultanistic regimes where there is neither (divided elite); totalitarian or post-totalitarian regimes where there is strong unity but narrow differentiation (ideocratic elite); and unconsolidated democracies, possibly oscillating with short-lived authoritarian regimes, where there is wide differentiation but weak unity (fragmented elite). These regime types also reflect Frederic Fleron and Lester Seligman's ideas on recruitment.[29] By locating the elites in a power index, we can obtain some indication of how the elite is institutionally structured.[30]

Chapter Three assesses the social background in an attempt to see whether certain groups dominate over others. Different stages of develop-ment or different regime types appear associated with the dominance of certain social backgrounds. The Communist Comparative Leadership School, [31] spearheaded by the work of Carl Beck and James Malloy, did much to place the comparative study of communist elites in the broader po-litical system. Its work on the Soviet political system explicitly drew on the findings of David Easton, David Apter, Karl W. Deutsch, Gabriel Almond and G. Bingham Powell and Herbert Spiro.[32] Beck and Malloy sought to illustrate social, economic and political relationships between elite social background criteria and broad socio-economic developments, how the elite's behaviour fitted into the political system's wider goals. They offered dynamic analyses, describing elites as both catalysts of, and respondents to, political change.[33]

The implications of homogeneity[34] have been assessed by the classical theorists, Vilfredo Pareto, Gaetano Mosca and Robert Michels and, more recently, by Harold Lasswell who, we shall see, have all been interested in what is termed the 'genetic aspect of elites'.[35] In the context of increasing our understanding of the elite system as a whole, the implications of Chapter Three can only be limited, however. We will not be able to conclude from this chapter alone whether a person's demographic or professional background was the determining factor in recruitment, nor the nature of elite-elite, elite-society relations.

One key criticism of elite studies around the world has been the absence of testable propositions that link the background and career characteristics of elites with their orientations. Authors differ on whether they believe there is a link. Reinhard Bendix argues that knowledge of the 'social composition of the members and leaders of different political organizations' will 'provide a clue to the political goals which their leaders are likely to pursue'.[36] By contrast, Lewis Edinger and Donald Searing say there is no provable link between social background, on the one hand, and elite-elite or elite-mass relations, on the other.[37] Milton Lodge's work on Soviet elite attitudes similarly found intervening variables of career more important than social background.[38]

Nor can the link between an individual's social background and that person's attitudinal orientation be assumed. In seeking statistical relationships between socio-economic variables and the social backgrounds of political leaders, the researcher is entering a field where data, while assembled with much effort, care and perseverance, will remain somewhat incomplete.

In the context of a system undergoing such structural changes, its legitimation becomes crucial, a process explored in Chapter Four. This legitimation process in the first ten years of Kazakhstan's rule has been only partly about striking a psychological and a material relationship with the population: the former, in terms of identification and the latter, in terms of distributing the gains from economic growth. This chapter underscores the contradictions of elite nation-building policies in Kazakhstan, and focuses in particular on how the elite legitimation process itself is a factor behind these contradictions. Specifically, the inability and often unwillingness of the elite to define an inner cultural core has blurred the boundaries between who is 'in' and who is 'out', making the content of nation-building policies blurred. This may well have been a factor in the maintenance of interethnic harmony between the titular and non-titular groups.

Chapter Five assesses the extent to which the elite, once it had been granted independence, set about establishing a system by design rather than default, the product of the elite's ability to bargain and influence its composition and its institutional structure. It examines the methods used by elites to achieve and maintain their predominant positions, what Beck and Malloy term 'techniques of power maintenance', whether by winning through the ballot box, the use of mass physical terror, or control over and manipulation of the flow of information.[39]

Chapter Six, by contrast, focuses on the structure of constraints and opportunities within which the elite acts. The policies identified in Chapter One, and agency as identified in Chapter Five, can reshape the environment; the chapter thus emphasizes both the general system attributes and the systemic policy outcomes. Establishing the nature of such constraints and opportunities is important in our understanding of why particular groups were able to maintain power. Various scholars have argued that institutions are a product of culture.[40] In this path-dependent version, institutional design is best served and explained by legacies, initial conditions and cultural patterns; they routinize tasks and lower transaction costs and strengthen existing orders. We look therefore at how both elite-elite relations and elite-society relations are structured, defined and legitimated.

# FRAMEWORK AND APPROACH

The focus on *elite system* is informed by a central debate in social, political, economic and, more recently, international relations theory: the relationship between structure and agency.[41] Beck and Malloy employed four categories to identify and understand the characteristics of the three basic types of elite system: elite perspectives, techniques of position maintenance, elite structure, and behavioural norms and dispositions. They hypothesize that perspectives and techniques have a determining effect on elite structure and elite behavioural norms.[42] This book takes an agency-structure approach not to add to the theory of this relationship, but because it captures the conceptualization explained earlier of the elite as part of a wider system.

In simplified terms, the political system may be seen as structure and the elite as agent. Structure refers to the social, economic and political environment in which relations have acquired meaning and order. These meanings and orders both empower and constrain actors since they provide templates to which actors can refer and impose barriers and limit the agency of actors. 'Agency' refers to political conduct, and here the capacity of decision-makers to shape the course of events is emphasized. Whilst unintended consequences may be a component of structure, intended consequences are of agency.[43]

The structure-agency relationship was usefully analysed and refined by

Colin Hay in his work *Political Analysis: A Critical Introduction*, [44] and issues raised by Hay weave through the approach adopted in the following pages. First, ideas and identity matter in the structure-agency relationship. Second, agency and structure are empirically inseparable. Third, power is as much a process as a resource.

Ideas shape the preferences and behaviour of actors as well as the structures within which culture becomes embedded. Institutions can be created to provide symbols, scripts and routines, and in doing so provide strategically useful information which can affect how actors represent themselves. In Peter Hall and Rosemary Taylor's terms, culture 'emphasizes the extent to which individuals turn to established routines or familiar patterns of behaviour to attain their purposes', [45] a practice heightened in a transitional era. Which networks and patterns, if any, the Kazakhstani political elite has depended on for its formation and functioning forms part of this enquiry.

Second, agency and structure are conceptually separable but empirically blurred. They do not form a neat dichotomy. A particularly useful way of conceptualizing this relationship is, as Hay points out, Bob Jessop's strategic-relational approach, [46] which gives agency to structure and structure to agency. It acknowledges, for example, that, on the one hand, an environment is not static or exogenously fixed but can be shaped by individual actors (an action setting); and, on the other, that an agent is shaped and constrained by the environment, and (un)consciously incorporates this setting when deciding on a course of action (a situated agent). This approach emphasizes the dual importance of contingency and unintended consequences. While Chapter Five assesses how the behaviour and policies of the elite shape the environment in which they act, Chapter Six analyses how this environment constrains or empowers the action of the elite.

Finally, power is conceived as a process, 'involving the exercise of control, constraint and coercion in society.'[47] Following Hay, power is here understood to operate on all three dimensions of the so-called 'faces of power' controversy.[48] The first, pluralist dimension of power focuses on the decision-making process, is actor-centred and assumes that power is zero-sum.[49] Power is conceived here as the individual's ability to make decisions and to influence outcomes. The second dimension of power is instead process-centred and emphasizes the importance of influencing what is on the political agenda. The third dimension, as put forward by Steven Lukes in 1974, concentrates on the ability to shape preferences, to manipulate consciousness. His analysis suggests that asymmetrical power distribution is the result not of the system but of institutionalized manipulation, 'the many ways in which potential issues are kept out of politics, whether through the operation of social forces and institutional practices or through individuals' decisions'.[50]

# ...ND LOCATING THE POLITICAL ELITE

...n of system and power determine how we go about
...e political elite. In general, the tendency is to define
... functional way but to operationalize 'eliteness' on
...al position. Either way, the approach focuses on the
...sion of power, i.e. who matters in the decision-making process.
While institutional roles are an important starting point in the location of
the political elite we also need to go away from looking at elites formally
and institutionally in an attempt to appreciate also the non-active and
potential elites from which subsequent elites are drawn, in the ways that
they affect both the second and third dimensions of power.

While the search for political elites and the problems associated with
such an undertaking have provided cause for concern, disagreements
over whether or not an elite has been located arise frequently from the
use of different definitions. As Alan Zuckerman highlights, 'in some cases,
the definitions chosen make it impossible not to find a political elite. In
others, the criteria used make it impossible to find one.'[51] Dahl's definition
may exemplify the second problem, since it seeks to locate 'a minority of
individuals whose preference regularly prevails in cases of differences in
preferences on key political issues'.[52] C. Wright Mills defined it as 'men
... in positions to make decisions having major consequences ... [T]hey
are in command of the major hierarchies and organizations of modern
society.'[53] James Meisel, however, framed it as 'the collective manipulation
of the masses by a small leadership group or by several such groups ... To
put it into a formula, all elites shall be credited here with what we should
like to call the three C's: group consciousness, coherence and conspiracy.'[54]
Mindful of the view of power as a process and its three dimensions, the
political elite here is considered as those who exercise 'preponderant
political influence'[55] (the core political elite) but who may or may not be
the institutional 'power holders of a body politic'.[56]

This definition still leaves the empirical problem of identifying those
individuals who in fact exercise 'preponderant political influence' in
Kazakhstan's political system.[57] A brief word on the book's methodology
is therefore appropriate.[58] Broadly speaking, social scientists have to date
used three strategies for identifying elites: positional, reputational and
decisional analysis.

Positional, or locational, analysis assumes that powerful people are
located in the institutions of government. In other words, people derive
power from institutional roles. The key treatize on this topic is C. Wright
Mills' *The Power Elite*: 'To be celebrated, to be wealthy, to have power
requires access to major institutions, for the institutional positions men
occupy determine in large part their chances to have and to hold these
valued experiences.'[59]

Because formal institutions usually keep records, positional analysis is the most common technique for finding the powerful. It is not without its flaws, however. This type of analysis assumes that we know which institutions are politically significant, but potentially neglects individuals who merely rubber-stamp decisions. As noted, this method also ignores the indirect influence of those figures not located in governmental institutions.

The reputational approach is closely associated with Floyd Hunter's study of communal power structure.[60] Reputational analysis relies not on formal organization charts, but on informal reputations of power. Usually a 'panel of experts', or 'informants', deemed to have either been involved in or closely observed political change. This technique presupposes that participants in a system can judge who is powerful and who is not. It incorporates powerful figures whose influence is also indirect or implicit. But reputational analysis also has shortcomings. Any researcher using this method must decide whom and what to ask. Errors in choosing informants may bias the results but, with a large membership, the 'panel of experts' expands the selection and intensifies the cross-referencing of those thought to be members of the elite.

The reputational approach is also related to the third main technique for identifying the powerful – decisional analysis. This method – sometimes called event analysis – is based on the assumption that, if political power is defined in terms of influence over government activities, we can detect it by studying the means by which specific decisions are reached and, in particular, by identifying the individuals who successfully initiate or veto proposals. In the best-known application of decisional analysis, Robert A. Dahl studied decisions (in New Haven, Connecticut) on three issues: urban redevelopment, public education and nominations for public office.[61] Again, there are several significant limitations. Only a few decisions can be studied in detail, yet patterns of power often differ from issue to issue.[62] Access to records detailing the process of and actors involved in decision-making is extremely difficult. Decisional analysis is probably best suited for studying matters that have already become recognized public issues.[63]

Because methods of locating the powerful have certain limitations, some analysts have merged several different approaches. For example, in a pair of studies of Yugoslav and American elites, Allen Barton and his collaborators combined positional and reputational analysis in the so-called 'snowball' technique.[64] In each country, incumbents of key formal positions constituted the initial elite, as defined operationally. Respondents from these positions were then asked for the names of others to whom they looked for advice or whom they thought to be generally influential. People receiving at least five such nominations were themselves added to the elite sample, and they in turn were asked for further nominations.[65]

The present study also adopts this 'snowball' technique. On the basis of positional analysis, an initial list of the political elite was compiled.

The names on this list were then submitted to an independent panel of experts consisting of 41 individuals who remain anonymous. They are referred to in the text as Expert (E) and as belonging to one of four groups: Group A (Local Academics); Group B (Local Journalists); Group C (Transnational Corporations); and Group D (International Organizations and Foreign Government Representations). Weights were assigned to the various power groupings and individuals and the rankings arranged in a power scale. Both experts and elite members were asked at the end of the interview to give their opinions on who should be included in the political elite. Additionally, some text-based analysis of elites were used.[66]

Through the cross-referencing of these techniques, 383 members of the political elite were identified for the combined years of 1995 and 2000 but, since 139 of these were the same individuals, 244 represented the study on which the social background analysis was based. In this analysis, attempts were made to compare 1995 and 2000 as well as provide aggregate data. Time and money constraints did not allow for an interviewing of the political elite in 2000 and only a part of the panel of experts (20) was re-questioned. Supplementary media sources were, however, used as in 1995 to establish rankings, as were polls on elite attitudes, opinion polls and other survey data.[67] Thus, although the 2000 data is not directly comparable to that of 1995, its use does at least offer a sense of trends in the 1991–2001 period. It is not by chance that the study of a single political unit at a single point in time is the most common type of study of political elites conducted by social scientists. The gathering of data, and gaining access to members of the elite, is difficult and time-consuming.

Of the 244 identified, 37 were interviewed between October 1995 and December 1996. Data cited in the text is sourced as 'Political Elite' (PE) and a number, referring to the number in which they appear in the Appendix.

In the same period, 42 members of three regional elites (including the three regional governors in the central sample above) were interviewed. This study, as explained, focuses on Kazakhstan's national or central elite and thus the concern is not on how micro-regional environments had an impact on *regional* recruitment processes. Most experts included regional governors as part of the central elite, however, by virtue of the fact that they were appointed by the central elite and were a result of or affected national policy. While the emphasis therefore was to secure interviews with the centrally appointed regional governor, other top-ranking members of the regional administration were interviewed to gain a regional executive perspective on the central recruitment process.[68]

The regions of Pavlodar, Shymkent and Uralsk were partly selected for their differing geographies, economies and demographics. While the cities of Pavlodar (head of Pavlodar region in the north-east) and Uralsk (head of West Kazakhstan region) were both founded as Russian forts (1861 and 1613 respectively), Shymkent (capital of South Kazakhstan region) was established as a staging post on the Silk Road in the seventh century. South Kazakhstan region, the only major cotton-growing area in Kazakhstan and home to the country's largest oil refinery, has both well-developed industry and agriculture. Pavlodar is an industrial region, housing one of the world's largest open-cast coal mines, a thermal-electric power station, the republic's only tractor factory, a significant aluminium plant and oil refinery. In the mid 1990s Pavlodar was providing over half of Kazakhstan's energy. Agriculture here was intensively developed since the opening up of the 'Virgin Lands' in the 1960s. Western Kazakhstan's economy is based on gas, condensate and oil reserves and grain production. While Kazakhs form the ethnic majorities in southern and western Kazakhstan, Pavlodar is Russian-dominated.[69]

The 37 top-ranking members of the elite interviewed included: the Prime Minister and members of his chancellery (6); Ministers and First or Deputy Ministers (8), top-ranking members of the presidential administration including members of the National Security Committee and Heads of Economic/Legal Departments (7), regional governors (4, including of Almaty), other members of executive power (7), legislative power (3) and members of the counter-elite (2).[70]

We cannot call those interviewed a strict representative sample of the political elite (e.g. by nationality or, say, gender, in per centage terms as reflected in the 244) since access played a significant role in regulating which members of the political elite were interviewed. The sample is placed in the context of the broader 244 and an analysis of trends offered.

The elite members interviewed requested anonymity which has, of course, been respected. The question of anonymity is not, however, a problem in the context of the book's stated aims. These are not to provide particular information about individual members of the elite but instead to gain a sense of their collective identity, interests and institutions. The Tables at the end of the Appendix give anonymized social background data of those interviewed.

Causation between the elite and system change is very difficult to make. We can contrast personnel changes and changes in the background, activities and/or attitudes of major political leaders, but instead there may simply be a functional relationship between the requirements of the political system and the composition of the elite. We need to distinguish between identifying and attendant characteristics of change. We also have the problem of excluding potentially important intervening variables. With all the caveats of the Introduction in mind, we begin with an assessment of the context of transition from communist rule.

# Chapter One

# THE CONTEXT OF TRANSITION, 1991–2001

## LEGACIES AND POLICIES

The nature of Kazakhstani independence and the elite's assumption of power is intimately related to the territory's history and its landlocked geography between China and Russia. The interaction with Russia brought intense Russification economically, socially and culturally, and is punctuated by a series of major events, profound tragedies and remarkable achievements. These revolutionized Kazakhstan's traditional pastoral steppe society and bequeathed major legacies for the contemporary political elite. This chapter begins with a brief historical excursus and proceeds to analyse the major legacies for the elite.

Contact with Russia, begun minimally in the seventeenth century, intensified in the eighteenth. On the one hand, in 1716–1718 the Russians introduced a string of forts, the so-called Orenburg fortified line, on the edge of the steppe. As part of Russia's expansion southwards, settlement of Russian peasants in the Kazakh steppe intensified, particularly in the late nineteenth century, encroaching on sacred nomadic migratory routes and the increasingly scarce pastureland. On the other hand, Kazakhs approached Russia for imperial protection. In 1723 the Kalmyks of the Volga had raided settlements in the Kazakh steppes to link up with their kinsmen from Zhungaria. Caught by surprise as they prepared to leave their winter campsites, the Kazakhs fled, leaving most of their possessions and livestock. This Great Retreat of 1723–1725 (*Aqtaban Shubirindi*),[1] which was to imprint itself into Kazakh epic literature, prompted Kazakh tribes, hitherto long divided, to form a common front and, in 1728, to vote for a supreme chieftain, Abulkhair. To secure his political position and to gain Russian protection from further such encroachments and land pressures, in 1730 Abulkhair requested Russian suzerainty (*poddanstvo*).[2]

Granting suzerainty a year later, imperial Russia saw in this relationship the possibility of further securing its trade routes to the south. In the 1820s these trade interests strengthened and European settlement on the steppe continued. Increasingly concerned about the security of Russian trading interests to Central Asia and as part of their larger goal to establish fully fledged colonial rule throughout the steppe and Turkistan areas, Russian authorities annexed the Syr Darya region, at that time under the rule of the khan of Kokand, and finally in the 1860s acquired control of the khanate of Kokand itself. As part of the Steppe Statute, [3] three governor-generalships were established on the steppe.[4]

The continued settlement of Russians in the region led to the further displacement of Kazakhs from their pasturelands and, combined with several harsh winters, to the famine of the 1890s. During this same period, contact with Russian and European settlers was leading both to acculturation and the formation of a small group of bourgeois nationalists who established the *Alash* movement, which became a moderate nationalist uprising in 1905.[5] Maintaining its loyalty to the Tsarist authorities during the First World War, the movement after the 1917 February revolution formed the Alash Orda government which lasted until 1920. At the same time, Kazakhs were deported after 1916 when an anti-Russian uprising in reaction to forced conscription failed and was followed closely by famine and disease.

The national delimitation of Central Asia by the Bolsheviks in 1924–1925 established the five main administrative-territorial units of Kazakhstan, Kyrgyzstan, Tajikistan, Turkmenistan and Uzbekistan, and in 1925 the 'Kirghiz' ASSR was officially renamed the 'Kazak' ASSR; in 1936 this was amended to 'Kazakh', 'in order to reflect more closely Kazakh pronunciation'.[6] Also in 1936 the Kazakh ASSR was elevated to full Union republic status, which it retained until it declared independence in December 1991. The territory covered by the Kazakh ASSR was slightly larger than that over which traditional Kazakhs roamed.

The consolidation of Soviet rule involved repression, sedentarization and collectivization. Soviet power liquidated the intellectual and political elite through three main waves of terror in 1928, 1937–1938 and 1949–1950. Many well-known members of the Kazakh intelligentsia were among them. The traditional Kazakh pastoral-based kin-based nomadic economy, already under attack in the Russian period, was destroyed through the twin policy of collectivization and sedentarization. The number of Kazakhs resultantly had fallen by 39.8 per cent, from 3, 637, 612 in 1926 to 2, 181, 520 by the time of the 1939 census.[7] Stalin deported various nationalities (such as Germans, Koreans, Poles and Chechens) and, between 1954 and 1956, a large influx of settlers from the Slavic and Baltic republics arrived as part of the Virgin Lands campaign. Launched by Nikita Khrushchev this campaign sought to transform the steppe into a major grain-producing region, again driving Kazakhs away from lands in northern regions.[8]

In this period the appointment of Dinmukhamed Kunaev as Kazakh First Party Secretary in 1960 was to prove instrumental for the consolidation of the Kazakh SSR.[9] As a protégé and friend of Leonid Brezhnev he had by 1971 become a full member of the Politburo of the Central Committee of the Communist Party of the Soviet Union, uniquely amongst Central Asian party leaders. Kunaev built up an ethnic Kazakh, largely politico-administrative, cadre and helped sponsor the educational and cultural development of ethnic Kazakhs.

In December 1986 Kunaev was removed from his post as Kazakh First Party Secretary and an ethnic Russian from Moscow, Gennady Kolbin, was parachuted in from Moscow. Crowds of youths congregated in the streets demanding an explanation, and, after some hesitation from the leadership, three top officials were appointed to liaise with the crowds. One of these was Nursultan Nazarbaev.[10]

Born in 1940 in the southern village of Chemolgan, near Alma-Ata (now Almaty) city, Nazarbaev attended a local Russian-language school and went on to complete a technical degree in the Ukraine city of Dneprodzerzhinsk. He began his career as a metallurgist in the Karaganda Metallurgical Combine in Termitau, central Kazakhstan and it was here that he first became active in politics. Having served his time in the Komsomol and the local Communist Party of Kazakhstan (KPK), by 1979 he had already been appointed to second secretary of the Karaganda regional committee. A year later he was appointed Secretary for Industry on the republic's Central Committee. In 1984, Nazarbaev was appointed chairman of Kazakhstan's Council of Ministers, effectively the number two position in the republic after Kunaev. This meant that at the age of forty-four Nazarbaev was the youngest among all Soviet republic chairmen.[11] As chairman of Kazakhstan's Council of Ministers and the second most prominent Kazakh in the party, Nazarbaev may well have had expectations that he would be picked to replace Kunaev.[12] Moreover, his criticism of Kunaev during the period between March 1985 and December 1986 indicated the reform-mindedness that should have made him a member of the Gorbachev-Ligachev-Ryzhkov reform team.

After several attempts by Nazarbaev to 'save' the Soviet Union, the Slav republics gathered in Minsk on 8 December 1991 to declare the Union defunct, creating a Commonwealth of Independent States (CIS) in its place. Just over a week later, as the last republic to do so, Kazakhstan declared its independence on 16 December. On 20–21 December another meeting of the CIS was arranged, this time in Alma-Ata (now Almaty), and, in addition to seven other former Soviet republics, Kazakhstan was admitted.

The legacies of this Russian-Kazakh interaction confront the contemporary elite, the full implications of which can only be understood in the context of how this interaction transformed traditional Kazakh society. The three key legacies are economic industrialization and urbanization; acculturation; and the establishment of administrative and cognitive borders.

The steppe was revolutionized from a largely nomadic pastoral economy to a settled, urbanized and industrialized society. The traditional Kazakh steppe tribes were predominantly pastoral nomads, and the primary socio-economic unit in Kazakh nomadic society was the encampment, or *aul*. Several encampments would come together for the long summer migration; they would also unite in time of internal conflict or external aggression. During the winter, to improve their chances of discovering good pasture, they would separate again into their original units.

The construction of the Orenburg fortified line allowed for the expansion of Russian trade with Central Asia and many wealthier Kazakh nomads became middlemen, a cash-based economy emerging from a barter-based one. The settlement of Russian peasants encroached on key nomadic migratory routes and increasingly scarce pastureland. The introduction of a *kibitka* or tent tax (a tax on each household, irrespective of number in household), exacerbated inequality among nomads. The reduction in pastureland robbed nomadic life of its self-regulatory mechanisms, since scarcity constricted the nomads' ability to change to other groups.

Already under attack in the Russian period, the traditional Kazakh pastoral-based nomadic economy was destroyed through the twin policy of collectivization and sedentarization. The Soviet era bequeathed huge industrial complexes to the elite, built entire new cities, created the Baikonur cosmodrome and ensured that upon independence Kazakhstan had become one of the economically most viable republics. A clear divide between urbanized, industry-employed Russians and rural Kazakhs had resulted. Mass literacy was achieved.

Escaping economic dependency on Russia, in the context of Russian withdrawal from the region in the early independence years, underpinned an essential part of the early independence economic reform strategy (below). The inheritance of a viable economic unit (Introduction) and the ability therefore, on the one hand, to attract investment and, on the other, to gain substantial profits from the sale of its resources, was to prove decisive both in the consolidation of Nazarbaev's power in the early period and the increased elite fragmentation visible by the end of the decade (Chapters Five and Six).

The sharp drop in the Kazakh population and the continued influx of non-Kazakhs noted earlier had made Kazakhs a minority in their Soviet republic. The 1959 census showed that Kazakhs had now been reduced to a mere 20 per cent of their population, compared to Slavic and European settlers making up as much as 60 per cent.[13] The settlement of Slavs in both the Russian and Soviet eras brought intense acculturation, albeit to different degrees depending on the region. From 1789, Russo-Kazakh primary schools were opened in all districts, and some institutions of higher education were specifically designed to offer Russian education to children of Kazakh khans.[14] The literacy level among the sedentary population grew rapidly, in both the Kazakh and Russian languages and around the 1860s Kazakh was being written, and in the Arabic script. Acculturation processes between Russians and Kazakhs significantly outpaced those in the southern areas, due to the northern areas' geographic proximity and its longer incorporation under Russian rule. The Junior and Inner Zhuz, closest to European Russia, and most exposed to contact with Russians, witnessed an even more marked degree of acculturation. In the southern areas the Uzbek influence remained stronger. Writes Lawrence Krader: 'A Middle Horde Kazakh could adopt a 'Russian' point of view and have the public opinion of his community support him in it a full generation anterior to even a remote envisagement of such a situation in the Great Horde'.[15] Acculturation was also seen through the growth of the national bourgeoisie and its flourishing in Alash Orda. As Chapters Four and Six intimate, regional differences persist and Russia's proximity and acculturation processes are an important factor in explaining some of the contemporary elite's legitimation process (Chapter Four), recruitment decisions (Chapter Five) and broader environment (Chapter Six). These involved crucial dilemmas of how to establish an identity separate from Kazakhstan's 'other', Russia, and the extent to which, in a modern state, this identity should or could draw on traditional referents of tribe and clan.

The north/south contrast was seen, for example, by the way in which Islam was transmitted. In the later eighteenth century, Catherine the Great had employed Tatar mullahs to proselytize in the northern steppe areas; by contrast in the south, Central Asian missionaries arrived of their own accord and the Kazakhs of the Senior Zhuz were converted under the rule of the khan of Kokand. Islam in the south was more conservative and also anti-Russian.[16]

Finally the Russian and Soviet eras established administrative and cognitive borders of belonging. The borders of the Kazakh steppe were fluid, subject to encroachments by the Russian and Chinese empires. Imperial policy introduced to the steppe a fundamentally different conceptualization of power, one defined by territory, regulated by procedural elections and supported by a bureaucracy.

The tribal-clan structure gave the Kazakh steppe tribes both day-to-day meaning and their very livelihood. Nomadic society was not based on a tributary mode (where the elite coerces) or a capitalist mode (where labour is bought and sold), but on a kin-ordered mode.[17] Kinship-centred production was based on the opposition between those who belonged to the group, by virtue of lineage or clan for example, and those who did not. At the same time, however, the rigid structural hierarchies were offset by the principle of exogamy and the inherent mobility of nomadic life which meant that any one encampment did not necessarily include nomads of the same kin. In reality, therefore, these clans were often not based on lineage. Clans formed the aul and consisted of 'an extended patriarchal family network':[18] maternal relatives from other clans (the Kazakhs were exogamous up the preceding seven generations);[19] freed slaves; poor nomads who had become isolated from their communities became dependent on new households. However fictional the tribal genealogies were, they nonetheless provided the framework of group belonging.

The borders of the three governor-generalships established by the 1867–1868 Steppe Statute did not necessarily coincide with those of a zhuz and nor did the borders of the newly established Soviet fourteen administrative-territorial units. Nevertheless, the Soviet period saw an increased salience of the zhuz as a unit of identification, partly through Kunaev's use of this identification, a point explored in Chapters Four, Five and Six. After the dismissal of Janin Shaiakhmetov from the post of First Secretary, Kunaev's recruitment policies strengthened the status of the zhuz, because he played zhuzes off against each other and promoted his own Southern Horde in whose hands more and more power became concentrated.

The ruling stratum did not belong to this clan tribal system. Kazakh traditional society was a textbook example of Khazanov's 'differentiated segment society', in which 'the ruling segment ceases to be a replica of the other segments, fully or partially falls away from the genealogical cliché of the given society, acquires distinct laws of kinship and descent and, most importantly, turns into a distinct estate.'[20] Traditional Kazakh society was, according to Elizabeth Bacon, 'conical' in shape, or 'pyramidal' to use the typology developed by Meyer Fortes and Edward Evans-Pritchard.[21]

The narrow segment at the top comprised the Kazakh hereditary estate, the aq su, or white bone, whilst the lower part consisted of the non-hereditary masses, the qara su, or black bone. 'Bone' denotes lineage, and the use of the colours white and black come from traditional Mongol practice. The sultans of the white bone, or tore were directly descended in the male line from Mongol princes, most often those who could claim descent from Chingiz Khan. Only sultans possessed the legal right to compete for the leadership title of khan, or ruler. Although a hereditary estate, members of the ruling elite had to earn their title through charisma or military skill and periods of succession involved bitter power struggles between the khans.[22] Khans were weak;[23] they did not preside over a defined area (at no time in Kazakh steppe history did a zhuz concord with the territory over which the khan ruled),[24] tribe, slaves or standing army and did not command a tax-collecting bureaucracy. They often had to entertain lavishly to maintain the support of these tribes.

The black bone had its own leaders: the *bai* (the wealthier stratum who often acted as heads of auls); the *batyr* ('hero') and the *bii* ('interpreter of customary law' or 'judge'). Their role and influence depended on the specific situation and their character. Each clan also had its *aqsaqal*, or elder. Nomadic respect for social authority was higher (in the form of the *bii*, 'judge' or the *aqsaqal*) than their respect for political authority (in the form of the khan).[25]

Ultimately, kinship served different functions for the white and black bone. At the lower level, kinship acted as an organizing principle, determining issues, for example, of inheritance, property, and material help on birth, weddings and funerals. For the white bone, by contrast, genealogy was emphasized and was the basis of legitimation for khan power and the maintenance of their rule. We shall assess what units of belonging the contemporary elite uses for its legitimation primarily in Chapter Four.

While the borders of the governor-generalships did not necessarily coincide with clans, those of the newly established Soviet fourteen administrative-territorial units did acknowledge clan divisions. Concludes Pauline Jones Luong: 'Kazakh clans remained essentially intact while larger traditional configurations (i.e. tribes, historic regions, and hordes) were divided.'[26] As we shall note in Chapter Six, however, both Russians and Kazakhs were included in clan networks. Borders and settlement changed but on the whole strengthened the role of kinship at lower levels of society.[27] Bacon notes how sedentarization strengthened the unit of the clan by giving the unit fixed borders – a point to which we shall also return in Chapter Six.

The 'larger tribal configurations' to which Jones Luong refers include the 'horde'. The appearance of the horde, or zhuz (meaning 'hundred' in Kazakh) was first reported in the sixteenth or seventeenth century. Although the origins of the zhuz are hazy, their name suggests Mongol influence and reflects the importance of units of decimals in Altaic steppe politico-military organization.[28] Independent of each other, the zhuz were known as the Senior (*Uly*) Zhuz, Middle (*Orta*) Zhuz and Junior (*Kishi*) Zhuz.[29] Their labels indicate their chronology of formation, the Senior having been formed first. The Senior Zhuz covered the most extensive territory in the east and south-east of the country. The Middle Zhuz, geographically closer to Russia, covered the northern and central regions (and a part of south-eastern Kazakhstan), and the Junior Zhuz in the west around the Caspian Sea, Aral Sea and Ural river. The approximate boundaries of the zhuz have remained more or less unchanged.

Evidence provided by scholars such as Bacon and Lawrence Krader suggests that the three units also differed in some aspects of political and cultural life.[30] Legends hold that each is associated with a different symbol: the Senior with sheep (symbolizing wealth); the Middle with a pen (signifying knowledge); and the Junior with a weapon (symbolizing a warrior culture).[31] V. V. Vostrov and M. S. Mukanov, for example, contend that the three zhuzes were offshoots of one whole.[32]

This tripartite geographic division into zhuz and the horizontal division into clans and tribes coexisted with the perceived common line of descent of all Kazakhs from one ancestor. Precisely when and how Kazakhs began to be known as a distinct set of these pastoral groups remains unclear, as does the order in which tribes appeared on the steppe.[33] The term 'Kazak' was apparently used in the thirteenth century by the Chinese, and peoples of the Caucasus and Volga-Don region.[34] As Martha Brill Olcott writes: 'The consensus is that the Kazakh people or Kazakh nation was formed in the mid-fifteenth century when Janibek (Dzhanibek) and Kirai (Girei), sons of Barak Khan of the White Horde of the Mongol empire, broke away from Abu'l Khayr (Abulkhair), khan of the Uzbeks.'[35]

The folk derivation *qaz* (goose), *aq* (white), links it to a popular legend of a white goose that turned into a princess, who in turn gave birth to the first Kazakh.[36] It is impossible to say how ordinary Kazakhs at the time interpreted their identity. In any case, as part of their process of self-definition Kazakhs appear to have discovered their descent from a common ancestor.[37] The most popular related legend is that of Alash, viewed as the original ancestor of the Kazakhs and his three sons – Uisun, the eldest, Aktol, the middle, and Alshin, the youngest – who formed the Ulu, Orta and Kishi Zhuz respectively.

The development of a sense of 'Kazakhness', begun under the Russian imperial era, grew in the Soviet era when, through the establishment of a Kazakh Soviet republic, ethnic Kazakhs were given a territory that was clearly defined and that bore their name. Soviet nationalities policy consolidated both Soviet identities and individual republican identities. Not only mass literacy and education created a bond between rulers and ruled but also the nurturing of simultaneous 'identification with the Soviet state and with the national group'.[38] The national group was also granted the ability to use the Kazakh language as an effective medium of communication.[39] And in the 1924 Kazakh Constitution the status of state language was granted to both Russian and Kazakh. The sense of 'Kazakhness' was also strengthened through the creation of a national, albeit Soviet republican, elite. Kunaev was able to build up largely southern-based recruitment networks that operated independently of Moscow and increasingly of society, benefiting from the material privileges that had accrued to the nomenklatura class more generally. As elsewhere in the Soviet Union, elite building was given its own institutional network for the first time. The demonstration between 16 and 18 December 1986 broke out in the context of this heightened national self awareness. But, as Shirin Akiner explains, the catalysts remain unclear.[40] In any case, in December 1986 Kunaev was removed from his post as Kazakh First Party Secretary and an ethnic Russian from Moscow, Gennady Kolbin, parachuted in from Moscow. Gorbachev's decision to bypass Nazarbaev for a Russian from outside Kazakhstan broke the traditional rules of Soviet society. As Martha Brill Olcott writes:

> What may have seemed rational cadre politics in Moscow – a means of reducing local political influence, of increasing integration into the greater union, and also of avoiding falling into the clutches of any local faction – looked from Central Asia much more like Great Russian chauvinism.[41]

The legacy for Kazakhstan's post-Soviet leaders was how best to use the state that the Soviet Union had created and how to find new political direction and content in the ideological vacuum left by the collapse of Soviet-style communism and the banning of the KPK.

Although independence was declared in December 1991, the late Gorbachev years are essential in understanding how Nazarbaev had already managed to consolidate his leadership prior to independence. As Martha Brill Olcott highlights, Nazarbaev's election as First Secretary of the KPK's Central Committee in May 1989, and his co-chairmanship of the Supreme Council between February and April, allowed him to consolidate power. In September 1909 he became chairman of the Supreme Soviet. Once elected First Secretary, Nazarbaev sought to avoid the weaknesses of Kolbin who had been unable to build up his own cadre and worked to secure the administration under his control. He moved to conciliate with other officials, including in April 1991 with Kunaev himself, whose brother he had criticized as anti-reformist. Following the example set by Gorbachev in Moscow, Nazarbaev in March 1990 converted his chairmanship of the Supreme Soviet to a presidency confirmed by parliamentary election. Nazarbaev's key contender for the post of president was an individual who had been closely involved in the 1986 riots, Khasen Kozha-Akhmet. Collecting his signatures from inside a traditional yurt set up outside the State Supermarket of Alma-Ata's busiest pedestrian mall, Kozha-Akhmet practically obtained the required number to compete for presidential office. As the election date approached, his yurt was ransacked leaving no record of the signatures. Nazarbaev now stood alone and on 1 December 1991, under the slogan of 'Want a Flag for Kazakhstan? Cast Your Vote for Nursultan', won outright with a reported 98.7 per cent of the vote.

## INDEPENDENT KAZAKHSTAN[42]

With independence and the assumption of the presidency, the Nazarbaev regime was faced with the dual task of political and economic transition. The final section of this chapter periodizes this agenda and ends by underscoring three challenges that have shaped the 1991–2001 period: the links between central and regional power, between politics and identity and between domestic and foreign policies.

## Political Change in 1991–2001

Kazakhstan, it is suggested here, has passed through four main phases of political development since independence: liberalization between 1992 and 1994 with heightened institutional competition in 1994–1995; the legalization of presidential domination of the system, with the passing of Kazakhstan's second constitution in 1995; centralization and concentration in 1995–1998; and the onset of repression and intra-elite competition with open fragmentation in 2001.

While the first three years witnessed a liberalization of political activity, they also sowed the seeds of authoritarianism that had characterized the polity by the close of the 1990s. By 2001 Nazarbaev had survived four prime ministers (Sergei Tereshchenko, Akezhan Kazhegeldin, Nurlan Balgimbaev and Kasymzhomart Tokaev) and four parliaments (the 12th parliament, which 'self-dissolved' in December 1993; the 13th parliament, surviving for a year from March 1994); and the bicameral parliaments (Mazhilis and Senat as lower and upper houses respectively) of 1995–1999 and 1999–2004.

## 1992–1994: Liberalization

The period of 1992–1994 is influenced by the way in which Nazarbaev consolidated his rule in the late Gorbachev era. Already strengthened by the alliances and institutions built in this period, the president had forged an elite team which he carried into the early independence period. Unlike Yeltsin who immediately abolished the Communist Party, Nazarbaev chose to allow the KPK to proceed with a scheduled congress, signalling to the elite his wish for overall administrative continuity in the context of an anticipated new specific round of appointments to the government. In October 1991 the president appointed a number of economists to his cabinet, including Erik Asanbaev as vice-president, Uzakbai Karamanov (head of the Council of Ministers) as chairman of a new Council of Ministers, and Daulet Sembaev (former head of Nazarbaev's economic advisery council) as vice premier. Sergei Tereshchenko, a Russian-Ukrainian, was appointed to the post of Prime Minister. An agronomist by training and born in the Russian Far East, he had, while studying in then Chimkent, mastered Kazakh. Nazarbaev additionally appointed the first of several foreign economic advisers, including Grigory Yavlinsky, one of the authors of the 500 Days plan of economic transformation Gorbachev had commissioned, then rejected. Although Nazarbaev appointed this team directly under his control, it was located in the government, creating a dual executive.

Asanbaev was part of a significant number of reformers within this early presidential administration and government who promoted gradual liberalization. Nazarbaev initially sought their advice; in these early days he perceived their support as crucial to his presidency. As a key concession to the reformers, the president allowed Asanbaev to head the drafting of Kazakhstan's first post-independence Constitution, or as Duchacek calls this formal distribution of power within the state, the 'power map'.[43] The commission was initially headed by the vice-president. In May 1991 a round-table discussion involving commission members, deputies and parliamentarians from other Soviet republics debated the proposed draft, and in October the revised draft was submitted to a group of academics for comment.[44]

The twelfth parliament and president differed on whether the republic should be called parliamentary or presidential but overall the opposition from Supreme Soviet deputies on whether the republic should move to presidential was slight. Nazarbaev did not by then appear strong enough to impose a presidential republic, even if he was explicit that a republic with substantial presidential powers was his intention. Already in October 1991 in an interview with the Japanese newspaper *Hokkaido Shimbun*, President Nazarbaev stated: 'I see Kazakhstan as a democratic, presidential republic, with a professional parliament, elected on a multiparty basis, and with strong executive power in the centre and in the regions'.[45] By the end of December 1991 Nazarbaev had taken over the Constitutional Commission and persuaded former opponents to presidential rule to join him. Examples were S. Zimanov, M. Raev, K. Suleimenov and N. Shaikhenov. Nazarbaev ensured that the Constitution incorporated democratic rules and procedures and parliament was actively involved in its adoption.[46] Unlike Uzbekistan's Islam Karimov and Turkmenistan's Saparmurat Niyazov, Nazarbaev was not creating a cult of his own personality. The Constitution very clearly provided for mandatory succession by forbidding a president to serve more than two terms; it included a separation of powers between executive, legislative and judiciary and a legislature with real budgetary and law-making powers. Nevertheless, Nazarbaev was more successful than Yeltsin in negotiating approval for what he called a 'strong presidential republic'.[47] He successfully argued the need for strong presidential power which would enable the president to overcome the problems of a transition period demanding substantial and painful economic reform in a multiethnic state.[48] The document[49] was passed by an overwhelming majority at the ninth session of the Supreme Soviet of the twelfth convention on 28 January 1993.[50]

Despite his conviction that 'the stabilization of the economy and the transition to the market demand a categorical ban on any party, political, or ideological interference in this process', Nazarbaev began in early 1993 to create top-down political parties.[51] The key examples of these parties were, in the order of their formation, the Union of Unity and Progress for Kazakhstan, the People's Congress Party (PNFK later renamed SNEK), and the Union of People's Unity of Kazakhstan or UPU (renamed People's Unity Party or PUP). Of particular note was PNEK whose chairman Olzhas Suleimenov became an increasingly outspoken critic of the president. Suleimenov was also buoyed through metals trading, initial funds for which were made available from the Nevada-Semipalatinsk movement. Both Suleimenov and the head of UPU, Serik Abdrakhmanov, openly declared in 1994 their intention to stand for the presidency in the then scheduled 1995 presidential elections.

Differences between the twelfth parliament and the president were to emerge after the passing of the 1993 Constitution. They were dominated by a personality clash between the president and Speaker of Parliament, Serikbolsyn Abdildin. Parliamentary newspapers such as *Sovety Kazakhstana* and *Halik Keversi*, for example, published Abdildin's articles whenever the president was out of the country, which they would not dare when Nazarbaev was at home. One such interview was entitled 'one mountain, two peaks'. Parliament also represented distinct economic interests which fiercely opposed an IMF-backed stabilization programme, something which Nazarbaev and the government of Tereshchenko had tried to push through since the beginning of 1993. Nazarbaev was getting impatient; Kazakhstan had launched privatization back in 1991, but now the country was lagging behind Russia in its economic reform programme. The parliament's control chamber, headed by Abdrakhmanov, possessed compromising data on the executive elite.

Nazarbaev seized the initiative and 'invited' parliament to dissolve itself in December 1993. He justified the self-dissolution by stating that independent Kazakhstan had not yet held democratic elections, which would be scheduled for March 1994. At many key points in parliament's history, the president has been personally present and this was no exception. After hearing Nazarbaev's passionate appeal for self-dissolution, one deputy intervened to declare that Nazarbaev's actions were illegal. Nazarbaev left the chamber and returned only after a formal apology, and nearly all voted in favour of dissolution. Upon dissolution, the president decreed the status and income of the parliamentarians, and local commentators suspected a deal with parliamentarians had been struck.[52]

An additional decree granted the president plenipotentiary powers until the new parliamentary elections scheduled for 17 March 1994.[53] These powers included the unilateral right to make personnel appointments, to adopt a referendum and to declare a state of emergency without recourse to parliament until the first session of the newly elected parliament.[54] This law was in open violation of the existing Constitution, since it gave the president powers which, according to the Constitution, belonged exclusively to the Supreme Soviet.[55]

Of the 177 candidates for the parliamentary elections, 42 were picked from a 'state list' (*gosudarstvennyi spisok*) compiled by the president.

Nevertheless, the regional legislative bodies (*maslikhats*) in 1994 were not dissolved. Although partly handpicked, this parliament was not to prove subservient. The resistance to the draft second constitution was greater, however. Vitalii Voronov and Aleksandr Peregrin were the two deputies who actively opposed the draft Constitution in the twelfth Convention.[56] Both ethnic Russian, one a trained lawyer who had worked in the procuracy, the other a researcher, they were to become founders of what was then a key oppositional movement, 'The Legal Development of Kazakhstan'.

## 1995: Legalizing a Presidential Republic

In March 1995, the Constitutional Court, at the alleged prompting of the president, dismissed the thirteenth parliament on the basis of an alleged complaint lodged one year previously by an Almaty candidate, Tatiana Kviatkovskaia.[57] She complained that she had been disadvantaged by the large size of her own constituency, with smaller districts in Almaty enjoying disproportionately large voting powers. The Constitutional Court, on the basis of this single constituency, declared the entire 1994 parliamentary elections illegal. The dissolution of parliament automatically reinstated the president's plenipotentiary powers until December 1995, when new parliamentary elections were held. The alleged almost unanimous support for the president in the 29 April 1995 referendum granted him the powers to push through the new Constitution of August 1995 with substantially increased powers. This April referendum also extended presidential rule to December 2000, permitting the president to avoid the competitive presidential elections scheduled for 1996, which might have been contested by two candidates, Olzhas Suleimenov and Gaziz Aldamzharov, who, as mentioned, had become potential rivals to Nazarbaev.

The 1995 Constitution differed from its predecessor by establishing the dominance of executive power at the national level in both the government and presidential administration; dual executives in parliament and the judiciary prevented any meaningful separation of powers. Up to 1995 this executive dominance spanned government as well as the presidential administration, by 2001 power had been concentrated in one institution, the presidential administration.

*Azamat*, referring to a citizens' movement, was organized in 1996 by Petr Svoik, Galym Abilseitov and Murat Auezov. Petr Svoik was dismissed as chair of the Antimonopoly Committee in 1996, Abilseitov in 1995 and Auezov, who had been recalled from his post in Beijing as Ambassador to China in 1995, had not been offered an alternative position.

## 1996–1998: Centralization and Concentration

Once the new Constitution had been adopted, the Nazarbaev regime sought to consolidate its power through concentration and centralization.

This phase was to become the run-up to the calling of premature elections for 1999, which, in 1995, had been scheduled for 2000. To concentrate power in this phase, Nazarbaev weakened government and brought key actors into the presidential administration. Some important opposition media and actors were co-opted. To centralize power, Nazarbaev placed Erzhan Utembaev in charge of a thorough shake-up of both central and regional administrations.

Under World Bank recommendations, Utembaev halved the size of the presidential administration in spring 1997. The number of ministries fell from 19 in 1992 to 12 in 1998. The Cabinet of Ministers Administration was cut by 25 per cent. The most drastic changes occurred with the 4 March 1997 decree that reduced the number of ministries from twenty to fourteen and state committees from twelve to two.[58] Like other former Soviet states, Kazakhstan inherited a sprawling bureaucratic machine from the Soviet period. In its July 1996 report, the World Bank ranked Kazakhstan among countries with the highest level of government employment, with about 6.4 public employees per hundred – a total of some one million employees in a population which by 1998 had fallen from 16.1 on independence to 14.8 million.[59] Functions of the abolished ministries, state committees, committees and agencies were transferred to newly established ministries. In a decree of 22 April 1997, Nazarbaev transferred the powers to investigate corruption from the KGB-successor, the National Security Committee, to the State Investigations Committee of the Interior Ministry.[60] Furthermore, on 4 May 1997, regions were cut by five, from nineteen to fourteen, ousting 5, 000 state employees and saving US$20 million.[61] Further downsizing occurred in advance of the relocation of the capital from Almaty to Astana. In July 1997, Deputy Prime Minister Alexander Pavlov announced that 10, 000 more state jobs would be axed.[62]

Speaking on Kazakh Television Channel on 22 April 1997, President Nazarbaev stated: 'I have issued a decree to cut the staff of ministries and departments. By cutting numbers by half, approximately 0.5 billion tenge have been economized. Moreover, 93 fewer official cars will be needed. In Almaty alone, 1, 000 [public sector workers] have been made redundant'.[63]

In 1997 the tabloid newspaper *Karavan* was Central Asia's only newspaper to have its own printing press. 1997, however, witnessed the increased tightening of control over the media. *Karavan* was bought by the establishment and, although having changed ownership since the purchase, it remains in the hands of the incumbent elite. Independent regional radio and television stations were abolished and national television became increasingly monopolized by the state television company Khabar, run by the president's daughter, Dariga Nazarbaeva.

Other family members with prominent positions in the elite included two sons-in-law: Rakhat Aliev and Timur Kulibaev, who were appointed in

1997 as head of the Tax Inspectorate (later as Deputy Head of the National Security Committee) and Deputy Head of the then named Kazakhoil (the state national oil company) respectively.

Having consolidated his power, Nazarbaev in 1998 launched an informal election campaign for the 2000 presidential elections. Although Nazarbaev's televised national address on 30 September 1998 promised far-sweeping democratization measures and ruled out early elections, Nazarbaev had meanwhile struck a deal with parliament to call early elections for January 1999.[64] In return for their support, members of both houses of parliament would see their next term-of-office extended by one more year each (after the parliamentary elections of October 1999). New contenders would have greater impediments to elections as parties and movements participating in parliamentary elections in October 1999 would need to pass only a 7 instead of a 10 per cent threshold of the popular vote to sit in parliament. But the most important of parliament's amendments was extension of the president's term of office from five to seven years (effectively, then, until 2006). The president's required minimum age was increased from 35 to 40, and the age limit of 65 lifted.[65] All these amendments were incorporated in the October 1998 legislation and suggested Nazarbaev's hold on power was being institutionalized.

## 1999–2001: Elite Fragmentation and the Onset of Repression

The calling of early elections left only three months for campaigning, and only the incumbent president possessed the financial and organizational means to campaign. The election commission had barred the only serious contender to Nazarbaev, Akezhan Kazhegeldin (Prime Minister, 1994–1997) because of accusations of money laundering in Belgium and for participating in an unsanctioned meeting of the yet unregistered 'Movement for Honest Elections'. The commission claimed this was within constitutional practice since Clause 4.1 of the 8 May 1998 constitutional amendment to the electoral law stipulated that no one with a criminal record, including a minor offence, was allowed to stand for electoral office.[66] Deemed a dishonest election campaign by OSCE monitors, the elections also set a precedent in international monitoring when the OSCE refused to recognize the outcome.[67] The US and Germany (in its capacity as Head of the EU) both condemned the elections.[68]

Olcott concludes that the 1999 elections 'helped to transform Kazakhstan into the kind of country that President Nursultan Nazarbaev wants it to be, one with a strong president and an opposition that is sharply restricted in its freedom of action and range of activities.'[69]

Even so, in November 2001 Kazakhstan's political establishment unprecedentedly witnessed open disagreement between its members. On 14 November 2001, Aliev, Nazarbaev's son-in-law, resigned as Deputy Chairman of the National Security Committee. Most domestic analysts described the resignation as forced by an alliance of members of the elite unhappy with the influence he had amassed. Aliev remained an important figure through his substantial media and corporate interests. On 17 November, he was appointed deputy commander of the presidential guard, and Nazarbaev publicly defended him on national television. Aliev was also successful in his bid for a share in the National Savings Bank, Halyk. The apparent reconciliation between Nazarbaev and Aliev prompted an alliance of technocrats, businessmen and parliamentarians to announce the formation of the Democratic Choice of Kazakhstan (DCK) in November 2001. The key founding members of this new movement were Deputy Prime Minister Uraz Dzhandosov, Labour and Social Protection Minister Alikhan Baimenov, Deputy Defence Minister Zhannat Ertlesova and Pavlodar Governor Ghalymzhan Zhakiianov, as well as Kazkommertsbank head Serzhan Sukhanberdin and Temirbank head Mukhtar Abliazov, a former energy minister. On 19 November, Prime Minister Kasymzhomart called on Nazarbaev to dismiss Dzhandosov, Ertlesova, Baimenov and Zhakiianov, accusing them of intrigue and of using calls for further democratization as an excuse to build up their business interests. The premier threatened to resign if Nazarbaev did not cede to this request. It is likely that Nazarbaev staged Tokaev's intervention, since the president was able to express regret at then dismissing the ministers, who offered to resign following Tokaev's ultimatum, thus distancing himself from intra-elite rivalries.

## ECONOMIC REFORM

This political periodization is closely tied to the economic domain. Changes to the economic domain have been dominated by privatization policy, foreign investment (metals and minerals, oil and gas) and macroeconomic stabilization.

Privatization in 1991–2001 has passed through three stages: small-scale privatization, including housing (1991–1992); mass privatization and, at the same time, privatization of agriculture (which involved the privatization of livestock and equipment but not land) (1993–1995); and case-by-case privatization which under the premiership of Kazhegeldin (1994–1997) also involved the attraction of foreign management contracts.

In the spring of 1991, still under communism when 'privatization' was not a fully acceptable term, the Kazakh Supreme Soviet adopted a law on the more politically acceptable term de-statification. At the June 1991 plenary session of the KPK's Central Committee, Nursultan Nazarbaev declared: 'It is no secret that not everyone in our country supports this law. But answer this: Can we disperse a social market economy without de-statification and privatization? Can we increase production effectively without dispersing property?'[70] The law was adopted but in this first phase was limited to small- and medium-sized enterprises. By March 1993 about 30 per cent of trading companies had been privatized, 40 per cent of construction, 25 per cent of foodstuffs.[71] In this period it was fashionable in the local press to refer to the Chinese model and to East European countries that had pursued reform gradually. Considerable popular scepticism also existed about attracting foreigner investors on whom the newly independent republic might become dependent. This view, of course, suited national company directors who stood to receive not less than 10 per cent of the shares. Examples of well-known small companies in this phase were the furniture company Merei (Almaty) and the metals company Zhezkazgantsvetmet. In reality, however, productivity did not increase, and the period was instead characterized by high inflation, breakdown in traditional links with the collapse of Gosplan, and barter. Capitalization, moreover, was not occurring.

In March 1993 parliament passed a second law on destatification (*razgosudarstvleniia*) and privatization. Covering a two-year period (1993–1995), this second stage was largely based on the Czech voucher system which was later also used in Russia. All Kazakhstani citizens received vouchers representing a set value which they were able to invest in various investment privatization funds (IPFs). Fund managers would then use their vouchers to bid for up to 20 per cent of the shares in the medium-sized enterprises that were offered at privatization auctions. Of the shares, 51 per cent were to be auctioned, 10 per cent to be given to workers and staff, and 39 per cent went to the government. Although the aim was to spread the number of funds, vouchers remained lodged predominantly in ten of the two hundred or so registered. Olcott notes that the largest fund, Butya-Kapital, owned by a reputed relative of the regime, Bulat Abilov, 'received nearly 10 per cent of the republic's vouchers, making it by far the largest single actor in the second stage of privatization.'[72] But Nazarbaev faced broad-based opposition to market reform from the Twelfth Supreme Soviet and this was part of the reason for its 'self-dissolution' in 1993.

In December 1994, dissatisfied with the course of privatization and emboldened by their higher profile, leaders of these funds wrote an open letter to the president, urging him to include major, rather than simply medium-sized, industries in the privatization process. Only light industry had been privatized, they argued, and giants that could generate profits for the IPFs, such as the giant steel mill Karmetkombinat in Karaganda, were excluded. When no response from the elite was forthcoming, the IPF leaders decided instead to form a movement, *Novoe Pokolenie* (New Generation). The key leaders included: Kozykorpesh Esenberlin (Aziya-Leasing); Abilov (Butya); Nurlan Smagulov (Astana Motors); Nurlan Kapparov (Aktsept), Nurzhan Subkhanberdin (Kazkommertsbank); and Mukhtar Abliazov (Astana-Holding). Even with such seeming strength and organization, the movement placed the President and Prime Minister above recrimination. They instead blamed some state officials and above all conservative MPs who were unwilling to talk about the language law, the nature of the state and land privatization.

By contrast, the privatization of agriculture went at a breakneck pace, primarily because the central state wished to cut subsidies which were draining state coffers. Regional heads were asked to give monthly accounts of the agricultural privatization process. Olzhas Suleimenov of *Narodnii Kongress* went so far as to say that 'today's decollectivization has become for farmers as much a tragedy as Stalin's collectivization was then.'[73] The agricultural privatization process was equated by many as abandonment. The law in land, passed in December 1995, reintroduced private ownership, which was not fully extended to agriculture until 2000.

A third stage in privatization was introduced at the end of 1993 with case-by-case privatization. At the beginning it applied to companies with over 5, 000 workers and the first to be auctioned was the Almaty Tobacco Factory. The sale of the factory to Philip Morris was signed in November 1993, the same month that Kazakhstan's national currency, the *tenge*, was introduced. At the time this was the FSU's single largest foreign investment project signed, with Philip Morris earmarking $240 million over five years. Relations with the company, however, soured; the company accused the government of failing to provide fair operating conditions, such as the government's agreement in 1994 to allow RJR Reynolds to set up a competitive outlet at Shymkent's confectionary factory on, what Philip Morris argued, were better production terms. The government had, it said, also refused to include tax norms in the contract (taxes were raised from 20 to 30 per cent already in spring 1994).[74] The stand-off between Philip Morris, local management and government was resolved only when Nazarbaev firmly intervened. Unlike small and mass privatizations, these case-by-case tenders were dependent on personal relations between the investor and state official and needed a firm line from the latter. The incident was decisive for impressing on the president that Tereshchenko and his government were unable to deal effectively with foreign investors and had to be removed.

The appointment of the new Prime Minister, Kazhegeldin, marked a new phase in this third case-by-case stage by introducing management contracts. While such management contracts have been practised elsewhere in the post-communist world, Kazakhstan stands out in the number it signed. Whole sectors were given over to foreign management.

Examples of key management contracts were: the Joint Stock Company (JSC) of Pavlodar's Aluminium Factory (managed by Whiteswan Ltd); the JSC of Zhezkazgan's copper concern, Zhezkazgantsvetmet (managed by Samsung Deutschland); JSC Dansk Mining Corporation (managed by Japan Chrome Corporation); and the Sokolovsk-Sarbai Mining Facility (managed by Ivedon International Ltd). Most of these corporations were offshore investors.

Once entire economic sectors were handed to foreign management and, in some cases, eventually to foreign ownership, the process was stalled. Kazhegeldin's successor, Nurlan Balgimbaev, was appointed partly because he was a well-known opponent of privatization policies. Under Balgimbaev, the stock-market flotation of Kazakhstan's blue-chip companies was temporarily halted. The centre tried to regain control over enterprises in the provinces, not least because it needed their export revenues to finance a gaping budget deficit. Attempts to renationalize provoked disputes with some foreign investors, with even well-known western oil companies being charged with tax evasion. In contrast to Kazhegeldin's privatization policy, Balgimbaev's industrial policy, sponsored and developed by his Trade and Industry Minister Mukhtar Abliazov, promised a statist approach to reform. Balgimbaev's successor and former Foreign Minister Kasymzhomart Tokaev replaced Abliazov with a former northern-based akim Danial Akhmetov. To some observers, this suggested a mere gesture toward including regional representatives in central policy.

Between 1998 and 2001, while politically we saw the onset of repression and the management of elites, stagnation began in privatization. After all, by 1997, Kazakhstan had come to enjoy the highest per capita foreign direct investment of all post-communist states after Hungary.

The period of political elite infighting described in the previous section came at a time of unprecedented economic growth for Kazakhstan. In 2000, for the first time, Kazakhstan registered a budget surplus; part of the justification for the mass privatization programme had been to close the budget deficit. It was by now the fastest growing of all post-Soviet states. Kazakhstan had successfully implemented a macroeconomic stabilization programme and continued to offer incentives to foreign investors.

While the government succeeded in attracting major transnational companies and initially boasted a liberal foreign investment law, [75] the government was soon to have major disputes with each of the major transnational companies it attracted. The most notable were with Belgian company Tractebel, the Canadian company Hurricane Hydrocarbons and the American oil giant (then named) Chevron and the majority of disputes were over levels of tax obligations and profit repatriation.

By 2000, Kazakhstan's government and media had called publicly on foreign companies to increase their use of domestic Kazakhstani companies in the production process. In particular, foreign oil and gas companies were criticized for failing to subcontract to local food and construction companies, opting instead for imported products. By 2001, the economic debate had become focused upon the need to develop domestic business and to use domestic companies in the production process. In particular, foreign oil and gas companies were criticized for failing to subcontract to local food and construction companies, opting instead for imported products. Four principal factors explained popular, worker and government support for this increased use of indigenous light industry companies: greater availability of domestic sources of income were perceived to create possibilities for developing indigenous production capacity; the new Amnesty Law promised to bring in more indigenous capital; lobbying by local businessmen had strengthened; and political power had become dependent on good relations with domestic corporate groups. In short, both new domestic business opportunities and political constraints on the government meant that the development of domestic business was monopolizing the economic 'debate' in 2001. By also espousing this view, the government may have hoped to garner support both from the population at large and, crucially, from key economic groupings.

The political and economic transformation outlined above provided the backdrop to three major themes that have dominated Kazakhstan's independence: centre-periphery relations; the politics of identity; and foreign policy. By way of conclusion to this chapter they are briefly summarized here.

With the loss of Union transfers and Kazakhstan's decision to engage in rapid economic transition from plan to market, the nature of political and economic relations between the centre and the regions emerged as a major issue. Adjusting from being a centrally planned economy was extremely painful. The loss of substantial transfers from the Union government was accompanied by added responsibilities for defence and foreign debt service obligations. Traditionally, the north, central and eastern provinces had been more industrial, urban and Russian-dominated, whilst the southern and western ones have been Kazakh-dominated and largely rural. The years since independence have witnessed increased differentiation, but along new axes. The western provinces house substantial mineral resources and the expectant income gulf between these provinces has placed enormous strains on the centre's ability to manage the periphery.[76]

Although this new relationship had to be struck, it was not until 1997 that the centre undertook any administrative reorganization. Until then, Kazakhstan had retained the 19+1 formula of the Soviet era, which itself dates from the 1950s.[77] In 1997, the five regions of Taldykorgan, Semipalatinsk, Zhezkazgan, Kokshetau and Torgai were abolished. Termed 'regional optimization', the process fused these five provinces with adjoining territories (as shown in the above table). Taldykorgan and Torgai were joined in April 1997[78] and the remaining three in May of that year. The decree served to increase the average size of both district and province; northern provinces in particular have grown in geographic and population size.

Partly as an attempt to secure greater control over these northern border provinces, the centre literally moved northwards; in 1998 Akmola (renamed Astana) in north-central Kazakhstan replaced south-eastern Almaty as the political capital of the republic. The intention to relocate the capital was

announced in a presidential decree issued on 15 September 1995, Akmola
was decreed the new capital on 20 October 1997 and renamed Astana on
6 May 1998. Almaty in the process lost its capital status but managed to
maintain a status equivalent to regional status. New legislation in April
1999 incorporated the town of Kokshetau and several new districts
into Akmola, but Kokshetau was also made provincial capital in lieu
of Astana.[79] Kokshetau had been the former head of the now abolished
province. Kokshetau was partly chosen because it housed the Ministry of
Ecology. The majority of ministries had relocated by 1999 to Astana from
Almaty. Official motives for this decision emphasized how Almaty is both
situated in an earthquake zone and unable to expand physically because
of adjacent mountains. Most unofficial explanations linked the move to
a desire to increase the government's hold on the northern regions and
thereby the territorial integrity of the state, as well as to direct the process
of internal migration, particularly the encouragement of ethnic Kazakhs to
move to the northern regions.

## Kazakhstan's 14 regions including Almaty and Astana cities (June 1997–)

Akmola (incorporating part of Torgai)
Aktobe
Atyrau
Alma-Ata (incorporating Taldykorgan)
East Kazakhstan (incorporating Semei)
Zhambyl
Karaganda (incorporating Zhezkazgan)
Kostanai (incorporating part of Torgai)
Kzylorda
Mangystau
North Kazakhstan (incorporating Kokshetau)
Pavlodar
South Kazakhstan
West Kazakhstan

Just as centre-periphery relations were shaped by the growing
authoritarianism of the republic, so too were the elite's relations with its
new power container, the independent state. Neither a state (Kazakhstani)
nor a national (Kazakh) identity was readily available to the new nation-
and state-builders. It was possible in 1991 to question whether one or
two nations had been born, and the period between 1992 and 1994 was
dominated by discussions of the viability of bilingualism and dual
citizenship. The central Kazakhstani elite feared the possible union of its
northern provinces with Russia and attempted to construct a civic identity
which stressed affiliation to state rather than nation. It thus resisted dual

citizenship which it equated with dual loyalty and a possible north-south split. The choice of a unitary state further ruled out the granting of territorial mechanisms to maintain cultural differences, and the regime became significantly centralized. This centralization, as we have seen strongly associated with the authoritarian nature of the Kazakhstani regime, also aimed to stem the re-emergence of the traditional sub-national fault-lines of clan, tribe and horde, mentioned at the start of this chapter. These legitimation tasks were somewhat facilitated by the 1999 census results which declared Kazakhs now a majority at 53.4 per cent.

Vivid concerns of intra-Kazakh balance have often been greater than those of achieving some ethnic proportionality, partly because of the elite being confident that numerical superiority would be obtained after mass emigration and a relative ageing of the non-titular ethnic groups. The key discussion on intra-Kazakh relations as it relates to the elite concerned the degree to which, once again, clan, tribe and zhuz would be succumbing to transformation, and which of these levels, if any, would dominate and how they would relate to the nation.

Issues of identity were, finally, closely linked to Kazakhstan's relation ship with the wider world. A tension existed between, on the one hand, its multivector foreign policy and, on the other, its continued prioritization of Russia in this multipolarity. As mentioned in the Introduction, this was somewhat resolved in spring 2001 when the multivector policy prioritized contiguous powers, particularly Russia, China and Central Asia. As in domestic politics, Kazakhstan's foreign policy has been multifaceted, straddling various interests, its direction devoid of strong ideological content.

This 'multivector' foreign policy, as it came to be known, was primarily motivated by the republic's need to secure alternative oil pipeline routes. Astana has pursued a multiple pipeline policy, and the government has not ruled out options in its search for oil export routes to world markets. The full launch of the Caspian Pipeline Consortium line from the giant Tengiz field to the Russian Black Sea port of Novorossiisk occurred in October 2001, nine years after the project to complete a half-built Soviet-era line was first approved formally. Work on the Baku-Tbilisi-Ceyhan (BTC) oil pipeline began in 2002, promising to be the first pipeline in the Caspian region to both run direct to a deepwater port on the high seas and to bypass Russia and Iran. With the discovery of crude oil at Kashagan, investors appear to have shown interest in a Kazakhstan-Turkmenistan-Iran line.[80]

While Kazakhstan has since 1991 pursued its multivector foreign policy, professing to seek allies in several different directions, including the West, Middle and Far East, Russia remains its priority partner. During the Yeltsin era, Kazakhstan was keen to escape from Russia's orbit, partly because of Russia's own disengagement from Central Asia. Since the advent of Putin, however, Kazakhstan has welcomed Russia as its close ally: Russia's pragmatic re-engagement in Central Asia and the Caspian basin coincides with increased instabilities from Kazakhstan's southern neighbours, particularly in the form of porous borders and perceived threats of Islamic fundamentalism, insurgencies, and drugs trafficking. These issues led the political and military leadership in 2000 to identify a set of possible short- and medium-term threats to national security. These included local conflicts or instability in neighbouring countries affecting Kazakhstan's internal situation and posing the risk of spill-over; infiltration of 'religious extremist' or 'criminal' armed groups into Kazakhstan; and dissemination of inflammatory religious or nationalist propaganda. Russia's pledges and its foreign policy in the short term have promised a proactive policy.

Regional challenges have been exacerbated by an increasingly unilateralist government of Uzbekistan. Tashkent's inclination towards unilateralism is an attempt to reassert its regional hegemony. Uzbekistan is the most populous Central Asian state and has pretensions for regional dominance. In 2000, Tashkent unilaterally demarcated its border with Kazakhstan in the Saryagach area of the South Kazakhstan region, despite the absence of any border agreement between the two countries. Given the presence of strategic Uzbek communities in regions of neighbouring states – such as South Kazakhstan – there were fears that Tashkent might feel justified in expanding its borders. The presidents reportedly shared a personal rivalry which reflects their states' competition for regional leadership in Central Asia.

International problems become domestic ones and, by the same token, with its limited defence possibilities, Kazakhstan has often been forced to internationalize a looming domestic issue. In the immediate term, the reaction of Kazakhstan to security threats, as with other states, has been to close borders and tighten security.

Despite short-term temptations to become self-reliant and self-protective, Kazakhstan nevertheless continued to cooperate with outside powers. In particular it participated in the cooperation between China and Russia. The Shanghai Five, comprising the five states on the former Soviet-Chinese border (Kazakhstan, Kyrgyzstan, Tajikistan, China and Russia), was enlarged in June 2001 to include Uzbekistan and its functions expanded to include cooperation on regional security threats. Without such interlocking agreements, Kazakhstan's external sovereignty would probably have been severely diminished. The full repercussions of September 11th are of course outside the scope of this book because we end in November, but initially September 11th did seem to divert the regime's attention temporarily from domestic politics, giving the backdrop for an open expression of elite disagreements and prompting the events of November 2001.

# CONCLUSIONS

All five policy spheres indicated contradictory processes. In terms of the elite's relationship to political institutions, the regime has seen policies of both liberalization and authoritarianism. In the centre's relationship with the regions, the polity is a *de jure* unitary state that has witnessed *de facto* decentralization. The elite's policies of nation- and state-building have swung between ethnic and civic nationalism (with all the problems that this dichotomy involves). Economic policy has embraced privatization and foreign investment but the primary beneficiary of this process has been the state, not the market. Finally, foreign policy was not unidirectional or ideological but 'multivector' and pragmatic, and also simultaneously encouraged foreign investment and stalled, attempting populism through the introduction of an industrial policy. Overall, oil revenues were increasing the political stakes for all actors, domestic and foreign.

These inconsistencies have therefore also shaped the environment (see Chapter Six), and their effects have been: the unintended de facto and perceived decentralization and alienation of the regions; the alienation of non-Kazakhs, and the delegitimation of the regime in their eyes; the unintended revival of sub-ethnicity at the regional level; elite struggles between professionals and loyalists, between interest groups, and between centre and region; and the loss of popular legitimacy by the government, in terms of absence of leadership, ideas and policy.

This heterogeneity, as we shall see in the coming chapters, is the product of both agency and choice. Various opposites, fragmentations or cleavages have spun and are rooted in elite policies. The state was pulled in various directions and causes and consequences in the regime's politics were thus often complex and contradictory. Bargaining by forces within and outside the state demanded balance, negotiation and measure in ideology, practice and policy.[81]

# Chapter Two

# ELITES, CAREERS AND INSTITUTIONS

In a study of cities in the American state of Georgia by Floyd Hunter, the investigations generally concluded that a small number of people, mainly from upper- or upper-middle-class backgrounds, and/or representing business interests, were predominant in the community. C. Wright Mills applied these findings to the national level in the United States. In his influential study *The Power Elite*, Mills argued that three interlocking groups dominated the 'command posts' of American society: political leaders, corporate leaders and military leaders. Dahl challenged these interpretations, arguing that the image of a closed power elite should be replaced by that of a relatively competitive environment in which there are dispersed inequalities of power.[1] Additionally, Suzanne Keller has argued instead that society is governed by strategic elites which 'consist of the minority of individuals responsible for keeping the organized system, society, in working order, functioning so as to meet and surpass the perennial collective crises that occur.'[2] Does the Kazakhstani case suggest that members of the elite were associated predominantly with one formal institution, or were they spread more evenly across various institutional locations?

This chapter outlines elite structure in institutional and career terms.[3] To recall, interviews with the elite were conducted predominantly at one period in time, namely over an eighteen month period between late 1995 and early 1997. As explained in the Introduction, for temporal comparisons other opinion polls are employed as are the ratings of (part of the) panel of experts (within time and money constraints).

# INSTITUTIONAL RANKING

Control over recruitment is an extension of elite power. Not only can certain formal qualifications be imposed, but so can other selective devices to establish the appropriateness of any particular candidate for entrance. Elites, psychologically and politically, tend to recruit like-minded individuals; often this is more a question of values and behaviour than of social origins. This means, of course, that the elite is by definition and by practice an exclusive group. The nomenklatura system allowed the CPSU to maintain its self-appointed prerogative of the selection, training and allocation of cadres, [4] and this task now fell after independence to the selectorate of the Kazakhstani elite, that small number around and including Nazarbaev that could appoint and dismiss senior political advisers to officials.

Monocratic regimes are usually characterized by a selectorate of one. In the difficult years after the Turkish revolution of 1919, Ataturk, undisputed leader of the new regime, took personal charge of nominations to the Grand National Assembly.[5] There is some indication that Nazarbaev's recruitment became increasingly monocratic from 1991, even if many informal accounts described a president who continued to be influenced by advice from an inner circle of advisers.[6] That inner circle, in line with the developments among the political elite, underwent some changes.

Between 1991 and 2001 the selectorate became smaller, more homogenous and centralized. This would confirm the general tendency we noted in the two preceding chapters. The selectorate by 1998 was immediate to Nazarbaev: it was composed of family, relatives, close friends and loyal colleagues. The move to Astana appeared to have abetted the narrowing of the selectorate and political elite, as former members of the elite not selected by the president often remained in Almaty. This narrowing of the selectorate is significant. It implies that the elite as a whole was likely to become smaller, more homogeneous and centralized, which is again borne out by the data.

The panel of 41 experts (see Introduction) was asked to rank, in terms of power and influence, both the members and the institutions of the political elite in 1995. Different respondents emphasized different individuals according to the issue areas with which they were familiar, but the panel of experts deliberately represented a broad spectrum of issue areas. They expressed the following institutional ranking and positional structure of the elite.

### Table 1. Institutional Ranking of Influence: 1995–1996[7]

Level 1:
President

Level 2:
Head of Presidential Administration, Prime Minister, Deputy Heads
of Administration, Individuals close to the President either within the
Presidential Administration or outside formal structures
Level 3:
KNB (Kazakhstan National Security Council), the State Oil Company
Kazakhoil, Presidential Advisors, State Secretary, Some Party Leaders
Level 4:
National Bank, Tax Police, Regional Heads, First and Deputy Prime
Ministers, Ministry of Interior, Ministry of Finance, Ministry of Foreign
Affairs, Key Presidential Administration Departments, Security and State
Committees, other key positions in Presidential Apparat, Procurator General,
some Members of Parliament
Level 5:
Other Presidential Administration Departments, other Banks, Speakers of
Parliament and Mazhilis, Presidential Spokesmen, Supreme Court, Ministry
of Information and Social Accord
Level 6:
Ministries of Economics, Agriculture, Defence, Justice, Transport, Other
State and Economic Committees, Prime Ministerial Advisors, Chancellories,
Parliamentary Committee Chairs, Regional Courts, Government Committees
Level 7:
Low Ministries: Labour, Science, Education, Ecology; Arbitrage Court; some
Ambassadors, some Opposition members

At the top of the hierarchy (Level 1) was the president.[8] Levels 2 and 3
consisted principally of individuals in the presidential administration who
were associated with issues of domestic security and economic reform,
and individuals close to the president who enjoyed personal influence and
might or might not be associated with the formal institutions of power.
Most often, the less visible men or women behind the scenes were either
family or close friends of the president or those of foreign economic
advisers or investors. By definition, they lay outside the formal structure
of power and were therefore often beyond detection. Level 2 also included
the key gatekeepers.

Top-level figures in the presidential administration included: the vice-
president (an office abolished in 1995); the presidential security council
head (by 2001, outside the structure of the presidential administration);
and presidential inspectors (modelled on their Russian counterparts, these
presidential-appointed officials, based in the capital, were responsible for
reporting to the president on developments in their appointed region). The
second-tier officials in the presidential administration were department
and committee heads, presidential advisers and assistants. Presidential
assistants were legally higher in rank than advisers, but advisers were

often cited as equally influential. Levels 1, 2 and 3 may be viewed as coterminous with what Putnam identifies as the proximate decision-makers in his pyramid of power.[9]

Level 4 encompassed the office of the Prime Minister and those actors in government dealing with economic reform and domestic security. They exercised the power to make and implement decisions and they sometimes set the agenda. The deputy prime ministers often also held the post of Minister. In 1995, the panel of experts identified the following institutions as the key ministries: the Ministry of Oil and Gas, Ministry of Finance, Ministry of Trade and Industry, Ministry of Foreign Affairs and the Ministry of the Interior.

Level 5 was less institutionally coherent and drew actors from the presidential administration, parliament, government and procuracy as well as the heads of some regional administrations. It also included key diplomatic appointments, notably those assigned to Russia, China and the US, and some members of the cultural and private business elites.

Levels 6 and 7 were also drawn from various institutions but were political elite players predominantly in their own policy area. The principal departments at the regional level were those of the Interior, Economics and Finance. Anyone below these positions in the regional administration appeared to influence only regional politics. In March 1995, there were 20 regional governors, or akims, including the capital (then Almaty city). By 2000, their number had fallen to 14, including the new (Astana) and old capitals, as several were amalgamated.

Three main points may be noted about this institutional affiliation of the political elite. First, barring certain exceptions, the vast majority of the political elite was linked to a formal political institution, even if positional analysis formed only one part of the methodology of locating the elite (see Introduction). The additional use of reputational and decisional analysis still led us to find in 1995–1996 that members of the political elite were more often than not associated with certain institutions. There was no clearly discernible self-contained business or cultural elite. This suggests that in 1995–1996 political and social status was attached to the formal positions of office.

Second, the structure in 1995–1996 did not suggest a pluralist elite which, as depicted by Dahl, would consist of a relatively competitive environment with dispersed inequalities of power.[10] Moreover, while superficially the concentrated structure of the Kazakhstani elite bore more resemblance to Mills' power elite, it displayed two important differences. First, while in Mills' US power elite the military, large-scale corporations and the political directorate occupy the 'strategic command posts of the social structure'[11] and 'religious, educational, and family institutions are not autonomous centers of national power,'[12] in Kazakhstan, the weak military had no independent authority: only three of the 244 members were military officers and only by virtue of their holding a political, not military, post.

While the three domains of Mills' power elite, although interlocked as they 'tend to come together',[13] are initially separate, in Kazakhstan, the political subsumed the economic and cultural and were often at the outset fused, even if more fragmented by 2001. The three primary constituent groups of the political elite can be labelled political-administrative, economic, and cultural.

The fusion of economic and political power still applied in 2001, but it was more fragmented. (This is not shown by this data but by other opinion polls and commentary to which we return later.) By the end of the decade, most analysts agreed on the existence of at least six, if not eight, of these state economic groups, headed by the following individuals or organizations: Alexander Mashkevich, Oleg Li, Nurzhan Subkhanberdin, Mukhtar Abliazov, Nurlan Balgimbaev and Rakhat Aliev. Discussions about which groups were more influential than others became almost as popular as those surrounding zhuz or clan membership of individual members of the elite.

Third, Table 1 is a snapshot of the institutional architecture in 1995–1997. As suggested here, this architecture has been far from static. Departments, agencies, ministries and even regions have been dissolved or fused, and some entities even resurrected. But we can say that if institutions have intrinsically strengthened or weakened, then relationally the hierarchy of influence between these branches of power was more or less maintained until the close of 2001. For example, the apex of the presidential administration has narrowed in structure and strengthened over time, while parliament was weakened between 1995 and 1999, strengthening again thereafter. Relationally, however, the presidential administration has remained considerably stronger than parliament.

If, as we noted in the previous chapter, a dual executive was established in the early independence period, the influence of the government had overall decreased by 2001. We have instead seen an overall strengthening of the presidential administration with respect to other branches of power, as well as a strengthening of particular state organizations dealing with security and economics: the most notable being the National Security Committee (KNB) and related security agencies, others being certain institutions of economic management, such as the National Bank and the Ministry of State Income.[14] Kazakhstan's Anti-Monopoly Committee, resurrected in June 1998, continued the long line of agencies that would thereafter report directly to the president instead of to the government. Other agencies that had shifted from governmental to presidential responsibility included the National Statistics Agency, the Agency for Strategic Planning and Reforms, and, to some degree, the Strategic Investment Committee.

# INDIVIDUAL RANKING AND INSTITUTIONS

For this study, the Panel of Experts was also aked to suggest names of the ten most influential players in the republic and they produced this list for the following two time periods:

## Table 2: Core Elite Identified by the Study's Panel of Experts

| 1992–1994 | 1995–1996 |
|---|---|
| Nursultan Nazarbaev | Nursultan Nazarbaev |
| Sara Nazarbaeva | Sara Nazarbaeva |
| Nurtai Abykaev | Nurtai Abykaev |
| Sergei Tereshchenko | Akezhan Kazhegeldin |
| Erik Asanbaev | Marat Tazhin |
| Olzhas Suleimenov | Olzhas Suleimenov |
| Serikbolsyn Abdildin | Abish Kekilbaev |
| Zamanbek Nurkadilov | Daulet Sembaev |
| Daulet Sembaev | Tulegen Zhukeev |
| Kairbek Suleimenov | Marat Tazhin |
| Syzdyk Abishev | Sat Tokpakbaev |
| Nagashbai Shaikhenov | Nigmatzhan Isingarin |
| Nigmatzhan Isingarin | Vitalii Mette |
| Serikbek Daukeev | Aleksandr Pavlov |
| Uraz Dzhandosov | Sarybai Kalmurzaev |
| Grigorii Marchenko | Zhanybek Karibzhanov |
| Oleg Soskovets | Serikbek Daukeev |
| | James Giffen |
| | Kairbek Suleimenov |
| | Saginbek Tursunov |
| | Aleksandr Mashkevich |
| | Erzhan Utembaev |
| | Uraz Dzhandosov |
| | Grigorii Marchenko |

The above names were consistent with the following ratings poll conducted by VIProblem over two different time periods. Asked to rank 'influential people with prospects', their panel of experts offered:

## Table 3: VIProblem Ratings of 'Influential People With Prospects'

| August 1996 | | October 2001 | |
|---|---|---|---|
| Nursultan Nazarbaev | 38 | Nursultan Nazarbaev | 44.2 |
| President | | President | |

| | | | |
|---|---|---|---|
| Murat Auezov, Oppositional Leader 'Azamat' | 32 | Zeinulla Kakimzhanov National Savings Bank | 25.6 |
| Marat Ospanov Chairman, Mazhilis | 25 | Danial Akhmetov First Deputy PM | 23.3 |
| Akhmetzhan Esimov State Secretary | 22 | Altynbek Sarsenbaev Minister of Information | 23.3 |
| Marat Tazhin Deputy Head, Presidential Administration | 22 | Kasymzhomart Tokaev (PM) | 20.9 |
| Imangali Tasmagambetov Deputy PM | 20 | Rakhat Aliev Deputy Head, KNB | 20.9 |
| Petr Svoik Oppositional Leader 'Azamat' | 20 | Dariga Nazarbaeva Daughter of President; State Media Company | 16.3 |
| Akezhan Kazhegeldin Prime Minister (PM) | 18 | Imangali Tasmagambetov (PM) | 14 |
| Erzhan Utembaev Deputy, Higher Economic Council | 18 | Marat Tazhin Security Council Secretary | 14 |
| Nagashbai Shaikenov Deputy PM | 12 | Uraz Dzhandosov Deputy PM | 14 |
| Baltash Tursumbaev Security Council Secretary | 12 | Sarybai Kalmurzaev Head, Presidential Administration | 11.6 |
| Uraz Dzhandosov First Deputy PM | 12 | Gani Kasymov Head, Party of Patriots | 11.6 |
| Kasymzhomart Tokaev Minister of Foreign Affairs | 12 | Galimzhan Zhakiianov Akim, Pavlodar | 9.3 |
| Bulat Abilov Head, Butya Company | x | Nurlan Balgimbaev Oil Infrastructure Committee, ex-PM | 7 |
| Nigmatzhan Isingarin Head CIS Committee | x | Alikhan Baimenov State Service Agency | 7 |
| Saginbek Tursunov Head, Pres Admin | x | Grigorii Marchenko Head, National Bank | 7 |
| Altynbek Sarsenbaev Head, Information Agency (ex-Ministry) | x | Karim Masimov Minister, Transport & Communications | 7 |

Tulegen Zhukeev            x        Viktor Khrapunov        7
Ambassador, Korea                   Akim, Almaty

Gaziz Aldamzharov          x
Head, Dostyk Company

Source: Adapated from *Dinamika 1* and *Dinamika 2*.[15]

The ratings of individuals illustrate two main points about their relationship with institutions. In 1994–1996 there were more individuals rated who
were outside government structures e.g. Murat Auezov, Petr Svoik, Gaziz
Aldamzharov and Bulat Abilov. By implication, then, individuals may have
been better placed in the early independence years to influence institutions
than the other way round. This may also suggest the importance of the
individual in an under-institutionalized setting. An individual who has
the respect of his peers, has economic resources at his disposal, and enjoys
cultural and social status, may be strong also because of his personality
or psychological orientation. The panel of experts uniformly remarked
that it was very often impossible to separate an institutional index from an
individual index in this earlier period. By contrast, by 2001, in the VIProblem
Survey none of the individuals noted as influential and promising was
situated outside of government structures, and the individuals listed were
nearly all associated with strong institutions.

This leads onto a second point, namely that while, in 1995–1996,
individuals within executive power might have been linked to a weak
institution, this appeared to be no longer the case by 2001. Instead the
individuals selected by VIProblem in 2001 confirmed both the predominance of executive power and the relative strength of certain branches within
that executive power. Level 4 (primarily economic and security) increased
in influence between 1995 and 2000, becoming increasingly important in
setting the agenda. By contrast, the role and status of the Prime Minister
and Foreign Minister decreased. (The Ministry of Economics remained
a weak ministry). This is not to deny that influential individuals could
considerably strengthen institutions, such as Rakhat Aliev and the Tax
Police (first in Almaty, then as Head of its National Committee first under
the Ministry of Finance between November 1997 and October 1998, then
under the Ministry of State Income between October 1998 and September
1999). Those institutions which were given more financial and functional
responsibilities could in turn strengthen the individual and the indication
is that by 2000–2001 individuals were increasingly deriving their influence
from their institutional location. Simultaneously, the functional needs of
the system were giving certain individuals more influence than others.
Functionally, as we noted in the preceding chapter, the system prioritized
issues of security, nation-building and economic reform.

# CAREER STRUCTURE OF THE ELITE
## Typologies and Sequencing

While the career paths of individuals from the Soviet into the post-Soviet period were fairly uniform, those within the post-independence period were more varied. If we take first the sequencing between the Soviet and post-Soviet periods, the following represents the Soviet-era positions held by our 244 members of the political elite:

## Table 4: Elite and Soviet Occupation

| Position | Numbers |
|---|---|
| *Party or Soviet Government apparatus* | |
| Executive (administration and management) | 86 |
| Party | 54 |
| Legislature | 28 |
| | 168 (68%) |
| | |
| *Outside Soviet Party/Government Apparatus* | |
| Research | 34 |
| Students | 16 |
| Professional Positions | 13 |
| Industrial Management | 8 |
| New Economic Associations | 7 |
| Military | 4 |
| Agricultural Management | 2 |
| | 76 (32%) |

Of the 244 elite members identified in 1995–1996, nearly two thirds had served in either an executive or party post in the Soviet era, and the majority of those in an executive position. Just over a third had come from outside the nomenklatura, primarily from research. Several have argued that significant elite continuity is typical of post-communist states generally.[16] By contrast, David Lane has argued that elites are not a reproduced nomenklatura by demonstrating how, for Russia's political, regional and parliamentary elites, a majority came from outside the nomenklatura, and indeed to a great extent from an academic background. Lane has also stressed the importance of unpacking the concept 'nomenklatura'.[17] The figures here for Kazakhstan lie somewhere in-between. They suggest how a large proportion come from the Soviet executive and also that in the late Gorbachev period Lane's 'acquisition class' was comparatively weaker in Kazakhstan than in Russia. As James Hughes showed for the sub-national Russian elite in 1991,[18] Kazakhstan's Soviet-era officials were bifurcated in that they are recruited from a *common* source of leaders drawn from two main occupational categories: senior administrative officials, and senior managers of economic enterprises (economic). Consequently, occupational boundaries became blurred between these two groups.

Those members with prominent positions in the Communist Party of Kazakhstan (KPK) came to occupy some of the most influential positions in the initial post-independence presidential administration or parliament. Elite members who had their origins in medium-ranking executive posts in the Soviet era transferred primarily to the government. By contrast, only 23 per cent of the 1994 parliament consisted of members of the 1990 parliament.[19]

Typically, those members of the 1995 elite in top positions within the presidential administration were top CPSU and government executive officials pre-1991, either at national or regional level. Of the identified political elite, 28 per cent had worked at the regional *obkom* level. A distinctive feature of both the presidential administration and the cabinet of ministers is that their officials were drawn from a wide band of the top jobs, ranging from the Council of Ministers to the position of party writer. The majority came from political rather than economic jobs. Many in the presidential administration who had worked in the oblast administration had been first or second *obkom* secretaries. The bureaucracy was the main recruitment channel, even if some lateral entry was possible.

When those interviewed were asked why they thought they had been given their job (with the caveat expressed in the Introduction that the aim cannot be to uncover specific reasons why a particular individual was chosen or survived), they almost all Kazakhs and non Kazakhs alike – referred to their occupational experience. One member of the elite stressed that the president personally had been particularly impressed with his hands-on experience, first in a factory and then in regional administration; another that the president had approached him given his considerable experience in Gosplan and the energy industry (indeed the same speaker mentioned that these occupational criteria had been important in the choice made by Kunaev earlier). We noted a particular functional continuity in posts dealing with CIS relations, with many of those in leading positions on inter-CIS or Customs Unions, tending to have held positions in the Soviet era which demanded close relations with Moscow, such as Nigmatzhan Isingarin, Head of Integration Committee Belarus, Kazakhstan, Kyrgyzstan and Russia (1996–),[20] or Kalyk Abdullaev, Chair of State Committee for Relations with CIS countries (1995–1996).

The continuity between the Soviet and post-Soviet elites was also observed in terms of career sequencing: those in the judiciary tended to have served in the Soviet judiciary (more than half of judicial figures worked in the judiciary in the pre-1991 period, primarily in the procuracy), those in the presidential administration tended to have served in the party, and those in the Cabinet of Ministers tended to have served in the Council of Ministers. If members of the judiciary worked in government, they were also likely to have worked in the security services.[21] The political elite in security posts showed a large degree of continuity (e.g. former

KGB and Ministry of Internal Affairs have remained in these revamped organizations). This institutional continuity was sometimes diluted by disciplinary concerns: economists and lawyers were employed in all branches of government. Occupational continuity was also found amongst the industrial executives, both state and private. They had been either 'red directors' in the Soviet period or heads of new economic enterprises in the Gorbachev period.

Just prior to independence, six of the 19 ministers in 1995–1996 had been working as CPSU *apparatchiki*, four at ministerial level in the Kazakh SSR government, three as industrial executives, two as researchers, another two as USSR Ministry officials, one in a town administration and one in the military. Most of the Deputy Ministers or Heads of Department in 1995 had worked in Soviet government institutions.

Little occupational homogeneity was observed among parliamentarians, who ranged from the first cosmonaut of Kazakhstan, Kenes Aubaliev, to the chief national Greco-Roman wrestling trainer, Daulet Turlykhanov.

Overall the trends in Soviet to post-Soviet sequencing seem to be mirrored at the regional level, although the party seems to have provided a more direct route to a place in the 1992 elite. Of the twenty in 1992, nine had been Obkom First Party Secretaries and the remaining either *raikom* or *gorkom* heads. 'My experience as head of this oblast in the eighties, ' explained one former *Obkom* First Party Secretary, 'has served me very well in my present job. I rely still almost exclusively on the contacts I had in that period.'[22] Nevertheless, nine of the twenty had been employed in alternative jobs: four in the executive, two as heads of state collective farms, two in central government and one as state company director. For example, Vladimir Gartman and Andrei Braun, two ethnic German heads of regional administrations in the north in 1995, had formerly been state collective farm directors. By contrast, all three regional governors interviewed in this study – Kabibulla Dzhakupov of West Kazakhstan, Danial Akhmetov of Pavlodar and Zautbek Turisbekov of Southern Kazakhstan – had ended their Soviet careers in their respective regional branches of the KPK. Of the total 54 regional governors in the period between 1992 and 1995, most had worked in either the government or party structures of the Soviet era. Only seven of the 54 had been so-called 'red directors'. Three quarters of regional akims had served in their respective regions in the Soviet period.

## Independence Period[23]

Into the post-Soviet era, five main occupational categories were discernible: official, economic, professional, technocratic and business. These five career typologies expand on those that Frederick Frey found for his study of the Turkish political elite.[24] The 'official' refers to senior administrative positions in either a state or party position in the Soviet or post-Soviet period or both. The 'economic' refers to state company managers in the

Soviet or post-Soviet period or both. The so-called 'professions' refer here by definition to training in one of the three learned professions of law, theology or medicine. The fourth, 'business', refers to those who operated as businessmen outside of state structures either in the Gorbachev or early independence period or both.[25] The fifth, 'technocratic', refers to those who have come directly from education into government and have been hired for their (usually either legal or economic) expertise. Individuals may belong to more than one of these segments.

These categories were explained by various trends in career paths discernible in 1991–2001. The first was an intense institutional and elite reshuffling, so that one individual might have served in several institutions either simultaneously or sequentially. This institution hopping includes from centre to region and vice versa. Second, although the number of individuals with engineering degrees declined, those with technical specializations, noticeably in finance and law, rose. Third, between 1995 and 2000 the proportion of leaders from the professional stratum decreased by 12.2 per cent. The highest proportional decrease in the number of professionals occurred in parliament. Finally, businessmen (who started their enterprises in either the late Gorbachev period or independence periods) were incorporated into all branches of government.

## Elite Reshuffling, Simultaneous and Sequential Overlap

Different institutions and different hierarchies of power were associated with different rates of turnover, but overall the central elite has been subject to an extraordinary degree of reshuffling in 1991–2001. For example, between 1991 and 2001, under four Prime Ministers (Sergei Tereshchenko, 1991–1994; Akezhan Kazhegeldin, 1994–1997; Nurlan Balgimbaev, 1997–1999; Kasymzhomart Tokaev, 1999–2002), there have been eight First Deputy Prime Ministers each lasting on average a year. In 1994 alone, Kazakhstan had three Ministers of Economics; the Ministry was then abolished in 1997,[26] only to be first resurrected again in 1999 and then renamed Ministry of Economics and Trade in 2001.[27] The First Deputy Head of the Kazakhstan National Security Committee was rotated several times over 1997–1998.

The turnover of regional akims was often even more intensive than at the centre. This is shown below, with some stabilization in turnover noticeable by the close of the 1990s:

## Table 5: Regional Elites: The Turnover of Akims

| | Number of Akims per oblast, 1991–2001 | Number of years each akim in post , 1991–2001 |
|---|---|---|
| Aktubinsk | 3 | 1, 2, 1995– |
| Almaty | 4 | 2, 2, 2, 1997– |
| East Kazakhstan | 5 | 2, 1, 1, 1, 1997– |
| Atyrau | 4 | 2, 4, 1, 2000– |

| Zhambyl | 4 | | 3, 1, 3, 1999– |
| Zhezkazgan | 4 | | 2, 1, 2, 1. Abolished. |
| Karaganda | 3 | | 5, 2, 1999– |
| Kzylorda | 4 | | 3, 3, 1, 1999– |
| Kokshetau | 4 | | 1, 1, 3, 1. Abolished. |
| Kostanai | 4 | | 1, 2, 3, 1998– |
| Mangystau | 5 | | 2, 2, 2, 1, 1. 1999– |
| Pavlodar | 3 | | 1, 4, 1997– |
| North Kazakhstan | 3 | | 5, 2, 1999– |
| Semei | 3 | | 2, 1, 2. Abolished. |
| Taldykorgan | 3 | | 1, 3, 1. Abolished. |
| Turgai | 3 | | 1, 2, 2. Abolished. |
| West Kazakhstan | 2 | | 1, 1992– |
| Akmola | 3 | | 5, 1, 1998– |
| South Kazakhstan | 5 | | 1, 4, 1, 1, 1999– |
| Almaty City | 3 | | 2, 4, 1998– |
| Astana City | 1 | (since 1997) | 1997– |

The average number of akims in a region was three; the average number of years an akim has remained in his position was between two and three. The longest serving akim was Kabibulla Dzhakupov in West Kazakhstan. Some stabilization of rotation appears to have occurred by around 1998. Both of these trends will be explored (especially in Chapters 5 and 6). Higley et al posit the following implications of high elite reshuffling: 'Moderate degrees of elite continuity are compatible with, and apparently conducive to, democratic politics in the postcommunist period; really high degrees of continuity are associated with serious shortcomings in democracy.'[28]

The institutional continuity observed in the first half of the decade had by 2001 been punctured by increasing instances of sequential overlap, where more individuals had served in different institutions, perhaps moving from government, to a bank, then to presidential administration and then back into government. For example, as many as 50 per cent of the 1995–1999 parliament were former state officials, compared to 22 per cent in 1994–1995 and 28 per cent in 1999–2003 parliaments.[29] This overall phenomenon of sequential overlap in the post-independence period is illustrated also in the recruitment crossovers of central and regional elites.

## Centre-Regional Crossovers in Recruitment Patterns

Prominent figures of the national elite who had served in the provincial administrations included Akhmetzhan Esimov, Talgat Mamashev, Garii Shtoik, Gaziz Aldamzharov, Alexandr Pavlov and Asygat Zhabagin. The two prime examples were Kazakhstan's two first Prime Ministers, Sergei Tereshchenko and Akezhan Kazhegeldin. Zamanbek Nurkadilov, as mayor of Almaty city, also became a prominent member of the elite.

Around 1997, several members of the national elite became regional governors; examples included Imangali Tasmagambetov (Atyrau), Umirzak Shukeev (Kokshetau), Vitalii Mette (East-Kazakhstan), Mazhit Esenbaev (Karaganda), Sarybai Kalmurzaev (Zhambyl), Viktor Khrapunov (Almaty), Serik Umbetov (Zhambyl), Liazzat Kiinov (Mangystau) and Kalyk Abdullaev (South Kazakhstan), became regional governors.

In the early years members of the provincial elite sometimes enjoyed a meteoric rise in the national corridors of power. Viktor Khrapunov, who served as first deputy to Nurkadilov in the Almaty city administration and his successor Shalbai Kulmakhanov, temporarily became Minister of Coal and Energy before returning to become their successor as Almaty town akim in 1997.

Regional state company directors also enjoyed a meteoric rise in the early days of the post-communist elite, such as Oleg Soskovets (head of Karaganda Steel Works, Karmetkombinat between 1987 and 1991) who became First Deputy Prime Minister and Albert Salamatin (head of Karaganda Coal, 1989–1992) who became Minister of Industry (1992–1994). Both later emigrated to Russia (in late 1992 and 1994 respectively).

## Co-optation of Corporate Actors

Occupational boundaries became further blurred through the appointment of businessmen to prominent positions of power. A number of younger businessmen who had established themselves in business already in the Gorbachev era were brought into government in the period primarily of 1994–1997, mainly as heads of regional administrations. Examples included Semei's Galymzhan Zhakiianov (1994–1997), East Kazakhstan's Leonid Desiatnik (1995–1996), Aktobe's Savelii Pachin (1993–1995) and former Zhezkazgan's Nurlan Nagmanov. One notable exception was Akezhan Kazhegeldin who, instead of stepping from business into regional government, went on to be appointed Kazakhstan's second Prime Minister (1994–1997). It was under his premiership, then, that businessmen were first prominently incorporated into government.

A second round of businessmen was appointed into government around 1997–1998. Unlike those of the first round, by virtue of their commercial successes these were already prominent figures in the republic. They included Mukhtar Abliazov (former head of company Astana-Holding, appointed Minister of Energy, Industry and Trade in 1998), Erkin Kaliev (former head of company Glotur, 1991–1996, appointed Minister of Transport and Communications in 1997); Sauat Mynbaev (former co-head of Kazkommertsbank, appointed Minister of Finance in 1998). Most of these appointments in government lasted no more than a year, the individuals then being appointed to a lower-ranked government agency or returning to business. A notable exception was Mynbaev who, after a spell as Deputy Head of the Presidential Administration, was appointed Minister of

Agriculture. The number of individuals in parliament with a background
in business also rose within 1991–2001: while in the 13th parliament (1994–
1995) 13 per cent came from private business, this number had risen to 22
per cent in the 1995–1999 parliament and to 28 per cent in the 1999–2004
parliament.

At the same time as incorporating businessmen, government institutions
were going through a process of de-professionalization. For example,
while 37 per cent of the 1994–1995 parliament came from the fields of law
and medicine, this number had dropped to 7 per cent in 1995–1999.[30] As
we shall note in the next chapter, the younger members of the elite tend
to have been educated in finance or economic management, although
it is premature to say that the Kazakhstani government had become
'professional' in the sense of having its origins in economic management,
diplomacy and the former security services.

At the end of 2001, VIProblem asked a panel of experts: Which of these
social groups play an important role in the formation of the Kazakhstani
state?

## Table 6

| Group | Astana respondents | Almaty respondents |
|---|---|---|
| Workers | - | 8 |
| Intelligentsia | 5 | 16 |
| Businessmen | 40 | 44 |
| Heads of State Companies | 20 | 20 |
| State Officials | 80 | 68 |
| Pensioners | - | 4 |
| Democratic Political Leaders | - | 16 |
| Communist Political Leaders | - | 4 |
| Nationalist Political Leaders | - | 12 |
| Military | 10 | - |
| Security Organs | 60 | 52 |
| Mafia, criminal elements | 45 | 44 |
| No group plays significant role | - | 8 |

State Groups: April 2000[31]

The table confirms some of the developments we have noted: institutions
of government were composed primarily of state officials, with a strong
security arm and a considerable number of businessmen. The state was
perceived as highly corrupt and as a collection of groups struggling
amongst themselves to obtain private goods rather than as one group
which provides public goods. Several indigenous analysts have claimed
that the state is an arena for competition between various lobbying groups

D. K. Satpaev has argued that these lobby groups, as in other post-Soviet republics, are both based on Soviet-era networks (he cites the military, agrarian and energy lobbies as examples) and on post-Soviet ones (in particular what he calls the *biznes-lobbi* of which he cites six).[32]

## Consolidation of a Technocratic Sub-Elite

Finally, a number of technocrats earned high-ranking posts in key economic institutions, notably Uraz Dzhandosov (including as Head of National Bank, 1996–1998 and Head of State Committee of Investments, 1998–1999); Grigorii Marchenko (Deputy Head of National Bank, 1994–1996 to become its head in 1999); Zhannat Ertlesova (Deputy Minister of Economics, 1993–1995, Head of Centre for Economic Reform, 1995–1997, Deputy Finance Minister 1997–1999); Zeinulla Kakimzhanov (Head of National Savings Bank, 1994–1997, Minister of State Income from 1999); Erzhan Utembaev (Head of Agency for Strategic Planning, 1997 and 1998–1999); and Daulet Sembaev (Head of National Bank, 1993–6). For most of the 1990s these technocrats worked as a team, either formally or informally. Many of the economic agencies were in this period transferred from ministerial to presidential control. In a further development around 1999–2000, however, many of them were repositioned from these technocratic posts to more political posts primarily in the presidential administration or prime minister's office. A number of less well-known, younger technocrats had also joined the elite by 2000.

In 1991–2001, then, the top elite was concentrated in the executive; where in the early years this executive consisted of positions in both government and the presidential administration, by the close of the decade the presidential administration dominated. Second, while sequential continuity characterized the transition from Soviet to post-Soviet rule, the 1991–2001 period was characterized by sequential overlap with intense reshuffling. Third, occupationally all branches of power included among their ranks young businessmen and early indications suggested a slow de-professionalization of institutions of government. Fourth, despite repeated attacks on the institutional framework through repeated opening and closing of agencies, a technocratic sub-elite was allowed to operate.

# ELITE: INSTITUTIONS, THE CONSTITUTION AND ATTITUDES TO THE PROCESSES OF GOVERNMENT

These trends allow us to make some preliminary observations on the relationship between elites and institutions. It already appears that elites were shaping new institutions, whilst institutions furnished the setting within which elites rise and act. Even when relatively inchoate, institutions can shape elite composition, favouring the rise of some groups and individuals to power over others, and influencing the strategies and tactics employed by those seeking to win or keep power. The thirteenth parliament (1994–1995) was an example of this trend. Elites have changed significantly when institutions have not.

Second, institutions can change their names without changing their activities (such as the security police), while institutions retaining their old names (parliaments, for example) may acquire very different functions in substance. Repeated alterations to the institutional architecture carried policy implications. A number of ad hoc duplicate and parallel administrations sprang up largely to deal with economic policy. It seemed to indicate more of a hand-to-mouth response to post-Soviet problems, and indicated some difference from the Soviet era when, in principle, the Soviet administrative structure was rather clear and well-established.

Third, unlike in Eastern Central Europe where important institutional decisions were made very early in the transition process – especially in the roundtable negotiations between representatives of the opposition and the old regime – in Kazakhstan the institutional architecture came after the change in regime, namely post-1991.[33]

Fourth, initial decisions on formal constitutional and statutory provisions were only the starting point in a continuing competition among leading political actors. In reality, then, Kazakhstan's Constitution between 1991 and 1998 has functioned decreasingly as a state code and increasingly as a loose frame of government. Constitutional development conformed to a top-down model, [34] that is, it stemmed largely from the initiatives of leaders rather than as a response to popular demands.

The elite has been able to justify executive dominance in this regime by referring to the 1995 Constitution. Replacing the republic's first constitution of 1993, the 1995 Constitution decreed domination by executive rule and, in so doing, departed from its predecessor in three areas: the status of executive power; court reform; and the function of parliament.[35] First, the president's powers increased vis-à-vis other executive power branches. Whilst in 1993 the president was the 'single executive system', in 1995, he ceased to be even *part* of the executive system. He stands as independent arbiter and guarantor of both the Constitution and the state's territorial integrity. Whereas the 1993 Constitution provided checks and balances on the powers of the president, its successor did not make him accountable to any institution. The powers of the president were further strengthened by the constitutional amendments of 7 October 1998 under which the age restriction of 65 was lifted and the presidential term of office extended from five to seven years. In addition, the president could now hold early presidential elections and call a referendum to override any parliamentary law without any need for parliamentary approval. The perception of the panel of experts was that only members of the executive exerted a real effect on decision-making.

The president's powers in relation to the other branches of power also increased in 1995. He now directly controlled the successor to the Constitutional Court and the Constitutional Council (CC), the six members of which are nominated by him, the senate and the regional parliaments.[36] The Arbitration Court was abolished in 1995, and the Prosecutor's Office restructured with part of its functions transferred to the newly established State Investigation Committee, which was also now subordinate to the president. The judiciary lost the relative independence it enjoyed prior to 1995.

The bicameral parliament also emerged the paler in comparison with its unicameral predecessor, the Supreme Soviet. In the 1995 constitution, parliament's size was cut from 177 to 114 members, with 67 members of the Lower House (*mazhilis*) and 47 of the Upper House (*senat*). Of these 47, 40 represented the provinces (two from each) and seven were appointed by the president. While the seven remain for the entire term of the senat, half of the remaining 40 are re-elected every two years. The first bicameral parliament was elected in December 1995 and its successor in October 1999. Deprived of the Audit Chamber, which was dissolved along with the last Supreme Soviet, and deprived of the right to appoint the Prosecutor General, parliament lost all its levers of influence on the presidential office in 1995.

Constitutionally, the dominance of the executive branch of power was mirrored at the regional level which was again reflected in the Constitution. The executive dominates the local level; it is unaccountable to the legislature and monopolizes all decision-making. Article 87.2 lists the jurisdictions of the provincial administration which include: the development of a province's economic, social and budgetary programmes and their means of finance; the management of public property; and the appointment or dismissal of heads of lower-ranked executive bodies. By contrast, maslikhats can take decisions 'only according to their competencies' which effectively is open to interpretation and usually means only in relation to the development of the provincial budget. But even here their powers are curtailed as the budget is centrally administered and is subject to 'agreement of the akim' (Article 88.2).

While the maslikhat is permitted to remove a city or district akim, it is not allowed to remove a provincial akim or the akims of Astana and Almaty who enjoy provincial status (Article 87.5). Even the maslikhat's ability to remove the local akim is subject to parliament's approval. The akim 'is a representative of the president and the Government of the Republic' (Article 87.3) and is 'appointed to office by the president of the Republic on the recommendation of the Prime Minister' (Article 87.4). This suggests possible contradictions, as the akim effectively answers to both president and government. The akim's right to appoint lower akims was reduced in the October 1998 amendments: the president decides whether a lower-ranking akim will be elected or appointed. Nevertheless, the president has only used this right once, with respect to a district in Almaty. The 6 May 1999 amendments to the electoral law further boosted the powers of the provincial administration by giving it the sole right to compose the regional electoral commissions (Article 13.3), a right previously shared with the maslikhat. The akim's resolutions may be respectively annulled by the president, government or, in the case of a lower akim, by a senior akim (Article 88.4). The maslikhat, in turn, can be annulled by the *senat*, the effective territorial representation at the centre, if it considers the maslikhat is failing to fulfil or has outstripped its functions.

What, finally, of elite attitudes to this institutional architecture? On the one hand, the elite displayed considerable attitudinal congruence on the rules of the game. Even regional elites, who we shall see had a number of policy disagreements with members of the central elite, did not support federalism or the election of the akim. Said one: 'We do not have the geographic and demographic basis upon which to become a federal state. This is quite different in Russia' (PE, Shymkent, 11).

Respondents felt that parties exerted a very weak influence, primarily because of a lack of popular interest in their activities: 'In Kazakhstan, the mentality of the average citizen is strongly influenced by the leadership' (PE, 21). This dovetails with a VIProblem 1995 survey which cited the main reason for the weakness in the party system as the political apathy of the population (54 per cent), followed by the absence of charismatic party leaders (26 per cent).[37] On elite attitudes to public participation, the respondents considered that society was too immature to participate. 'This is not the time for political parties, political parties will only develop if they are needed by the people' (PE, 18). One top leader remarked that 'the whole of society has a poor understanding of what is necessary' (PE, 8) and a leading parliamentary representative of the Communist Party lamented that: 'People are indifferent to politics; society is not politicized. I understood that I had to go to the people myself' (PE, 6).

Although the majority blamed the population itself for the absence of participation, it also did not view the absence of pluralism as negative. The overwhelming majority agreed with the proposition that 'although political parties and groups play an important role in a democracy often they uselessly exacerbate political conflicts.' The majority of those questioned argued that the development of political elite groupings was detrimental to the stability of the state, and that particularistic interest groups undermine the moral health of the nation. The majority viewed conflict as both weakening society and as dangerous to society. With the exception of political leaders outside the government, the Kazakhstani elite did not appear to view conflict as functional, and strove for consensus.

There appeared, however, a large degree of mistrust between players in the system, notably between region and centre, and between different branches of central government. The mistrust between centre and region was supported by a May 1996 VIProblem survey in which 62 per cent thought that regional state capacity was low. The principal reasons given were: corruption of lower organs (48 per cent), 'serious slippage on cadre politics' (44), 'absence of a regional development concept'(36), 'stagnation' (32), 'weak control by society of their actions' (30), 'insufficient powers' (26), 'lack of coordination between central and regional organs of power' (24), 'weak central control of regions' (10).[38] The election of the akim, even though 70 per cent of VIProblem respondents supported it, would not, they thought, solve these problems. In another study around this time, central elite members criticized the local elites for their lack of effectiveness: 62 per cent thought that problems in the effectiveness of regional state capacities were the major ones facing Kazakhstan. 46 per cent felt that there were problems in the capacity also of central organs of power.[39]

Surveys in 2000–2001 indicated, however, that more members of both the central and regional elites were advocating substantial and immediate change, suggesting impatience with the current system and a sense that it had become dysfunctional. A VIProblem poll taken immediately after the November 2001 open elite fragmentation suggested that a considerably larger per centage than those polled in 1996 criticized the leadership and considered policy ineffective. Many felt that economic reform had simply ground to a halt.[40]

The majority of the elite interviewed did not see the unitary system as working to their satisfaction. This did not necessarily imply a desire for federalism, however, even if a majority supported the election rather than appointment of the akim. By the close of 2001, according to VIProblem, while some members of the central elite had also come to support the election of regional leaders, neither central nor regional elites thought that the election of the regional leader would be a panacea.[41]

# Chapter Three

# SOCIAL BACKGROUND

The focus on career and demographic attributes in other studies has traditionally been justified on three grounds: the absence of social homogeneity has been said to explain elite conflict; social background characteristics have been said to be accurate predictors of elite attitudes and values; and certain demographic and career attributes have been associated with certain systems. Elite social background can thus be seen as a set of social resources converted into positions and influence. If some patterns in occupational backgrounds were discernible, can the same be said for demographic attributes?

The analysis here focuses on six demographic attributes: age/year of birth; gender; the nature and amount of formal education; family social background and standing; place of birth (urban/rural and region), with some reference to zhuz membership; and ethnicity. It needs to be emphasized again that this is only a small sample and that the availability of data, particularly on family social background, is uneven. Without analysing the determining factor behind each individual's appointment it is impossible to say with complete certainty which factor matters more than another and, indeed, whether other factors, such as personality, friendship or even money, matter more, or at all. The data here does not offer specific information on this differentiation. Instead we can, at best, offer some hypotheses suggested by the data that there might be strong correlations, in terms of their relationship with career typologies, level and duration. At points, comparison will be made with Turkey; in the early reform years Nazarbaev regarded Turkey as a model secular regime that had achieved rapid political and economic modernization.

# AGE

The age variable was divided into four categories: those under 36, 36–45, 46–55, and those over 55. This enables us to study characteristics such as the addition of younger generations, which *might* indicate revitalization, and continuity of dominance by older generations, which *might* indicate conservatism and elite adaptation to transition.

## Table 7: Age and the Elite

|        | 1995          | 2000          | 1995 & 2000   |
|--------|---------------|---------------|---------------|
| < 36   | 12            | 18            | 15            |
| 36–45  | 30            | 37            | 32            |
| 46–55  | 44            | 36            | 41            |
| > 55   | 14            | 9             | 12            |
| n      | 209 = 100%    | 174 = 100%    | 244 = 100%    |

It is often contended that younger people rise rapidly to elite positions during regime transitions, and the sample here would confirm this trend less for 1995 but increasingly for 2000.[1] In 1995, the majority of the elite falls into the 46–55 age bracket. If we take comparisons between those who were members of the political elite only in 1995 and those who were members in 2000, the elite is considerably younger overall in 2000. The majority of those who joined the elite in 2000 were under 36. This confirms a trend criticized in 2003 by analyst Sabit Zhusupov, who notes that 'it is simply absurd when three quarters of the leadership is made up of under 30 year olds'.[2] While the central elite had become younger the regional elite governors had become slightly older. 70 per cent of the 1995 akims were aged between 46 and 55 rising to 75 per cent by 2000.

The advent of a group of younger 'technocrats' and businessmen bring to mind comparisons with Ataturk's 'Young Turks' or the rise to power of Hassan Ali Mansur in Iran. Despite this younger elite, the average age of the Kazakhstani elite might still be slightly higher than in some other Soviet republics.[3] Overall, however, the average age of the elite is lower than that of heads of government worldwide. The youngest tended to be concentrated in the presidential administration and economic agencies, the eldest in parliament.

The age distribution of the Kazakhstani elite is thus less different from that of the general Kazakhstani population than is often encountered amongst other elites. In 1990, only 10 per cent of the total population was over 60. By 1995, this had reached 12 per cent, and the forecast in 1995 for 2000 was 17 per cent, with as many as 26 per cent forecast for 2050.[4] In more traditional, non-western societies power is often a concomitant of age, and while that was certainly true for the Soviet era, it did not appear to apply as yet to what was still early post-independent Kazakhstan.

# GENDER

'In statistical terms, ' Putnam has remarked, 'women are the most under-represented group in the political elites of the world. In most areas of the world – "developed" or "undeveloped" – there seems to be marked incompatibility between the female role in society and certain occupational roles, especially that of the politician.'[5] The data for Kazakhstan does not contradict this finding, despite supposed Soviet-era emancipation.

## Table 8: Gender and the Elite

| GENDER | 1995 | 2000 | 1995 & 2000 |
|---|---|---|---|
| Male | 94 | 93 | 94 |
| Female | 6 | 7 | 6 |
| n | 209 = 100% | 174 = 100% | 244 = 100% |

Of the elite in 1995 and 2000, 94 per cent are male, with only a 1 per cent rise in women by 2000. There was not much variation across institutions, although women tend to be found more frequently in government or parliament. There was only one female minister in 1995, and three in 2000. All 54 regional governors have been male. Out of this study's regional elite respondents, only 6 of 42 were female. Some prominence was given to women's issues in 1998 when a specific ministry was assigned the portfolio of women's affairs. At both central and regional levels, women tended to be employed in departments dealing with social, cultural or socio-economic issues; for example, the Minister of Social Support in 1995 was female, and the heads of the socio-economic departments of all three of this study's regional administrations were women. The higher the status of the position, the lower the inclusion of women.

Women interviewed would often compare their contemporary situation to that of their predecessors. In the pre-Soviet era, a woman was mistress of, and often owned, her yurt, which was usually included in her dowry along with household equipment, clothing and jewellery. Kazakh women were not veiled, and girls associated freely with young men, in horse races, singing contests, and other diversions. As Winner has pointed out, in the traditional heroic epics of the Kazakhs, the heroine was 'usually endowed with qualities similar to those of the *batyr* (hero)', and was 'depicted as the equal of her husband or lover in moral worth and intelligence.'[6]

The Soviet government strove explicitly to 'rescue women from bondage' and established specific quotas for particular jobs. In 1934, non-Kazakh women predominated: 'Of the total number of women employed in all institutions, only 7 per cent or 557 were Kazakhs.'[7] In 1960, there were higher per centages of Kazakh and Kyrgyz women who had specialized education or were enrolled as students in higher education than of any other Central Asian nationality.[8] One parliamentarian stated: 'I used to be in a top regional executive position. Now I got into the thirteenth parliament but see little chance of this channel surviving. I think that women should form political parties to boost their participation' (PE, 6). The UNDP 1997 report states that 'An illustration of the growing inequality between men and women can be seen in employment and political administration.'[9]

Other than their gender, there was little that unified the females in the identified political elite together as a sub-elite, characterized instead by high occupational and social diversity. They were born in various parts of the country, had different discipline specializations (generally economics, law, sociology), and either made their way through regional party organs or as professionals. It does seem, however, that the party route had been the most assured for females, and those who had reached the higher ranking posts tended to be ethnic Kazakh.

# EDUCATION

Statistically speaking, there is a stronger correlation between education and membership of the political elite than between social origins and membership of the political elite (note, of course, that the two indicators can be interrelated).[10] In discussing political stratification in developing countries, Suzanne Keller argued that: 'Formal education is the single most important entrance requirement into the higher circles.'[11]

In describing the career paths in the previous chapter in terms of social backgrounds, university education immediately comes to mind. There is evidence, from Turkey and from other nations, which suggests that attendance at a distinctive secondary school is the most important educational experience in terms of influence upon subsequent political behaviour.[12] Unfortunately, we do not have such information for the Kazakhstani elite but correlations between higher education and elite membership can be observed.

Unlike Turkey's Ataturk, Kazakhstan's Nazarbaev inherited a well-developed modern educational system with the result that educational distinction could not play the same role in Kazakhstan that it had in Turkey.

## Table 9: Education and the Elite (per centage)

| Principal Institution of Education | 1995 | 2000 | 1995 & 2000 |
| --- | --- | --- | --- |
| Other | 5 | 7 | 5 |
| Higher Technical Institute (Almaty) | 19 | 17 | 17 |
| Higher Technical Institute (Kazakhstan) | 10 | 10 | 11 |
| Higher Technical Institute (Moscow) | 14 | 12 | 14 |

| | | | |
|---|---|---|---|
| Higher Technical Institute (Russia) | 7 | 3 | 6 |
| Polytechnic (Almaty) | 8 | 9 | 8 |
| Polytechnic (Kazakhstan) | 5 | 6 | 5 |
| Polytechnic (CIS) | 1 | 1 | 1 |
| Kazakhstan State University (Almaty) | 15 | 17 | 17 |
| University (Kazakhstan) | 3 | 3 | 3 |
| University (Moscow/St Petersburg) | 9 | 11 | 9 |
| University (Russia) | 1 | 2 | 2 |
| Military | 3 | 2 | 2 |
| n | 209 = 100% | 174 = 100% | 244 = 100% |

Adult literacy rose from 8.1 per cent in 1897 under Tsardom to 83.6 per cent in 1939 in the Soviet period.[13] From 1933 a comprehensive policy of development of secondary and higher education was introduced. Thus Soviet elites did not try to perpetuate social inequalities. Formal education had been an entrance requirement into the higher circles in the later Soviet period (the concentration in the early Soviet period had been on the social mobility of peasants and workers, as elaborated below). While Frey's identified Turkish parliamentarians were, in terms of their education, 'about as atypical as they could be',[14] Kazakhstan's highly educated Soviet elite mirrored a well-educated population. Thus, although a member of Turkey's political elite might draw status from education, this was not always the case for a member of the immediate post-independence Kazakhstani elite. This places Kazakhstan outside the hitherto observed trends for developmental states to consider education more important by and for elites, and for the gap between an educated elite and an often poorly educated mass to be significant. Precisely because the overwhelming majority of the elite have received higher education, and come from a society which itself was highly educated, education did not appear to be a key differentiating criterion in selection for the vast number of politico-administrative posts in the transition from Soviet to post-Soviet rule.

The overwhelming majority of the Kazakh political elite identified here had undergraduate degrees. Fifty per cent of the elite in both years combined have some form of postgraduate education. Of this about one third are candidates of science and nearly one fifth hold doctors of science. Nearly all members of the elite had attended some form of higher education institute. Most Kazakhs in higher education had also attended Russian schools. Of the central elite, over a quarter had attended either a university or a higher education institute in Russia. Of these, a fifth had studied in either Moscow or St Petersburg. Almaty was the town next most frequented by the elite for either university or technical education. Regional elites in Pavlodar had most frequently attended institutes in Russia; otherwise the majority of regional elites interviewed tended to be regionally educated, with the majority again having attended a higher institute. In terms of discipline studied, engineering saw a drop, and economic management and finance a slight increase.

Frey concludes for Turkey that 'we see in this non-western "developing" society with its relatively newly formed parliamentary institutions the same over-representation of the legally and administratively trained that we so frequently observe in the more established parliaments of the West.'[15] When compared to western public administrations, law and political science in Kazakhstan are still *under*-represented in power, and the elite is dominated instead by the sciences and economics.

The considerably high level of education in Kazakhstan is unsurprising, testimony to the remarkable development of the school system and the rise of literacy during the Soviet period. By the 1950s, the per centage of literacy in Central Asia was much higher than elsewhere in the Muslim Middle and Near East. While in 1940 Kazakh students made up only 30 per cent of the total at the Alma-Ata State University, by the mid 1990s the majority of the student body were ethnic Kazakhs. The creation of a native Muslim technical and scientific elite can be counted as another achievement of the Soviet regime, one that was championed by former First Regional Party Secretary Dinmukhamed Kunaev. Strong incentives for native students, including such explicit privileges as easier admissions, more available scholarships, and more lenient grading, had begun to bear fruit. Rasma Karklins points to a survey conducted in West Germany among Volga German émigrés from Kazakhstan and Central Asia. An overwhelming majority of the respondents mentioned nationality as a key factor in admissions to institutions of higher education in those republics.[16]

With higher education so commonly shared, other skills, especially in the context of new demands, assumed added importance. A minority of the political elite declared knowledge of a foreign language. This is largely because the graduates of Kazakhstan's best Soviet-era linguistics school, the Foreign Languages Institute, have sought employment with foreign companies rather than in the government. Unsurprisingly, those with intelligence service training or, among the younger cohorts, those with business or international organization experience, often had foreign language knowledge. The most-widespread foreign language spoken was English, although several members' biographies also indicated German, French and Turkish. Very few listed Chinese or Arabic, although knowledge of these languages has tended to secure ambassadorial appointments abroad.

Many members of the political elite had sent their children abroad to gain a western education. The number of elite members who receive high-level training at western faculties is likely to grow. Some of the most popular destinations included North America, Turkey, and the EU. By the end of the decade a large number of training programmes were also taking place in China. In addition, some high-level government members have also been trained by foreign governments and companies, the West being a more popular choice in this regard than Asia. At least one fifth of Turkey's Kemalist Assembly had received high-level training at western faculties.[17]

## PARENTAL BACKGROUND

Mosca argued that to look at education as a significant social background characteristic misses the point, however. This is because education itself is determined by what he perceived as a far more powerful social background characteristic: social class. The higher the social class, the greater the access to education, Mosca contended. A direct correlation between social class and education has indeed been shown for many countries;[18] can we say that today's political elite is highly educated *because* its members come from families who were also educated?

To reach an answer, we must first consider the relationship between an individual's social status and that of his family of origin: that is, his/her social mobility. The political importance attached to social mobility inevitably varies from polity to polity and ideology to ideology. Perceived mobility is as important as actual mobility but there is a link between the two. In any investigation of the relative social statuses of a man and his parental family (such as educational levels of parents, nature of dwelling, area of residence), a variety of indicators should ideally be employed. However, when the use of only a single indicator is possible, the indicator most commonly employed is the father's occupation. It is the one measure with which all others seem to correlate most highly. Often then, a single indicator, the father's occupation, is used and this is what is used here.

Putnam writes that virtually all the existing evidence states that political leaders are drawn disproportionately from upper-status occupations and privileged backgrounds. This makes sense; family status should open doors, increase the individual's confidence, even their distinctive set of political values. But Putnam also notes a highly significant exception here: the absence of such a correlation for communist regimes. It has been estimated, for example, that more than four-fifths of the Soviet Central Committee were the children of workers or peasants. Harasymiw also found that a large proportion of the top elite came from low status families.[19] Evidence from Yugoslavia indicated that 38 per cent of the party and legislative leaders came from proletarian families and another 31 per cent from the peasantry.[20] This needs, however, to be qualified with the recognition that there was considerable pressure exerted on the Soviet political elite to make themselves look 'proletarian' in roots.

The data for Kazakhstan[21] appears to substantiate the findings for other communist regimes. There is demonstrable evidence in support of the substantial social mobility of those members of the elite born before the 1960s, particularly for those members of this study's Group 4 (the over 55s) and the upper end of Group 3 (46–55) who will have been born at the latest in 1940 (see Table 7). These tend to be the children of fathers who were peasants, agriculturalists and workers and whose main adult status remained unchanged. President Nazarbaev in his official biography proudly states: 'It used to be that people boasted about their "proletarian" origins. Now the trend is to find some aristocratic blood among their ancestors. Well there was never one aristocrat in my background. I am the son, grandson and great grandson of shepherds.'[22] Many of those interviewed related how their parents did not have access to the educational opportunities that they themselves enjoyed. Typical answers included: 'My parents were workers. Of course they didn't do my type of work – I'm the first to be an economist!'; or, 'They were peasants.'; or again, 'My father was killed in the Great War and my mother had to feed the children. I am the first trained economist in the family' (PE 17, 20, 9). So, it is largely men currently in power, rather than their fathers, who have had the chance to be the 'new men' of their time. Already in the Soviet era they were better educated, more physically (and socially) mobile, urban-based, relatively wealthy and working in occupations with decision-making responsibilities.

The decline in social mobility in the later Soviet era is visible and likely to continue, however. In 1991 to 2001 some members of the elite have fathers who remained workers, some now have fathers who were part of the elite. The older members of the political elite have backgrounds less diverse than those of their fathers, who in turn had less diverse backgrounds than the population at large. There are many indicators of this diminution of social variety and the accompanying diminution of the bases from which movement to political power is possible. Social status is a prerequisite for a certain type of education – a degree from one of the elite schools of economics, or some western postgraduate training, for example – which is only available to those who can pay. The effect of social standing, as well as wealth and education, on political stratification is likely to rise.

Because membership of the political elite might no longer confer the sort of social status once enjoyed by membership in the Soviet era, it cannot be taken for granted that the offspring of the incumbent elite will choose to echo the career choices of their fathers. Governmental positions, with their low state salaries, might not, therefore, be sought by the vast majority of educated Kazakhstanis and it may be that many will, as in other post-communist countries, opt instead for the greater job security offered by a career in business.

The picture is still far from simple. In the early independence era, while a poor family background did not constitute a serious handicap, a good family background seemed an advantage, but still no guarantee of success. It would thus be misleading to say this is another ruling class – the situation is more fluid than that. Having parents recently or currently in the elite helps but does not guarantee access to the elite, and certainly not to the top positions. If we compare this to Iran where, in Marvin Zonis' study, some 64.4 per cent of the elite for whom data were available had fathers who held posts in the government or Imperial Court,[23] the figure is likely to be considerably lower in Kazakhstan. Putnam writes that generalizations on family background 'are supported by virtually all the existing evidence'[24] but it seems premature to draw this conclusion for Kazakhstan.

We can, however, observe over this period an increased tendency for relatives of Nazarbaev and his core selectorate to be given important positions in government. As noted in the previous chapter, his daughter, Dariga Nazarbaeva, was appointed head of the State Television Company Khabar in 1995; and his sons-in-law, Rakhat Aliev and Timur Kulibaev, were appointed respectively head of the Tax Inspectorate in 1996 (assuming chairmanship of Kazakhstan's National Security Committee in 2000) and vice-chair of Kazukhoil in 1997 (becoming chair of Kaztransoil in 1999). A reported relative of the president's wife Sara Nazarbaeva, Nurtai Abykaev, became through his appointment as head of the presidential administration between 1994 and 1995, one of the most influential members of the selectorate. The prevalence of the president's 'own', partly a consequence of the narrowing of the selectorate (see Chapter Two), led some commentators, notably V. N. Khliupin, to nickname the political elite Nazarbaev's *bolshaia semia* (big family).

## BIRTHPLACE AND THE ELITE

Social status is intimately linked to the discussion of the degree of correlation (and even causation) between an individual's membership of a zhuz and their having gained a place in the elite. Professor Nurbulat Masanov is a key exponent of this thesis. He has argued not only that zhuz membership is the decisive factor behind recruitment but also that specific zhuzes are associated with specific levels and types of appointment (see Chapter Four).

Masanov emphasized not only inter-zhuz rivalry but also intra-zhuz rivalry. He contended that tribes have a definite hierarchy within a zhuz and that competition for positions occurs also at this level. In particular, he contended that Nazarbaev had appointed individuals from the village of his birthplace, Chemolgan, leading to the Chemolganization of the elite

Masanov also contended that it would be unacceptable for top-ranking regional members not to be members of those clans with the highest status.

Correlations between patterns of recruitment and zhuz membership are difficult to uncover, not least because place of birth does not necessarily equate with zhuz membership. For example, the forefathers of urban Kazakhs will almost certainly not have come from an urban setting, not least because of Soviet-era migration. The equation between birthplace and zhuz background is more reliable for rural-based Kazakhs, but even here we cannot exclude the possibility of migration or the fact that some regions belong to two zhuzes, and those boundaries are not always clear from a bibliographical entry of birthplace.

With these qualifications in mind, the evidence – which relates to only just over half of the sample in both 1995 and 2000 since only that number are rural-born – suggests the continued dominance of the Senior Zhuz in the top positions of the political elite (54 per cent) but also a significant number of Middle Zhuz appointments (roughly 37 per cent) and only 9 per cent of Junior Zhuz appointments. The figures for 2000 are similar in trend (51 per cent, 39 per cent and 10 per cent). Relative to the per centage of zhuz membership for the population as a whole, these represent an over-representation of the Senior Zhuz, a near representation by the Middle Zhuz but an under-representation of the Junior Zhuz.[25] Although not strictly comparable, these figures are not dissimilar to those of another study (albeit lower here for the Middle Zhuz).[26]

With regard to tribal and clan belonging of elite members, we cannot look to elite biographies. Anecdotal evidence, and evidence gleaned from those interviewed, does suggest that members are aware of the hierarchy between tribes, that heads of regional administrations tend to come from the highest status clan and that intra-tribal rivalry does exist. These issues are briefly explored in the remaining chapters.

To go from this sort of correlation, then, to saying that an individual's zhuz affiliation is *the* decisive force shaping the recruitment of the Kazakhstani elite, is a step too far. As we shall see, other factors and the environment came to make recruitment much more complex, of which one part was the fact that the sub-ethnic identities that were spawned altered the environment and became local legitimating factors that central power had not envisaged (see Chapter Four). Whether deliberate or not, however, much of the population and key constituencies of intellectuals perceive both Kazakhization and tribalism to have been key features of recruitment. This perception has been sometimes exploited by the opposition.[27]

What we can determine with more certainty, however, are the rural/ urban and regional backgrounds of the elite.

## Table 10. Birthplace: Urban/Rural and the Elite

|             | 1995        | 2000        | 1995 & 2000 |
|-------------|-------------|-------------|-------------|
| Not Known   | 1           | 0           | 1           |
| Urban       | 42          | 48          | 44          |
| Rural       | 57          | 52          | 55          |
| n           | 209 = 100%  | 174 = 100%  | 244 = 100%  |

More members of the political elite were born in rural than urban areas in both 1995 and 2000, although slightly more were born in urban areas in 2000. The Pavlodarian elite interviewed was substantially more urbanized than its southern or western counterparts. In his study of comparative elites, Putnam highlights how elites are drawn disproportionately from the cities, in particular the larger metropolizes. The under-representation of villages and small towns, he writes, 'characterizes both developed and undeveloped countries, both capitalist and communist systems.'[28] The reverse appears to be the case for the political elite of Kazakhstan, where the majority are drawn from rural areas. According to the 1999 census, 56 per cent of Kazakhs now live in cities; 44 per cent in the country.[29] Some towns, particularly those in the south such as Tekely, Karatau and Kentau have seen rapid depopulation. This is still partly a function of the legacy of Soviet mobility, however.

## Table 11. Birthplace: Region and the Elite

|                    | 1995        | 2000        | 1995 & 2000 |
|--------------------|-------------|-------------|-------------|
| Almaty City        | 15          | 19          | 16          |
| Almaty Oblast      | 8           | 9           | 8           |
| South              | 23          | 23          | 22          |
| North              | 20          | 20          | 21          |
| Centre             | 14          | 10          | 13          |
| East               | 9           | 8           | 8           |
| West               | 9           | 8           | 9           |
| FSU except Russia  | 2           | 3           | 3           |
| Other              | 0           | 0           | 0           |
| n                  | 209 = 100%  | 174 = 100%  | 244 = 100 % |

Of Kazakhstan's five territorial zones, almost two thirds of the population live in the southern and northern regions, which make up about half of Kazakhstan's territory. Only one eighth of the population live in the western region, although it accounts for more than one quarter of the country's territory. The majority of the elite were drawn from the most densely populated regions: the South and North. The least represented of the provinces in terms of the birthplaces of the elite were the Centre, East and West. In short, there was domination by the South, followed by the North.

The majority of those who had joined the elite between 1995 and 2000 came from the South or North. The under 36-year-olds came overwhelmingly from the South and East, with a plurality from Almaty. The regional representation that has increased the most between 1995 and 2000 is Almaty city (up from 15 to 24 per cent).

For the post-independence elite, the most striking fact in terms of birthplace was perhaps that around 17 per cent of the 1995 political elite were born outside Kazakhstan, 13 per cent of them in Russia. Even if the majority of those born in Russia were ethnic Russians, a few top-ranking members were Kazakhs. Several members of the political elite, although born in Kazakhstan, had served their working lives in Russia and were called back from service in Russia or the Ukraine. In Turkey, as in most other countries, it was a definite political advantage to have been born within the national frontiers and to have strong ties with some important locality. Eighty-nine per cent of all deputies were born within the confines of present-day Turkey, even though the majority were born subjects of the much larger Ottoman Empire (just as Kazakhs were subjects of the Soviet empire) rather than citizens of the territorially reduced Turkish Republic.[41] To have been born or recently worked abroad does not appear to have been either a political advantage or disadvantage to becoming a member of the Kazakhstani elite. By 2000, the proportion of those born in Russia had in any case declined considerably.

The per centage of the political elite born in Almaty or Astana relates to 'metropolitanism,' or the domination of a country by its main city. Many developing nations currently confront this trend. In the West, commentators on French politics have pinpointed the focusing of French life on Paris as the main cause of alleged French political debility. Canadian historians have often espoused a 'metropolitan' theory of Canadian politics that considers the country exploited by the great eastern centres of Montreal and Toronto. In Turkey, during the Kemalist movement, the true power of the Turks was thought to lie in Anatolia, not in European Turkey. By contrast, in Kazakhstan, the capital has moved away from the South, traditionally deemed the centre of Kazakh power. As yet the majority of top positions have been retained by the Almaty elite; this is still early days, however, and it is possible that such a move could yet take place.

# ETHNICITY

## Table 12. Ethnicity and the Elite

|         | 1995 | 2000 | 1995 & 2000 |
|---------|------|------|-------------|
| Kazakh  | 76   | 85   | 78          |
| Russian | 18   | 12   | 16          |
| German  | 2    | 2    | 2           |

| Korean | 2 | 0 | 2 |
|---|---|---|---|
| Ukrainian | 0 | 1 | 0 |
| Other | 2 | 0 | 2 |
| n | 209 = 100% | 174 = 100% | 244 = 100% |

Taking 1995 and 2000 together, 78 per cent of the elite is Kazakh. Of the remainder, 16 per cent are Russian, 2 per cent German, 2 per cent Korean and the last 2 per cent of other European origin. In the 1995 elite, the number of ethnic Russians was considerably higher than that in 2000, at 18 per cent. Kazakhs held 73 per cent of the top positions in the presidential administration. According to the panel of experts, no new Russians joined the ranks of the top elite between 1995 and 2000. While other minorities had made up 13 per cent this had dropped to 4 per cent by 2001.

These trends concur with those cited by V. D. Kurganskaia and V. Iu. Dunaev who argue that the per centage of non-titular minorities occupying administrative posts has fallen from 42.5 per cent in 1995 to 33.3 per cent in 1999. They further argue that this trend is likely to continue since the number of non-titular representatives in the under-30 age group has fallen from 34.4 per cent in 1998 to 29.1 per cent in 1999.[31]

The degree and speed of this process of Kazakhization differed institutionally and regionally. If 60 per cent of regional (*obkom*) First Secretaries in 1991 were ethnic Kazakh,[32] 70 per cent of akims were in 1995 (14 of 20) and 88 per cent were by 2000 (14 of 16). Of the 54 akims between 1991 and 2001, 78 per cent were Kazakh; 12 per cent Russian; 6 per cent German, 2 per cent Ukrainian and 2 per cent Korean. The Soviet practice of diarchy (see Chapter Six), whereby a Kazakh head would invariably be deputed by a Russian or vice versa, was no longer a rule.

## Table 13. Ethnicity and the Regional Elite

|  | 1991 1st Sec/ Dep | 1992 Governor/ Dep | 1995 Akim/ 1st Dep | 2000 Akim | % of Ethnic Kazkahs 1999* |
|---|---|---|---|---|---|
| Aktubinsk | R/K** | K/R | R/K | K | 70.7 |
| Almaty | K/R | K/R | K/R | K | 59.5 |
| East Kazakhstan | R/K | K/R | R/R | G | 48.5 |
| Atyrau | K/R | K/R | K/K | K | 89.0 |
| Zhambyl | K/K | K/K | K/K | K | 65.5 |
| Zhezkazgan | R/K | R/K | K/K | Abolished | |
| Karaganda | R/K | R/K | R/K | K | 37.6 |
| Kzylorda | K/K | K/K | K/K | K | 94.2 |
| Kokshetau | K/R | K/R | K/K | Abolished | |
| Kostanai | R/K | K/R | K/R | K | 31.1 |
| Mangystau | R/K | R/K | K/K | K | 78.7 |

| | | | | | |
|---|---|---|---|---|---|
| Pavlodar | R/K | K/K | K/K | K | 38.2 |
| North Kazakhstan | R/K | G/K | G/K | K | 29.5 |
| Semey | K/R | K/R | K/R | Abolished | |
| Taldykorgan | K/R | K/R | K/R | Abolished | |
| Turgai | K/R | K/R | K/R | Abolished | |
| West Kazakhstan | K/R | K/K | K/K | K | 64.8 |
| Akmola | G/K | G/K | G/K | K | 37.4 |
| South Kazakhstan | R/K | K/K | K/R | K | 67.6 |
| Almaty City | K/K | K/R | K/R | R | 38.5 |
| Leninsk Town | R/K | R/R | R/R | | |
| Astana City | N/A | N/A | N/A | K | 40.9 |

* *Itogi perepisi naseleniia 1999 goda v Respublike Kazakhstan.* 1999. Almaty: Agenstvo respubliki Kazakhstana po statistike.

** G = German; K = Kazakh; R = Russian.

The Kazakhization of regional appointments is also shown by Kurganskaia and Dunaev who demonstrate that by 2001 in all of Kazakhstan's regions the non-titular population was, proportionate to their respective regional populations, under-represented in regional administrations.[33]

Similarly at the central level, Kazakhs had risen to dominate national and regional power structures to a degree that is disproportionate to their per centage of the population:

## Table 14. Population: Nationality Composition of Two Main Ethnic Groups[34]

| Nationality | 1959 | 1989 | 1999 |
|---|---|---|---|
| Kazakh | 30.0 | 39.7 | 53.4 |
| Russian | 42.7 | 37.8 | 29.9 |

The findings here do not depart from those of other countries; lower status ethnic and religious minorities are usually under-represented in the higher political strata. What *is* striking here is the extent of the under-representation. Although for most of the 1990s ethnic Kazakhs were a minority in their own state, this study suggests they dominated power structures at 70 to 80 per cent. Only the 1999 Census confirmed their recently acquired majority status, according them 53.4 per cent, with Russians forming now only nearly 30 per cent.[35]

Kazakhs were occupying elite positions and specializations formerly monopolized by Russians. This was particularly the case in the technocratic domain. While it was noted that at the regional level economic departments were still often directed or deputy directed by Slavs, the central elite now had a Kazakhized technocratic stratum. We return to this coincidence of class and ethnicity in Chapter Six and the Conclusion.

In socio-economic terms, very early signs are that the post-independent political elite is less 'modern' in the sense of being less highly educated and less dependent on salaried income than its predecessors – often only a generation away from the very different social backgrounds from which they have risen through education. It was in the Soviet era, and not yet in the post-independence era, that the revolution created the sudden changes in and opportunities for social promotion: permitting new roles; creating new classes; providing the basis for new struggles for succession and policy direction.

## SOCIAL BACKGROUND AND ELITE ATTITUDES

Did our sample of those interviewed detect any possible correlation between social background and attitudes? We can make these only tentatively because of the size of the sample and because members of the elite were understandably often unlikely to disclose policy disagreements.

The answers given by the interviewed elite did not suggest, for example, a female, ethnic Russian, or 'young' attitude on policies. The life and outlook of the intellectual professional female bore more resemblance to that of her male counterpart in education and vocation than to that of her uneducated sister. The group that joined the ranks of the elite during this period – young ethnic Kazakhs – also did not appear attitudinally uniform, falling instead into two main groups which could loosely be termed cosmopolitans and bourgeois nationalists. The social backgrounds of these two categories were not neatly identifiable, however; for example, those who had received an education abroad did not always fall into the cosmopolitan camp.

Importantly also, the economic sub-elite who wanted to see a rule-based, transparent economy did not always see this as democratization. Similarly, the regional elites were not always in favour of democratization or federalism. Promoters of civic nationhood were not necessarily democratizers; promoters of privatization did not necessarily wish to see the growth of participation. This picture of variegated attitudes suggested a number of cross-cutting rather than reinforcing attitudinal elite systems.

That said, a centre/region attitudinal axis did appear to be emerging. These disagreements arose particularly over the issues of foreign management of large state enterprises; the functioning – rather than existence per se – of the unitary state; and the pace of privatization. Both central and regional elites strongly supported the free market and were keen to see more free enterprise and individual initiative. The regional elites, however, were generally in favour of more state involvement in society.

A second axis along which disagreements were emerging was between, on the one hand, the technocratic sub-elite and, on the other, representatives of major interest groups in the government. The technocratic sub-elite has lobbied for increased transparency, accountability and efficiency in the policy-making process. But even these groups and their agendas have also been shown to be fluid. While the administrative elite favoured the increased regulation of economic actors, the business/technocratic elite were stronger supporters of state support for domestic industry (industrial policy). Whereas in the thirteenth parliament it had been primarily regional heads and deputies who had regularly called for a strengthening of state control of the oil and gas sector, and for massively redistributing resources from this sector to others that were unable to compete on the world market (especially agriculture) and to support social welfare, this agenda had, by 2000, been appropriated first by the business/technocratic elite and then by the administrative elite, with signs that the administrative elite were attitudinally less disposed to this than the business/technocratic elite. The two axes of centre/region and of technocrat/allies will be explained and further illustrated in Chapter Six when we discuss the policy environment.

Nevertheless, with the exception of some opposition leaders, neither the central nor regional elites desired fundamental change. While the regional elites were considerably more critical of current policies, and suggested that reform in some areas was needed, they did not question the system itself.

Oppositional leaders did not manage unity in this period. Whilst, for the Kazakh nationalists, the present system was acceptable as long as the government stepped up its protection of ethnic Kazakh cultural rights, those of the centrist oppositional parties, for example, advocated a federal, decentralized polity that could accommodate the country's multiculturalism: 'autocracy is not possible because we have a multiethnic country; governance here is extremely difficult' (PE, 3). The movement Azamat's platform promoted a significant change in the form of real democratization of the political system, independence of the electoral commissions and local self-government. But even among the opposition many advocated only evolutionary change: 'abrupt change would be bad for Kazakhstan – this country can only deal with soft, quiet change' (PE, 23).

Caution and incrementalism should not be mistaken for conservatism, however. A strong majority in all three regions and the centre emphasized the ability of their culture to absorb change from outside. A representative of the young Kazakh business sub-elite took this further:

> The social stratum to which I belong did not put the emphasis on Kazakh values. We do not use the Kazakh language. I cannot pretend that for me the history of the fifteenth and sixteenth centuries are important. My group is more mercantilized, not traditional; it doesn't feed on nationalism. This has its pluses and its minuses because the group is very malleable, and modern Kazakhs are experiencing problems with rural Kazakhs with new social cleavages emerging. But if we are speaking about Kazakhstan's future, this group should play a cardinal role (PE, 4).

While many other studies of elites have demonstrated how regional leaders display more parochialism and conservatism than central leaders, [36] there was no strong evidence of this difference in this study's respondents' answers. Only a minority spoke of the importance of traditions, on the lines of 'Know one's traditions, good or bad. Good tradition is respect of elders' (PE, Shymkent, 1), and tended to be ethnic Kazakhs of the older generation and from the South.

Finally, there was no necessary correlation between youth, reform and democratization. Most notably, the counterelite's platform in 2001 was primarily economic and not political. Only a minority has advocated democratization. A strong majority supported within-system change.

While our findings thus do not detect a direct linkage between social background and attitudes, this does not, however, necessarily confirm either that later socialization provides that link or that that social origins might become more important in defining attitudes in the future. Similarity in outlook might also be a function of institutional position, or indeed of wider environmental culture, both of which aspects we explore in Chapters Four and Five. Whether social origins become more important depends, moreover, on the degree to which intervening variables of recruitment and socialization prove strong enough to create a corporate identity. The persistence of a diversity of attitudes that will not neatly associate with one elite group or one social background group suggests that recruitment and socialization processes within each elite have not, so far, promoted and reinforced distinct group orientations.

Most also denied that place of birth was important: 'I consider myself from Almaty – although I was born in Semipalatinsk'; 'Because I have worked and studied in so many different places I am not particularly attached to the south.' Nor did whether an individual was born in town or country seem to exert an influence how they self-categorized their social background. Regional variations did have a weak impact on variations in how ethnic Kazakh female members of the elite perceived their cultural roles. In the more traditional South, influenced in its conservatism by neighbouring Uzbekistan, female members of the elite spontaneously referred to the importance of the home, oral history and language as means of cultural transmission. By contrast, a member of Uralsk's female political elite lamented the process of deculturalization that her ethnic Kazakh family had undergone.

The emphasis often placed in the interviews on the length of time served in the region may indicate the importance of later socialization. Lengthy socialization in a region was creating many stronger bonds with that region, often stronger than those that official or ethnic identities could supply. The interviewees suggested in 1995–1996 that Soviet occupation still had a more marked effect on perceptions of self and identity than the new post-Soviet roles.

The attempt here, albeit briefly, has been both to depict the social background, structure, values and attitudes of the political elite and to infer relationships between these variables. This chapter has given a sense of the permeability of the elites in question, and of whether the independence or agglutination model applies. As with all models, they represent extremes. In the independence model, the correlation between political status and socio-economic status is negligible, and there is no discrimination on the basis of, for example, occupation, education, family background, age, sex, religion, and ethnicity. By contrast, the agglutination model, as defined by Harold D. Lasswell,[37] posits a perfect correlation between an individual's place in the political hierarchy and his place in the social hierarchy, so that a socio-economically privileged class monopolizes political leadership. With important differences, the latter model more closely describes the Kazakhstani case.

The evidence here suggests that there is no necessary relationship in the Kazakhstani elite between the demographic attributes and particular career attributes of individuals. The analysis of social origins at this time period, when we are still feeling the effect of the strong Soviet institutions, is likely to be less revealing than in the coming years, as mobility slows and political institutions are still in flux. For the moment, the social background of elite members is relevant less as a predictor of individual behaviour than as an indicator of the structure of social power.

Nevertheless, this study shows that there is a strong correlation between one demographic attribute – ethnicity – and the ability to make it to the top. The overall predominance of male ethnic Kazakhs does suggest that being a member of this group gives an individual a considerably better chance of becoming a member of the political elite than would being non-Kazakh or female or both. But the existence of important exceptions to this rule also suggests that if a non-Kazakh male has particular educational or occupational attributes (the latter mainly Soviet-era socialization), or simply strong bonds from the Soviet era, he can also survive in power.

This chapter, then, has investigated the degree of elite cohesion along social structural lines. It indicates that we may have witnessed increased occupational differentiation between the younger and older members of the elite, as well as increased ethnic homogenization, as ethnic Kazakhs outnumber other ethnicities in all formal institutions of government. While later socialization, primarily in the Soviet period, therefore continued to be important in shaping the outlook of many of the elite members interviewed, the importance of region and ethnicity as an influence on self-categorization may grow. For example, already in 1995–1996 the importance of regional identifications was apparent, when in interviews it often appeared that, say, a Kazakh member of Pavlodar's elite might find more in common with his Russian regional counterpart than his co-ethnic in Shymkent. When asked to define their fatherland (*rodina*) those in Pavlodar tended to stress either the region or the Soviet Union, those in Uralsk and Shymkent both region and the state of Kazakhstan.

What this chapter cannot do is predict either elite attitudes (covered insofar as information is available) or policies. Even if members of the elite come from the same stratum, their attitudes vary. More broadly several scholars have questioned the importance of social background for elite behaviour[38] and the relevance of changes in an elite's social origins for shaping policy.[39] One study, for example, found that French elite preferences during the 1960s coincided with French government policy only about half the time.[40] This discrepancy may be seen here in the preferences of the elite with regard to Kazakhization policies, where many expressed misgivings about the pace of reform. In other words, just as we cannot predict attitudes from social origins, nor can we the outcome.[41]

Chapters Two and Three together have attempted to depict the institutional affiliation, career and social background of the elite and hinted at some attitudinal stances to both the form of government and the policies enacted. They have attempted to infer relationships between these variables. The remainder of the book now sets out to explain the reasons and explore the significance of this profile and characterization and begins with a better understanding of how the elite relates to its power containers, the nation and state.

# Chapter Four

# ELITE LEGITIMATION

The previous chapter focused on the primordial view of the nation, which argues that every person carries through life 'attachments', derived from place of birth, kinship relationships, religion, language, and social practices that are 'natural' for him/her, 'spiritual' in character, and that provide a basis for easy 'affinity' with other peoples from the same background.[1] This chapter looks at how the political elite has sought to construct a basis for its rule. Such an approach belongs to the instrumentalist school of nation-building, to a perspective that emphasises the use of cultural symbols by elites seeking instrumental advantage for themselves or the groups they claim to represent.[2]

Kazakhstan's legitimation process has been to a large degree about the self-legitimation of its rulers for its rulers. Ronald Barker usefully focuses on elite legitimation through the process of identification and this is the approach adopted here. The verb 'legitimate' conveys how governments actively go about winning and commanding authority (rather than simply the noun 'legitimacy' which can be viewed as a political resource). Barker writes: 'Since it is an activity, not a property, it involves creation, modification, innovation and transformation.'[3]

The self-legitimation of the elite refers to some of the ways in which the elite sees itself in its position of rule, and the extent to which the central elite is managing to legitimate itself with other centres of power. Reicher and Hopkins[4] illustrate the importance of a psychological understanding of nations and nationalism, and the ability of psychology to provide 'a bridge between the cultural and the personal by indicating how people can take understandings and values associated with large-scale social categories as their own.'[5] Social identity theory, by definition, emphasises the group over the individual or idiosyncratic, with in- and out-groups delimited according to the boundaries[6] created by the collective self – that is, according to a particular group's sense of belonging or not belonging.

In the wake of independence, Kazakhstan's political elite attempted to legitimate itself to three principal constituencies: the wider constituency abroad, notably to its 'other', Russia; to itself, including to its regions; and, to its population – both to its new titular ethnic group, the Kazakhs and to its non-titular groups, principally ethnic Russians. In the absence of free and fair elections, successful modernization and accountable institutions, legitimation through identification assumes added importance. In the context of Kazakhstan there was nothing automatic about this identity. Kazakhstan had no *Wendepunkt*, no national struggle and so the declaration of independence had to be justified. In most new states, elites have, to a great extent, relied on the identification of ethnicity when undertaking to build their followings, consolidate state power and legitimate their rule. When new rulers of new states are asked: 'In whose name do you rule?' the answer often confidently returned is: 'The Nation's!'. The weakness of Kazakh nationalism, the multifaceted identification processes underlying the political elites, and the nature of the relationship between elites and institutions, all promised to make the process of legitimation anything but that simple.

In order to accommodate these three constituencies, the top leadership thus legitimated a strategy that proposed simultaneously promoting internationalism and an ethnic Kazakh national-cultural revival. Two main elements in the elite's self-categorization and self-legitimation processes have assisted in this simultaneity: 'fuzzy' boundaries between the elite's two major ethnic groups, Russians and Kazakhs; and the tendency for ethnic Kazakhs at independence to display 'negative identity'. Both may be detected in how the elite interviewed categorized itself. These two factors might also partly explain the incompleteness and only partial intentionality of the Kazakhization process.

If the dual legitimation process has been possibly facilitated by fuzzy boundaries and a weak Kazakh prototype, it has also run into problems (both intrinsically in each of the projects and relationally). Four main problems complicated the simultaneous attempts to build an ethnic Kazakh nation and a civic Kazakhstani state: the process of restraint required for both projects to succeed hindered the process of Kazakh national-cultural revival; ethnic Kazakhs often unconsciously conflated the terms Kazakh and Kazakhstaniness, undermining the possibility of Kazakhstaniness becoming a shared mode of identification; the process has spawned and then denied sub-ethnic identifications, and the process often ignored strong regional identities (and important regional variations).

The caveats expressed in the Introduction hold again here. The respondents' answers can be only a snapshot of identity formation and these replies were often carefully crafted. The sample interviewed is not representative. Generalizations on identity formation are hazardous at the best of times. The use of the term 'non-Kazakh' or 'non-titular', sometimes used for the sake of simplicity, is problematic, since it covers a wide array of very different ethnic groups.

Political and cultural conceptualizations of the nation have often led writers to make a distinction between a typical republican, civic, French tradition versus an ethnic, organic German one. This dichotomy, as many have argued, may be false – for example, a civic nation may be based on an ethnic understanding – but the elite's nation-building project has arguably been built on the juxtaposition of these types of identities. The problems of the dichotomy are revealed later.

## INTERNATIONALISM

Internationalism may be understood in terms of the leadership's desire to reassure the non-titular population. Edward Schatz argues that the 'framing' of internationalism has contributed to the maintenance of interethnic stability.[7] The strategy of legitimation through the rhetoric of a multiethnic identity has provided some psychological comfort. One Russian central member of the political elite, explained: 'If we increase integration with Russia this will give psychological reassurances to those planning to emigrate and the situation would stabilize' (PE, 30). Another explained:

> We are also responsible for sponsoring the development of a new Kazakhstani form of identity. There was a very hard period in the first year of Kazakhstan's existence when we had to reassure Russians that their rights would be preserved. Simultaneously we could not ignore the fact that Kazakhs had been granted independence and were now first among equals. It was only after the situation had stabilized in the first two to three years that we were in a position to introduce a new Constitution on the basis of that multiethnic society (PE, 24).

A strong majority of those interviewed felt that ethnic differentiation should be downplayed not promoted, that the practice of defining people in terms of ethnic categories was a regrettable post-Soviet practice and that even speaking about ethnic differences could incite interethnic hatred. Since 1991, the president has stressed how the multicultural and multiconfessional nature of Kazakhstan determined the inescapable path

of civic responsibility and cross-national state identity.[8] This language
of internationalism served the legitimation process at home and abroad.
At home, it was directed to the non-titular groups who demographically
outnumbered the Kazakhs. Abroad, it was primarily intended to reassure
Moscow that Nazarbaev recognized the rights of Russia's co-ethnics
abroad. This emphasis on civic identification has been underscored by
policies of religion, language, citizenship and foreign policy.

Multiconfessional Kazakhstan, viewed by some indigenous commentators as a relic of the religious tolerance practised under the Mongol Empire,
was declared secular upon independence.[9] In 1995, President Nazarbaev
also told a Russian newspaper that 'Islam and Christianity are the two
flanks of Kazakhstan's spiritual legacy.'[10] The model often invoked, as
mentioned in the previous chapter, was modern Turkey, despite the fact
that there is no significant Christian presence in Turkey.[11] The elite did not
permit the registration of what they considered extreme religious groups,
such as the ethnic Kazakh movement *Alash*. The president warned against
the creation of parties of

> a religious nature – Islamic, Christian, Buddhist and so on...In a
> multiconfessional country, this might lead to grave disorder, fighting
> and bloodshed. Political parties should not be based on nationality
> [Recently] there was a report that there will be a Ukrainian party, and
> the creation of a patriotic party of Kazakhs began immediately. Do we,
> multinational Kazakhstan, need this? That is why the constitution bans
> parties of this kind categorically, and the law specifies it clearly.[12]

Nevertheless, authorities permitted a certain amount of freedom in the
registration of foreign religious organizations, such as the American Baptist
Group. The 'Islamic factor' was used only to an 'appropriate' degree.
Kazakhstan was alone among Central Asian republics in adopting observer
status in the Muslim-dominated Economic Cooperation Organization.[13] At
ECO's summits, Nazarbaev repeatedly emphasized the economic character
of this organization and how it would be 'categorically unacceptable to cooperate on an ethnic or religious basis.'[14]

Oumirek Kasenov, who in the early post-independence years headed
the presidential foreign policy think tank, the Kazakhstan Institute for
Strategic Studies, writes:

> Kazakhstan is not only a multinational state but also a multireligious
> one. Kazakhs confesses Islam, but a significant part of the population
> confesses Christianity and other religions. Because Islam is not so
> deeply rooted in Kazakhstan, its influence is not as strong as it seems
> to some observers in the West. Nevertheless, Kazakhstan takes
> into consideration the 'Islamic factor' in its foreign policy strategy.

to an appropriate degree. ... However there is little chance that Kazakhstan will join some sort of association of Muslim states, such as the Organization of the Islamic Conference.[15]

In 1994, as a sign of this balancing act, Nazarbaev travelled both on a hajj to Mecca and to the Vatican.

As regards language policy, although the Kazakh language was accorded state language status, the authorities trod carefully around the question of what status to give the Russian language. One member of the elite explained that they 'speak Russian at home with my daughter, and Russian and English at work. I support Kazakh language revival, but slowly; not these statements that by so-and-so month everyone should have learned Kazakh' (PE, 28); still another added: 'We need to create the correct conditions to allow Kazakh to be learnt. Without a dictatorship, there is no way that everyone will learn Kazakh... Politically, it is not wise to increase the salience of the language issue' (PE, 22).

The Russian and Ukrainian members of the elite interviewed considered the language law as a rise in status for Russian – which many mistakenly equated to elevation of the Russian language to official status – and as such the rhetoric seemed to be working:

> The granting of official status to Russian elevates the Russian language: no longer do we have the nebulous concept of state language. In many countries around the world, the official language means the state language anyway. This was just a lexical game and the compromise is a good one for both sides (PE, 33).

The authorities also refused to recognise groups based on ethnicities. Both the 1993 and the 1995 Constitutions banned parties based on ethnic lines.[16]

A third policy of legitimation through multiethnic identification was the republic's introduction of an inclusive citizenship law in 1993.[17] Kazakhstani citizenship derives from residency, not descent. Kazakhstan's 1993 citizenship law (incorporating the minor changes introduced in 1995), did not include naturalization laws, stiff language requirements, or stringent descent stipulations. Like Turkmenistan, Kazakhstan adopted a zero option policy, under which residents of the Kazakh SSR were automatically entitled to Kazakhstani citizenship but had to rescind any other. A deadline on citizenship adoption was imposed. The process ultimately proved more protracted than had been hoped, and although the deadline was thrice postponed, it was estimated that only 20, 000 Russians opted for Russian citizenship.[18] As a symbolic gesture to its Russian minority abroad, the Russian government, represented by the Chairman of the Commission on Citizenship, Abdulat

Mikitaev, embarked on a mission to 'persuade Kazakhstan to conclude an agreement on dual citizenship.'[19] Kazakhstan's elite, however, was united in its decision to permit only single citizenship,[20] believing that dual citizenship would breed split loyalties, something a young nation could not afford.[21] Defending his stance at Moscow State University in 1994, Nazarbaev referred to Kazakh poet Olzhas Suleimenov's reasoning that to accept dual citizenship would be like giving a parachute to only half the passengers on an airplane. Instead, argued Suleimenov, why not check that the airplane itself is in order and thereby guarantee the same standard of safety to all passengers?[22]

The elite interviewed seemed similarly united behind the principle of single citizenship and what was at the time the recently agreed Simple Exchange Agreement. This agreement was designed to facilitate the process for citizens of Russia and Kazakhstan, when settling in the other state, to take up the new citizenship. Explained one member of Pavlodar's regional administration: 'Now we have this principle: one wife, one citizenship. The formula is as simple as that' (PE, Pavlodar, 7).

The appointment of high-level Russians to ministerial posts, which have higher visibility than equivalent posts in the presidential administration, might have had the aim of legitimating the new government amongst ethnic minorities. A key example here was the appointment of Sergei Tereshchenko as Kazakhstan's first Prime Minister.

The rhetoric and some of the practice of multiethnicity have been achieved at little cost to state sovereignty. The rhetoric of multiethnicity has been intended as much for an external audience – Russia and the West – as for domestic consumption. Kazakhstan's geopolitical orientation took the middle ground. The leadership refers to its country as Eurasian, straddling East and West. Kasenov encapsulated the foreign policy and identity nexus thus:

> Although Kazakhstan is a multinational state, it was the Kazakhs who gave the state its name because it was created along primordial Kazakh ethnic lines. Nevertheless, Kazakhstan formulates and carries out a foreign policy that expresses the interests of the state as a whole rather than of any particular ethnic group, including Kazakhs.[23]

Nazarbaev has simultaneously stressed the Kazakhs' Turkic roots – 'our forefathers, as part of the single family of Turkic peoples...'[24] and the bloodties with Russia: 'I will develop Eurasianism...'[25] The leadership claims that Kazakhstan's uniqueness, which stems from being Eurasian, is symbolized by the Snow Leopard, an animal unique to the Kazakhstani mountains, fiercely independent 'but never the first to attack anyone.' The Snow Leopard is a combination of 'western elegance' and 'oriental wisdom',[26] embodying 'a space that links Europe to the Asia-Pacific region.'[27]

The content of Kazakh-conceived Eurasianism shows little resemblance to its Russian counterpart. Mikhail Alexandrov cites M. Titarenko, Director of the Russian Academy of Science's Institute of the Far East, who claimed that Nazarbaev's initiative for creating a Eurasian Union

> ... has very little in common with the spiritual principles of Eurasianism, and this is very clearly manifested in the light of the actual policy of administratively establishing domination by the titular Kazakh nationality, ignoring the multiethnic culture and multiethnic composition of the population of Kazakhstan.[28]

Eurasianists indeed promoted the idea of a common Eurasian nation, while Nazarbaev's plan did not include a common state nor even common union citizenship. Although internationalist, Nazarbaev was not prepared to countenance dual citizenship.

Ethnicity can serve to rationalize foreign policy direction to various audiences. Defending his absence from Moscow during 1996, Nazarbaev explained that Kazakhs 'have always been in favour of a multivector foreign policy.'[29] At any given time, Nazarbaev's rationalization was intended both for those partners he selected and, by way of apology, for those whom he did not. The president initially declared his country's intention to follow the Turkish model that would incorporate a Muslim heritage into a secular, Europeanized state. When Turkey failed to deliver on its economic aid promises, Nazarbaev saw more opportunity in accentuating the Asian content of ethnicity, emphasising how the authoritarian nature of his state and the political culture of his people might be more conducive to following an East Asian model of development. As echoed by Kasenov: 'As an Asian state, the Republic of Kazakhstan has also naturally made itself known in Asia.'[30] Nazarbaev again used ethnicity and historical ties to justify his relations with the South: '...it is important to note that the people of Turkey and Kazakhstan share common historical and cultural roots and traditions.'[31] Nazarbaev played the ethnic card most frequently when discussing Kazakhstan's relations with Russia. During his early presentations of the idea of a Eurasian union in 1994, Nazarbaev stated that Kazakhstan and Russia have 'blood interests' in working together.[32]

The elite's attitudes to Russia revealed here a fundamental ambiguity that is germane to a self-other relationship, in which the ethnie both embraces and fears the 'other'. Kazakhs continued to depend on Russia, but also sought differentiation from their northern neighbour. As we elaborate in Chapter 6, whereas the majority of both ethnic Kazakhs and Russians viewed the CIS and the Eurasian Union as their best guarantor of stability, as many as 31.6 per cent of ethnic Kazakhs viewed Russia as the principal threat (immediately below China), followed by the USA (8.8 per cent) and Iran (7.2 per cent). By contrast, non-Kazakh minorities regarded

Central Asia as the next biggest threat to Kazakhstan after China.[33] Regional differences over foreign policy direction were also significant. Ethnic Kazakh members of the elite interviewed in the North were less likely to view Russia as a threat than were their counterparts in the South, primarily because the northern communities had retained social, political and economic ties with the South of Russia.

# PROMOTION OF KAZAKH
# NATIONAL-CULTURAL REVIVAL

While the Republic's 1995 constitution guarantees equal rights to all minorities, and the state promises a national-cultural revival of all ethnic groups, a special place is reserved for ethnic Kazakhs in their new state. The 1993 Constitution designated the Republic as 'primordial Kazakh territory'. In his 1992 'Strategy for Creating and Developing Kazakhstan as a Sovereign State' Nazarbaev explained that it is

> quite appropriate even if the principle of equality of opportunities for all and equality before the law is valid, if in particular cases special provision is made for the interests of the native nation, the Kazakhs, as happens in many other states.[34]

This feeling is echoed by several of the interviewed ethnic Kazakh respondents, such as one who exclaimed: 'What was the point of forming the Kazakhstani state if not to give rights to the Kazakhs? If we had wanted to give equal rights to Russians then we should have stayed with Russia' (PE, Uralsk, 2).

National cultural revival has been sponsored through three main ways: cadre politics; demographic balancing (including the move to Astana); and the use of cultural referents and symbols to promote Kazakhness and distinguish it from the 'other', Russia.

One key way of legitimating Kazakh rule at home and abroad was to ensure that ethnic Kazakhs dominated political structures. This process was partly about ownership of the nation, in Anthony Cohen's terms, 'personal nationalism'. The individual is represented as the nation writ small, and the nation as the individual writ large; the nation 'conducts itself as a collective individual'.[35] Ethnicising the face of power was the quickest and most tangible way of presenting a new image of a new state. In this sense the ethnicising of the elite was partly intentional and comprised a wider power strategy, the subject of the next chapter.

The elite further legitimated the appointment of ethnic Kazakhs to top jobs in existential terms; if central power did not succeed in legitimating itself to the totality of Kazakhstan's regions then the country's new territorial integrity would be threatened. As part of this process, the central elite had to legitimate itself, on the one hand, to regions that had enjoyed preeminence in Kazakh recruitment in the Soviet period, mainly in the South, and, on the other, to those which in the Soviet period had answered not to Almaty but to Moscow (see Chapters Five and Six), mainly in the North. This dual necessity for continuity and change provoked three legitimation strategies: the initial employment of the zhuz template; the use of demographic balancing (including the move of the centre to the periphery by physically relocating the capital Almaty); and the use of cultural referents and symbols to promote Kazakhness and distinguish it from the 'other', Russia.

Nurbulat Masanov in this decade was the most vocal proponent of the view that an individual's zhuz affiliation determined the rank and type of political appointment.[36] Masanov explains the importance of the zhuz not just in symbolic but also in functional (Chapter Five) and historical (Chapter Six) terms. The Senior Zhuz, he contended, was accorded positions of low status but high influence. The Junior Zhuz, which has often acted as broker between the Senior and Middle Zhuzes, was appointed to positions of low profile, high status and relatively high influence. Finally, members of the Middle Zhuz – most notably members of its leading Argyn tribe – were placed in posts of lesser influence but that their influence was likely to grow with the move to Astana. In Erlan Karin and Andrei Chebotarev's terms: 'The republic's political system today is defined by paternal-clientelistic relationships and the division of Kazakhs into three tribal groupings [i.e. zhuz]'[37] and that zhuz membership is 'used as a mechanism for lobbying its interests in the organs of power'.[38]

This study's view is that while the regime's early legitimation strategies drew on zhuz memberships in central elite appointment decisions - quite simply because these were the templates that were readily available in the absence of a strong unified ethnic Kazakh identity - by the close of the decade these templates had been eclipsed by concerns of power maintenance and regime continuity. The environment had become too complex to allow recruitment to be dictated simply by zhuz affiliation (Chapter Six). Even in the early period in those, predominantly northern, regions where recruitment networks had been closely tied to Moscow, many non-titular members of the political elite, notably Germans and Slavs, kept their jobs – even to the level of akim.

Sub-ethnic identities have been referred to by the President as 'archaic solidarities that need to be eliminated'. Many members of the elite interviewed were keen to downplay the importance of the zhuz. Calling the zhuz factor an illness or curse (bolezn') one member of the central elite said: 'The zhuz system is much more important for the older generation because the CPSU exploited this zhuz system' (PE, 1). He was confident that young people would overcome zhuz identification by being educated abroad and he concluded that he would 'not talk to his own children about zhuz but instead about the seven to eight million Kazakhs who defended themselves against the Russian and Chinese empires' (PE, 1).

By contrast, regional interviewees, often united by the same zhuz, would refer to a lower level of belonging, the tribe or clan, as part of their self-legitimation. Kazakhs have nothing comparable to the national Kyrgyz epic, the Manas. The use of tribe and clan as referents in this regional self-legitimation process appears, as Schatz describes, to have been unintended by the centre.[39]

Second, the elite also used demographics and crude geography to legitimate ethnic Kazakh predominance in power structures. It sponsored a policy of repatriation of ethnic Kazakhs; it sought to show through the 1999 nationwide census that ethnic Kazakhs had reached a majority; and it deliberately repopulated ethnic Kazakhs to regions dominated by non-titular minorities, the move of the capital northward facilitating this at the elite level.

In the period under review, Kazakhstan's government reaffirmed its commitment to repatriating ethnic Kazakhs.[40] Since Kazakhstan became independent in 1991, its government has actively sponsored the return of ethnic Kazakhs from other parts of the former Soviet Union, China, Mongolia, Iran, Turkey and Saudi Arabia. The policy of giving citizenship rights to ethnic Kazakhs over other nationalities has been viewed as legitimating Kazakhs over Russians in nation-building. In September 1992, the government convened a worldwide *Qazaq kurultay* – the name given to the medieval meetings on the steppe – inviting representatives of the Kazakh diaspora from all over the world to Almaty. Many Kazakhs fled their native land in the 1920s and 1930s to these countries to escape agricultural collectivization and other policies imposed by the Soviet government. Even though the 1995 constitution stripped the Kazakh diaspora of its privileged entitlement to dual citizenship when living abroad, its members can still automatically become citizens of the Republic without any residency requirement, upon their return.[41]

The policy favoured ethnic Kazakhs abroad; Uighurs, for example, many of whom also fled in the Soviet period, were not automatically entitled to return to Kazakhstan. The policy, however, has not been without serious problems. Many of the newly arrived, having retained the Kazakh language, were sometimes regarded with suspicion by those who now predominantly spoke Russian. The government's policy also put considerable strain on the state budget. Returnees complained about not receiving allowances from cash-strapped regional authorities. Jobs were scarce and the prospects of those returning to agricultural labour were limited by a combination of lack of practical experience and the inability to speak Russian.[42]

The policy of encouraging repatriation was only partly responsible for the 1999 census figures, however. The main reason was continuing and substantial emigration by Russians, Ukrainians and Germans. As a result, Kazakhstan had seen a net drop in its population, from about 17 million in the early 1990s to just under 15 million by the close of the first decade of independence.[43]

As noted in Chapter One, the presidential decision of 1994, officially confirmed in 1995, to relocate the capital Almaty 1, 500 km north to what is now Astana (former Soviet Tselinograd and Kazakh Akmola) was officially explained by the need to move away from Almaty's seismic faultlines and limited expansion possibilities. Unofficially, most agreed that Nazarbaev had made a geopolitical decision. Movement to the centre possibly distanced ethnic Kazakhs from their traditional enemy, China. In theory, a central location enables the government to exert a tighter grip on the northern regions, which were dominated by ethnic Russians and open to possible secessionism, even eventual union with Russia.

Third, the elite legitimated its rule by its policies to transform the cultural markers of the power container which it now claimed to rule. As with recruitment policies more specifically, the realities of governing demanded both continuity and change: Continuity in the internationalism explained above, transformation in the need to give ethnic Kazakh content to a polity now ruled predominantly by ethnic Kazakhs. By transforming those cultural markers the elite would establish new boundaries between their Soviet and post-Soviet polities. With a predominantly ethnic Kazakh elite, this new construct would draw drew predominantly on cultural referents and symbols of Kazakh nationhood. The notion of a language law based on civic identity was most seriously questioned by the revised language law draft which was introduced in 1996.[44] Significantly, unlike the 1989 language law which originated in parliament, the brainchild of the 1996 draft was the government. Passed in 1997, the revised Language Law required Kazakh to be spoken fluently by Kazakhs by the end of 2000 and by non-Kazakhs by the close of 2005.[45] The 1995 Constitution had already stipulated that the major political offices in Kazakhstan require a knowledge of fluent Kazakh. Sergei Tereshchenko, considered at the time a rare non-Kazakh who was fluent in Kazakh, nevertheless had a Kazakh mother. The president outlined his plans:

> All schools in Kazakhstan should teach Kazakh properly and there should be a state Kazakh language examination to obtain the secondary education certificate. At higher educational establishments, Kazakh must be a compulsory graduation examination.[46]

In other words, a non-Kazakh science student, for example, would have to know advanced Kazakh to graduate from university. Many members of the elite interviewed were uncomfortable about the pace at which language reform was being introduced (partly because so many did not know the language themselves). For others, Kazakh had also become the language of emotion, the means of establishing an informal relationship between rulers and ruled. In defence of its use in such situations, Kazakhs would often explain that this practice was just as exclusionary to Kazakhs as 40 per cent did not know their own language.

Even if the state was multiconfessional, the elite used Islam to legitimate itself. The establishment in 1990 of a separate muftiat no longer under the jurisdiction of the Tashkent-based Muslim Spiritual Directorate of Central Asia[47] could be considered the first step towards official acknowledgement of the Islamic element in the national heritage. The political elite also accepted generous foreign donations, notably from Saudi Arabia, for the financing of mosques.[48] Only 63 mosques existed on Kazakhstan's vast territory before 1990 – by 1996, for example, there were more than four thousand. Almaty's only Soviet-era mosque, which lay deserted for decades, completed its extensive face-lift with Saudi Arabian money, in 1996.[49] Foreign donors also ensured the widespread distribution of Kazakh-language Korans.[50] Public gatherings often began with a short prayer, as on 16 December 1997 when President Nazarbaev opened a ceremony in commemoration of those who were killed in the Almaty riots of 1986.[51] Religious holidays were made public holidays; the Muslim festival of *kurbanbairam* as well as the springtime celebration of *nawruz* – commemorated by few Kazakhs during the Soviet era – are leading examples. The elite was thus using Islam to encourage among its citizens identification with state-sponsored religious institutions.

Furthermore, the elite consciously selected cultural references from the Kazakh tradition, creating templates around which a new republic could be identified. Historiography, public ceremonies, and, most effectively, the manipulation of symbols all contributed to this new identification.[52]

The changed pronunciation and transliteration of 'Qazaqstan' from its initial 'Kazakhstan' is a case in point. Between 1995 and 1997, the ethnic Kazakh elite insisted on foreigners pronouncing and transliterating their country the Kazakh way, with a definite emphasis on the Kazakh hard 'q'. One particularly high-ranking member interviewed insisted on the pronunciation of Kazakh as Qazaq, which set the group even further apart from non-Turkic groups. Kazakhstan was prevented by its multiethnicity from introducing such a policy immediately, and, since December 1997, with no official reason, has reverted to the old 'Kazakhstan'.

With regard to the collective rewriting of history, three main points stand out. First, the suffering that had been inflicted on the Kazakh population during the period of collectivization and sedentarization was openly acknowledged. This had, until then, been either ignored completely or trivialized with vague statements about mistakes and misunderstandings. Manash Kozybaev, Director of the Institute of History, Archaeology and

Ethnography of the Academy of Sciences of Kazakhstan, published a series of articles that revealed publicly for the first time that millions of Kazakhs had died at the regime's hands during the early 1930s. Zhuldyz Abulkhozhin, a key participant in the 1990 State Committee established to investigate Stalin's crimes, also highlighted the environmental devastation wrought by Khrushchev's Virgin Lands project of the 1960s. The Central Committee was more hesitant about a second reappraisal; in particular, the proposed rehabilitation of anti-Bolshevik Kazakh national communists. Nevertheless, the 'bourgeois nationalists' were now regarded with respect and the period of government by the Alash Orda praised for its example of independent government. Third, Kazakh-Russian relations were re-appraised and, although it was confirmed that the Junior Zhuz had asked to be admitted into the Russian Empire in 1731 in response to Chinese encroachments, it was now stressed that the Kazakhs had never invited either colonization or the Russian territorial-administrative system.

Second, we have referred to the introduction of Muslim ceremonies, but other public ceremonies were also integrated into the system of 'invented tradition'. The most important secular holiday in Kazakhstan is Independence Day, which combines official parades with unofficial popular festivities, such as fireworks and dancing in the streets. The official date of this holiday – 16 December – was moved forward to August because of the (largely unspoken) fear among the elite that popular turnout in winter would be low.

Third, as elsewhere in the FSU, a plethora of new symbols proclaimed the emergence of independent Kazakhstan: a national flag, a new anthem to replace the Soviet one, a constitution, a national bank, (embryonic) defence forces, a national currency, passports and other formal attributes of statehood. The cultural markers were drawn from Kazakh traditions. The new and elaborate flag, for example, includes a band of Kazakh ornamental motifs and an image of the steppe eagle, the Kazakhs' traditional hunting companion; the mythical winged horses and the smoke-hole wheel of the yurt form the centre pieces of the national coat-of-arms. The national colours of blue and gold symbolized the ancient Kazakh cult of the Sky. The flag is now mandatory at every civil wedding or ceremony. Linguistic disagreements also arose over the introduction on 15 November 1993 of the republic's sovereign currency, the *tenge*. It was only after considerable deliberation that the second batch of notes of the new *tenge* was issued in both languages. Prior to 1995, the notes were written only in Kazakh and both versions featured Kazakh folk-heroes.

Kazakhstan's nation-builders also sought more tangible, everyday ways in which to show that the political framework had changed. One method of achieving this was the commissioning of new statues.[53] Even for the founding fathers of the French Republic, money was scarce, and statues and buildings were ultimately often financed by private money, however, and the Kazakh situation was no different in that respect. For example, a former member of the elite, turned entrepreneur, provided capital for the construction of the House of Abai in London, named after the much-respected poet of Kazakhstan. A substantial museum and statue were also built to commemorate him in his hometown of Semei in 1996.[54] Zhambyl, one of the Kazakh steppe's most famous bards, had a yurt and statue erected in his honour outside the National Museum in Almaty in 1996. Situated prominently opposite the presidential palace is another notable statue, completed at the end of 1996 in commemoration of those who died in the Almaty riots of 1986 – an event whose official death toll still only stands at two.

A less costly and more effective means of altering perceptions was the elite's decision to rename streets, towns and regions to emphasise their Kazakh essence. The Caspian port of Shevchenko, for example, became Aktau; the Slavic-named cities of Gur'yev and Panfilov, Atyrau and Zharkent respectively. By 1995, over twenty streets had been renamed in the capital alone: Karl Marx was transformed into Kunaev; Kommunistichesky into *Ablai Khan;* and Kirov into *Bogenbai batyr,* both of the latter paying homage to the medieval and modern heroes of the Kazakh ethnos. The spelling of the names of several towns and provinces was also altered to reflect Kazakh pronunciation; the official designation of Chimkent, for example, became Shymkent; Alma-Ata, Almaty and Kustanai, Kostanai.[55] In 1996, Nurbulat Masanov wrote a letter to the Head of the Press Section under the president demanding an explanation for the absence of streets named after Russian heroes.[56]

# FACILITATING DUAL LEGITIMATION

Various factors facilitated the above dual legitimation process of simultaneously promoting internationalism and an ethnic Kazakh revival. For the period under review, Russians, by virtue of the history of their interaction and the contiguous presence of their kin state, remained the constituting 'other' for ethnic Kazakh elites. The Russian members of the political elite, in the framework of Benjamin Akzin's 'similarity-dissimilarity' pattern,[57] continued to share with their ethnic Kazakh counterparts many of the cultural norms of the Soviet period. In facing up to a past of simultaneous repression, collectivization, sedentarization and modernization, the ethnic Kazakh elite in interviews typically evaluated the Soviet political order as beneficial to their country, and often rationalized the past by presenting a balance-sheet of pluses and minuses: 'there was a lot of good and some bad' (PE, Shymkent, 16); 'Economically the Soviet period was just not quite long enough for us' (PE, 5); 'We had already ceased to write about communism in mid-1993. This was far too early' (PE, 19). Overwhelmingly, both (generally older) Kazakhs and Russians alike regretted the passing of the system which, they often felt, might have been saved if reform had come earlier and been better managed (with the blame on Gorbachev and, in particular, on his imposition of Kolbin), and a mixed reaction to Kunaev. There was only a weak correlation between negative attitudes to the Soviet era and personal or family experience of persecution, loss, or repression during the Soviet period. Those individuals who had lost family members (and nearly every Kazakh member of the elite asked had a personal experience to relate) were often as able to rationalize the Soviet past in terms of means-ends arguments as those who had not.

Russians and Kazakhs interviewed shared a similar view of the Soviet past possibly because both had benefitted and both had suffered at its hands: 'We must understand, ' explained one central elite member, 'that we were all opposed not to Russians but to the communist system. Russians also were victims of communism' (PE, 19). The Soviet era, explained another, had been 'good for many things, especially for the economy'(PE, 5).

Myths also paradoxically helped to feed this rhetoric of internationalism. Nations often feel a duty to at least partially fulfil their self-ascribed myths. The relatively liberal citizenship law probably reflected a part of the Kazakh mentality that considers itself genuinely tolerant. This came across very strongly in interviews with the elite. Many referred to the Kazakh tradition of hospitality in their self-definition, nurtured on a territory that has for centuries served as a crossing point and a melting pot of a myriad of peoples. Many illustrated their nation's generosity by pointing to the historically proven fact that it was only when travelling over that part of the Silk Road coterminous to contemporary Kazakhstan that merchants did not deem it necessary to carry extra foodstuffs, in the knowledge of the generosity of the Kazakhs.

In turn, Russians interviewed appeared often to have appropriated these self-ascribed myths. A Russian Minister explained how both 'Russians and Kazakhs are very hospitable' (PE, 30), and one of his Kazakh counterparts that: 'Good characteristics of Kazakhs include that they were never confrontational (we have the Bolsheviks to thank for that), and they helped others' (PE, 32).

As part of this acculturation process, the conversations with the elite suggested also a spontaneous and genuine reluctance to put their own nation forward at the expense of another. Both wished to downplay ethnic differences. Said one Kazakh: 'There is a certain Kazakhstani mentality: I don't place much emphasis on being Kazakh, but rather that I am a citizen of Kazakhstan. ...' (PE, 9) And another explained that when

> sitting in a room of Uighurs, Kazaks, Russians, you cannot draw attention to your nationality. In day-to-day conversation and dealings with people you need an identity that unifies. That will ensure high culture at the top and security and stability at the bottom (PE, 30).

Russian members of the elite appeared in their interviews almost resigned to the reality that the 'fate of this country' and the success of achieving a civic, Kazakhstani identity 'depends primarily on the fate of the core ethnos' (PE, 13). One Belarusan explained that his kin state 'had dumped them' (PE, 2). Simultaneously, ethnic Kazakhs interviewed were often sceptical that a Kazakhstani identity could be formed.

The dual legitimation process was also assisted by the difficulty of pinning down a prototypical 'Kazakh'. The category prototype 'is that position which best differentiates the in-group from the out-group, or to be more exact, which again maximizes inter-category differences compared to intra-category differences'.[58] The forging of a prototype as an exclusive type can be fostered by language and religion, neither of which for many ethnic Kazakhs readily constituted elements of what Michael Billig has termed 'banal nationalism'.[59]

Many ethnic Kazakh members of the political elite interviewed, especially of the centre and north, admitted that they did not commonly use the Kazakh language in their work or at home. None of the Russians interviewed had a working knowledge of Kazakh, and, as some of the bolder individuals were quick to point out neither did many of the Kazakhs working in government: 'Russian will be here for a long time to come'(PE, 30), another exclaimed: 'Why impose Kazakh? The key problem lies with the Kazakhs themselves they are not determined enough to learn their own language' (PE, 2). Even those Kazakhs interviewed who claimed to speak Kazakh at home with their children nearly always also said that they regularly spoke in Russian as well. The largest group consisted of individuals who, while not overtly opposed to the development and increased acceptance of the Kazakh language, wanted this to be a measured process.

Despite this lukewarm reception of the promotion of the Kazakh language, and despite the fact that the Kazakh language was often perceived to have little future,[60] Russians feared being linguistically isolated as the state begun to open Kazakh-language schools.[61] Part of this relates to the high-profile attention given to language policy – despite its incomplete implementation.

The importance of locational differences in responses should again be emphasized. A higher proportion of the Shymkent elite than the other two regional elites of this study had spoken Kazakh at home, gone to Kazakh-language schools in the Soviet era, and continued to use Kazakh at their workplace and with their children. Only two of the eleven ethnic Kazakhs interviewed said that Russian had been their language from birth, in school and subsequently; both these Kazakhs were born and lived in Russian-dominated South Kazakhstan towns. An ethnic Kazakh elite's command of Kazakh in the North depended also on the locality where he or she was raised, specifically whether that locality was urban or rural. Thus two of the four members of the Kazakh elite in Pavlodar spoke Kazakh at home because they came from rural areas with predominantly Kazakh-speaking communities. The other two had been raised either in a town neighbouring mines where Russian dominated or in Pavlodar itself. The same applied to Shymkent where the nine out of eleven who declared their predominant use of Kazakh were rural-born. In Uralsk the majority of rural-born Kazakhs had also used Kazakh as their dominant language. While one central elite member held that the Kazakh language should grow in status – 'in the South, for example, it is impossible to not use Kazakh' (PE, 27), a Kazakh member of Pavlodar's elite regarded Russian as a tool of interethnic unification: 'Discrimination, or differentiation is not possible in our country because we all speak the same language' (PE, Pavlodar, 6).

Almost all ethnic Kazakh members of the elite expressed their religion culturally not spiritually. Many explained that 'given that the majority of us were nomads, it was implanted to a very shallow degree... Missionaries had to be athletes to keep up with the nomads!' (PE, Pavlodar, 3) or that 'historically Islam has no real meaning. Remember that Kazakhs would read the Koran in Arabic but often not understand it' (PE, 5).

Of the regional Kazakh elites, those of the South displayed the most affinity for Islam but insisted again that their relationship was a cultural one, and a minority only practised the five pillars of Islam. Few members of the elite, outside the older generation of Kazakhs, stated that they could recite passages from the Koran or say the Islamic prayers (bata) correctly. The first Kazakh translation of the Koran did not appear until 1993, around the same time as the Uzbek and Turkmen translations. It may well be that if Kazakhstan had been a mono-national state, it would also have declared itself secular.[62]

The elite proclaimed publicly that it was proud of its nomadic past, oral traditions and elaborate customs. Nomadism is the most significant historical marker that divided the Kazakhs from their sedentary northern neighbours, the Russians. On the other hand, the elite recognized nomadism's awkwardness in a western-centric view of civilization. Nomadism, by its very nature, also lacks physical reminders of a great past. Kazakhs interviewed would often have a certain sense of inferiority with regard to their past. One minister explained that the elite should not 'praise everything which is nomadic. When I land in Paris I am faced with incredible buildings and memorials; we have nothing equivalent' (PE, 19). Another minister continued that 'to be Kazakh is to be a person of the contemporary world. One of the big negative legacies of Soviet rule, perhaps the result of colonialism, is our inferiority complex' (PE, 27). As Epstein has noted, 'elements of negative identity are nearly always present where ethnic groups occupy a position of inferiority or marginality within a dominance hierarchy.'[63] Negative ethnic identities are characteristic not only of dominant groups, but of subordinate groups as well. If extreme conformity is a typical reaction to domination among the co-opted elites of subordinate groups, then empathy with the demands of subordinate groups is one form of response to power among the dissenting elites of dominant groups: Said another member of the elite: 'I am first and foremost Kazakh before anything else. But we are not superior to Russians or others' (PE, 7).

If this dual legitimation process – of internationalism and an ethnic Kazakh national-cultural revival – has been facilitated by fuzzy boundaries and a weak Kazakh prototype, it has also run into contradictions. Four main contradictions complicated the simultaneous attempts to build an ethnic Kazakh nation and a civic Kazakhstani state: the process of restraint required for both projects to succeed; the tendency of ethnic Kazakhs often unconsciously to conflate the terms Kazakh and Kazakhstaniness and thus undermine the possibility of Kazakhstaniness; the spawning and subsequent denial of sub-ethnic identifications; and also the ignoring of strong regional identities (and important regional variations).

First, paradoxically Kazakh identity was partly being asserted by denying Kazakh nationalism. Most enthused were the younger generation but even those, as we noted in the previous chapter, were split between what might be loosely termed 'cosmopolitans' and 'nationalists'. Respondents seemed aware that they might be labelled prejudiced or intolerant if they were seen to believe in national character and to endorse nationalist sentiment. They seemed therefore wary of expressing such positions.

Second, the two projects were muddled through the conflation of the terms 'Kazakh' and 'Kazakhstani'.[64] The interchangeability of the terms concords with Billig's sense of the national – that it should be as unconscious, as unforced as possible. Explained one Kazakh: 'The idea of Kazakhstani citizenship will not be realized. Russians or Koreans, for example, will not subscribe to it, even if the Kazakhs do … We cannot insist that others also become Kazakh' (PE, 27). Consciously or unconsciously, the Kazakh interviewed has here equated adopting Kazakhstani citizenship with becoming Kazakh. This conflation is in part responsible for the failure of the Kazakhstani concept to reassure. One Russian explained how it was easier for him as a member of the elite to understand what Kazakhstaniness is but that as a member of the population 'many are afraid of this identity, do not believe in it, and emigrate' (PE, Pavlodar, 7).

One can therefore observe a tension between different formulations of nationality within the Kazakhstani debate. At one extreme, there was an attempt to formulate Kazakhstaniness as an inclusive nationality, within which the distinctions between Kazakh, Russian and German are entirely secondary. An associated position was to insist on Kazakhstaniness as an authentic nationality but to place it alongside ethnic identities such as Russian or Kazakh identity. There is no necessary contradiction in being Russian and stressing one's attachment to Kazakhstan, but the way in which ethnic Kazakhs 'own' Kazakhstan in their narratives seems to have created one. If 'Kazakhstani' is seen as merely a device to impose a hegemonic Kazakhness in which non-Kazakh reality is obliterated, then it becomes a mode of domination rather than a possible form of identification.

Third, the Kazakhstani central elite in its official rhetoric denied the importance of sub-ethnic sources of belonging. This is problematic for two reasons. On the one hand, the elite is then forced to find unambiguous national heroes. The key national heroes, as Edward Schatz has illustrated, are, however, associated with particular zhuz; the vague character of nation-building and the elite's failure to follow through on nation-building policies has left it up to the elite, especially the regional elite, to interpret the letter.[65]

In some regions, moreover, sub-ethnic markers of identity seemed to be powerful markers of belonging that could actually serve to strengthen the ethnic sense of the nation. The elite may thus have been denying itself an important legitimating tool. Although references to tribalism were banished from the official nation and although generally considered a taboo topic in the interviews (both the Pavlodar and Uralsk elites were keen to avoid the clan issue, claiming it to be a 'southern problem' PE, Pavlodar, 1, 2, 6 and Uralsk, 1, 5), they were frequent in the Shymkent elite's narratives. The Shymkent elite appeared to have a stronger sense of their ethnic self, their answers often replete with detail about ethnic stereotypes and values. An ethnic Kazakh heading a department in the presidential administration who was from the South: 'I don't just know my 7 generations back, I know 20 back. My family is of Turkic not Mongolian heritage. We are proud of our family relations' (PE, 24).

Finally, the interview answers suggested that it is erroneous to assume that identification will automatically be based on ethnic, or national, terms; the elite interviewed here and findings elsewhere suggest that regional identies were strong. In the past, it was often thought that those Russian officials in the USSR's non-Russian republics who spent their entire lives in that territory or were born there were likely to defend local interests with greater vigour than those who came to the republic at a later age. Similar local patriotism was apparent amongst, for example, the Ukrainian and Russian members of the Pavlodarian political elite. These individuals had often arrived in Kazakhstan as part of the Virgin Lands project of the 1960s. This portion of the political elite regarded itself as having actually built, constructed and promoted Kazakhstan within the Soviet Union. The implicit argument they made was that the relationship of their self with the nation was born in Soviet times; to strip them of that affiliation would be to strip them of their sense of belonging. In the words of one member of the regional administration in Pavlodar:

We have managers, leaders who are from Odessa, Leningrad, Moscow, like pioneers in America. I don't think that in England you would have been able to construct a town like this in 20 years. When I arrived it was a mere village, I was so shocked I immediately wanted to turn back. Where on earth had I landed, I asked myself, after the big town life of Sverdlosk? Serious construction began in 1970s. Before we arrived there was no tractor factory, no chemical factory, no refinery and neither of the two large electric power stations. The Soviet Union constructed this territory (PE, Pavlodar, 5).

While both the towns of Uralsk and Pavlodar were Russian and Soviet creations respectively, Shymkent's is a history with far less Russian content. 'I must point out, ' said one ethnic Kazakh of Shymkent's regional administration, 'that Shymkent was built before the arrival of the Soviets or Russians and is part of the ancient traditional Silk Road' (PE, Shymkent, 11).

The southern Kazakh elite interviewed was also the most negative about the Soviet period. Of the ethnic Kazakhs in Shymkent, a quarter viewed the Soviet period as negative, and they cited repression and collectivization, which this same elite said had killed at least half of the Kazakh population. This is despite the fact that the South was less affected by collectivization since it was already more sedentarised than the remainder of the Kazakh Republic's territory by the 1930s. While some more general positive features of the Soviet era, such as education, were mentioned, they were generally attributed to the actions of the former head of the Kazakh Communist Party, Dinmukhamed Kunaev. Kunaev received praise from ethnic Uzbeks and Kazakhs alike, being perceived as advocating the interests of southern Kazakhstan during the late Soviet period. Essential to the contemporary perception of the Soviet period by the southern elite was the impression that very little has changed, and that the power southern clans enjoyed continues.

Anthony Smith writes that 'collectivities in the process of "ethnic formation"' will generally aim to accentuate those attributes they feel are lacking.[66] This may explain why the elite's ethnic Kazakhs have sought to use Islam and language in their national-cultural revival programme; why they have often felt the need to compensate for their weak ethnic sense of self; why lineages and clans have sometimes become the solidifying elements in their identity; why historical heroes remain; and why the law on language, which elevates Kazakh above Russian, often makes emotional rather than practical sense.

The Kazakhs' fusing of the distinction between Kazakhs and Kazakh-stanis undermines the possibility of Kazakhstaniness becoming a mode of identification for non-titular groups. But negative identities and the fuzziness between boundaries may at the same time have contributed to a reduction in intra-elite conflict, as has the absence of emotional nationalism. There was deliberate self-restraint. Such observable negative identity means that ethnic Kazakh identity is *not* immune to counter positions, partly because its content is transparent. And, since the lines between ethnic, social and official nations are blurred, neat dichotomies are not possible. This makes it extremely difficult to assess where the ethnic narrative begins and the social narrative ends. Ethnic Kazakh assertiveness is not a product of democratic politics arising out of an advanced economy. It is the product of a weak ethnic sense of self that is being overcompensated for by a policy of territoriality.

The civic Kazakhstani state identity remained a strongly contested one, with doubters of its effectiveness among the ethnic Kazakh elite also. The difficulties of creating a normative state based on values and symbols encouraged the elite to opt increasingly for an instrumentalist approach, emphasising instead behaviour. Legitimation here is based on achievement and effectiveness, measured primarily in economic reform terms. This was embodied in *Strategy 2030*, Nazarbaev's equivalent of a state-of-the-nation address.[67] Delivered in 1997, it emphasized technocratic and managerial reform while diminishing reference to the consociationalism that had marked his earlier statements. This became part of a broader strategy of co-optation and compartmentalisation to which we now turn.

# Chapter Five

# TECHNIQUES
# OF POWER MAINTENANCE

The scarcity and frequent falsification of elections in Kazakhstan rendered recruitment an essential component of the political life of the country. Recruitment channels affect elite circulation and therefore power maintenance. Putnam has argued that '[M]odifications in recruitment channels, selectorates, and credentials can influence the composition of political elites independently of changes in socio-economic forces or functions, '[1] and that '[T]he changes embodied in the Communist and nationalist revolutions ... are explicable more easily in political than socio-economic terms.'[2]

Chapter Five focuses on agency, its intentionality and purpose. Specifically, it analyses the techniques that the elite has employed to keep itself in power. It assesses the extent to which the elite system in the first ten years of independence was a system by design rather than by default, the product of the elite's ability to bargain and influence its composition and institutional structure. Techniques of position maintenance, the term used by Beck and Malloy, refer to the methods used by elites to achieve and maintain their predominant positions. These techniques might include, but need not be limited to, competition through electoral procedures, the use of mass physical terror, or control over and manipulation of the flow of information.[3]

As explained in Chapter Two, in the early 1990s, the Kazakhstani elite's selectorate consisted of the president and a small coterie of his advisers. The primary aim of this selectorate was to maintain itself in power and to do so it attempted to: a) shape both the informal and formal opportunity structures; b) de-territorialize, centralize and de-institutionalize politics; and c) adopt a cadre policy of simultaneously seeking out allies and protecting technocrats as part of a broader patron-client network.

# LIMITING THE INFORMAL OPPORTUNITY STRUCTURE

Informal factors that increase the likelihood that certain individuals will consider themselves eligible for recruitment include the process of political socialization; various aspects of the social structure of society; the extent to which access to financial and other related resources is distributed evenly throughout the population; and the extent to which the prevailing societal norms encourage widespread office seeking.

Both Kazakhization and sub-ethnicity sit at the core of such an effective opportunity structure. One of the principal discussions about recruitment practice in Kazakhstan has been around the degree to which the political elite deliberately narrows the pool of eligible candidates by informally ruling out members of society who do not belong to a certain ethnic or sub-ethnic group.

To recall the findings in Chapter Three. With the caveat that it is difficult to uncover clan/zhuz membership because place of birth does not necessarily equate with zhuz membership, and the impossibility of stating conclusively whether ethnic factors determined every appointment (to do so would require the study of individuals in identical positions, differentiated solely by their nationality, rarely the case), the elite sample here suggested an overrepresentation of the Senior Zhuz, a near representation of the Middle Zhuz but an underrepresentation of the Junior Zhuz. In terms of ethnicity, this study found 78 per cent of the elite to be Kazakh in the 1995 and 2000 periods. It also found that the timing and number of ethnic Kazakh appointments had differed institutionally and regionally. This ethnic Kazakh monopolisation of power structures was found in other studies. Erlan Karin and Andrei Chebotarev argue that 'representatives of the indigenous population constitute 80 to 90 per cent of the administrative elite.'[4] A. Chubar posits the following figures: 85 per cent for the presidential administration; 72 per cent in the government and 77 per cent in the akimats.[5] According to Khliupin, the ministries with the most extensive Kazakhization have been the ministries of foreign affairs, oil and gas, information and press, and justice, all of which had become about 80 per cent Kazakh.[6]

This study argues that the appointment of ethnic Kazakhs is part intentional, part structural. Structural factors are explored in Chapter Six. In intentional terms, the appointment of ethnic Kazakhs, and specific zhuz representatives, may best be understood as only one of many techniques of power maintenance. This technique, essentially one of legitimation, was explored in the previous chapter which concluded that while both ethnic and sub-ethnic criteria mattered symbolically, in the period under review other techniques of power maintenance increasingly took precedence. Both ethnic and sub-ethnic criteria should in this sense be viewed in the context of power relations more generally; in one member of the political elite's terms, the appointment of ethnic Kazakhs was 'perceived as a necessary way of anchoring the post-independence elite in power.' (PE, 19). Or in opposition leader Petr Svoik's words:

> There is no defined border between Russians and Kazakhs in the oblast administrations. Of course, many Russians have left positions but some have got good positions. In North Kazakhstan oblast, for example, the akim is German. Most akims are loyal to the government which illustrates the ideology of nationalism is secondary to the ideology of power.[7]

These other techniques are explored in the remainder of this chapter.

However intentional, Kazakhs were occupying state positions disproportionate to their demographic weight in the early years of independence. The elite recognized that interethnic instability would threaten its control. Therefore the elite sought to minimise this scenario, as well as reduce alternative sources of authority, by de-ethnicizing the broader social and political opportunity structure.

The language of internationalism, described as part of the legitimating process in Chapter Four, contributed to just such a de-ethnicization. As a consequence of framing the legitimacy of the new state on civic rather than ethnic grounds, discussion of ethnicity became taboo and interethnic stability portrayed as the success of just such framing. In this context a de-ethnicization of the political space became easier. This discourse of de-ethnicization has helped the elite to remain in power because it disempowered alternative ideologies in the political space and slowed the formation of non-Kazakh movements because they already felt protected by the state. The de-ideologization of the political space has enabled the elite to concentrate on techniques of management. Elsewhere, Fleron describes the ways in which elites use technical and managerial skills in the process of governing.[8] In Expert, Group A's terms: 'Our government is not built on principals of politics but on the principles of "housekeeping" and "management".'

To 'de-ethnicize' the political space, the elite has also either placated or co-opted leaders of non-Kazakh movements or organizations. Several Slav directors of Soviet state enterprises were co-opted. The leaders of the National Cultural Centres (Chapter Four) were placated; the Slavic movement *Lad* was permitted actively to support Russians emigrating to Russia, and the Association of Koreans was allowed to participate in business initiatives where they might have been otherwise excluded. (This may partly explain the instrumental attitude of Koreans to the Kazakhstani state, as revealed in Masanov's survey on political culture analysed in Chapter Six).

The result of de-ideologization and co-optation was to steer the debate of issues often away from ethnicity to issues of loyalty and opposition. Movements during the 1995–1998 and pre-1999 presidential election period were primarily differentiated by whether they supported the incumbent regime. This two-bloc system was further encouraged by the 1998 electoral law with its single mandate and two-round requirements. Sixty-six of the MPs were to be elected on a first-past-the-post system in single-mandate constituencies, the other ten by proportional representation on the basis of party lists. Other than the Communist Party, Alash and Azamat, the movements were pro-executive. The party law and the electoral law also forbade the formation of ethnically based parties. Nearly all heads of National Cultural Centres supported the president in January 1999 and the pro-presidential parties of *Otan* and *Grazhdanskaia Partiia* in the parliamentary elections of Autumn 1999. The intended effects of the electoral system were thus to narrow the party system into two main blocs: those belonging to the opposition and those supporting the state.[9]

## LIMITATION OF FORMAL OPPORTUNITY STRUCTURE

The formal opportunity structure was transformed in other ways to control the channels of recruitment and severely limit the opportunity structure outside the executive power. The elite has limited formal institutional power both through legal and extra-legal means. Chapter One demonstrated the increased authoritarianism of the regime. The elite has attempted to create what Linz and Stepan term a 'within-type' regime change,[10] in which personnel replacement is likely to be less-substantial and the elite more able to control the accession of new leaders into the regime.

As noted in Chapters One and Two, the legalizing of the presidential republic through the passing of the republic's second constitution in 1995 established the presidential dominance in the regime. Few of those interviewed doubted the president's intention to establish such a constitution. The intentionality of the electoral system has been excellently analysed elsewhere by Pauline Jones Luong.[11] The president was personally involved in the final writing stages of the Constitution. A lawyer working at the time in the presidential administration explained how '[D]espite his busy timetable, the president played a significant role... We all took off for his country house and we literally worked through nights... He knew much about other constitutions and we used his information' (PE, 14). The upshot, explained an Expert, is 'a 100 per cent domination of executive power.' (Expert, Group A) Nazarbaev had at an early stage intimated his intention to establish a presidential republic with a bicameral parliament. 'Many deputies were dead against the project of a two-tiered parliament being prepared by Vice President [Erik]Asanbaev, ' explained another Expert. 'Already in this project autocratic tendencies were coming from the presidential apparat. So the president summoned me, along with others, and said: "Persuade me, opponents, I would like to listen to you again" and the project was shelved for a couple of years.' (Expert, Group B)

Chapter Two explained the various ways in which the president's powers in the 1995 Constitution increased vis-à-vis other power branches. The use of the Constitution to justify elite action suggests that elites are the originators of institutional design, and that they fashion constitutions to build up their power. Constitutions matter not only as power maps but also in that they provide a legal basis for extra-legal measures. Deliberate contradictions in the Kazakhstani Constitutions allowed President Nazarbaev to escape accusations of non-constitutionalism, while at the same time couching his actions in legal terms.

Extra-legal measures (described in Chapter One) have taken three main forms: the December 1993 self-dissolution; the March 1995 dissolution; and the calling of early elections in 1999, combined with the falsification of these elections' results. When in December 1993 the president 'invited' parliament to dissolve itself, a decree granted the president plenipotentiary power until the new parliamentary elections of 17 March 1994. The bicameral parliament was so established that of the 177 candidates for the parliamentary elections, the president was allowed to pick 42 from a 'state list' (gosudarstvennyi spisok). In March 1995, the Constitutional Court, at the alleged prompting of the president, ruled to dismiss this thirteenth parliament on the basis of a complaint lodged one year previously by an Almaty candidate, Tatiana Kviatkovskaia. The Constitutional Court, on the basis of this single constituency, declared the entire elections of the previous year illegal. The dissolution of the central Mazhilis reinstated the president's plenipotentiary powers until December 1995, when new parliamentary elections were held.[12] The allegedly almost unanimous support for the president in the 29 April 1995 referendum granted him the right to push through the new Constitution of August 1995 with substantially increased powers. This April referendum extended presidential rule to December 2000, permitting the president to avoid the presidential elections scheduled for 1996, thus allowing Nazarbaev to avoid standing against Olzhas Suleimenov and Gaziz Aldamzharov, two reportedly popular alternative candidates of the time.

Nor did the presidential elections of 10 January 1999 prove democratic. The calling of early elections left only three months for campaigning, and only the incumbent president possessed the financial and organizational means to campaign. More seriously, the election commission disqualified the only serious contender to Nazarbaev, former Prime Minister Akezhan Kazhegeldin. The commission claimed that it was within its constitutional right, since Clause 4.1 of the 8 May 1998 constitutional amendment to the electoral law stipulated that no one with a criminal record, including a minor offence, was allowed to stand for electoral office.[13] Kazhegeldin had been accused (but not convicted) of money laundering in Belgium, and of holding an unsanctioned meeting of his campaign movement, *For Honest Elections*. In response to this biased pre-election campaign, an exaggerated participation rate[14] and a falsified counting process, the OSCE and other observers declared the 1999 election results falsified.

The institutionalization process outside of the executive has been strictly controlled, in particular with regard to the judiciary and legislative spheres; party political formation; and the deliberate obstruction of the development of an indigenous bourgeoisie. 'If we take from 1994, since the dissolution of parliament, and compare the situation with what it was in 1991', said one Expert, 'then we can see that the division of power is far less clear and effective; we are now in the situation of a dominating executive power' (Expert, Group A).

## DE TERRITORIALIZATION AND CENTRALIZATION OF POLITICS[15]

Just as the regime sought to de-emphasize ethnic identities, so has it sought to downplay regional identities or interests. The centralization of politics has been achieved in a number of ways: by harnessing territorial representations through executive national institutions; by ensuring control over the economic reform process especially by centralizing case-by-case privatization between 1995–1998; and the centralization of the recruitment process which has involved the ethniccizationtion of power and regional-elite crossovers.

Politically, centralization enables the central elite to oust regional competitors and economically to monopolize regional resources. It has been achieved by emaciating regional powers; by weakening the regions through a process of regional consolidation; by moving the capital to the periphery; by creating top-down parties and by ensuring centre-regional crossovers in the recruitment process. These measures enabled central elites to buy off regional elites when they need them, such as during election periods. Economically, the elite's mass privatization campaign was centrally managed and exluded regional players.

In a federal system, the centre does not have the judicial right to abolish, amend or redefine its territorial units. As a unitary authoritarian state, Kazakhstan has done all three. Five regions were fused with their neighbours in 1997. The committees set up to enforce these changes were composed exclusively of members of the national elite. The move was presented as a means to rationalize and centralize government.

On 4 May 1997, Nazarbaev ruled out any further administrative changes. The political opposition group Azamat, as well as advocating the election of the akim, at the same time argued for the reduction of provinces to three to improve efficiency and to better express the country's regional geographies. Further elimination was unlikely, however. Significantly, no mergers occurred in the republic's western regions. Given the considerable resources shared by these regions, their union might have been perceived as destabilizing to the centre. By the simple law of competition and size, a system consisting of larger numbers of smaller regions would tend to have a stronger central government than one with a smaller number of larger regions. The government thus appears deliberately to have limited the number of provinces to twelve.

Ethnic homogenization and the de-regionalization of ethnic politics was further abetted by the physical relocation of the Centre (Chapter One). In a bold move, the centre was physically relocated to the periphery to create a new centre and to increase influence over peripheral regions. Relocated to the north, the president supposedly would be better placed to proffer patron-clientelism to the North and to distance himself from significant southern elite networks.

Provincially based movements have been curtailed by the creation of top-down, transmission-belt parties. These are parties created by the presidential administration. Their members and names have changed over the years. The most significant have been the Kazakhstan's Union of People's Unity (SNEK), formed in 1993 in the run-up to the 1994 parliamentary elections; the Liberal Party, headed by the president's then Press Secretary Asylbek Bisenbiev in the run-up to the January 1999 presidential elections; and, OTAN, whose campaign prior to the October 1999 parliamentary elections was managed by Kazakhstan's first Prime Minister, Sergei Tereshchenko. By creating a series of top-down centrist parties, the elite itself has firmly occupied the political space. In conversation in early 2002 with Foreign Minister Tokaev, US Assistant Secretary of State Elizabeth Jones recounts how she urged that Kazakhstan's 'elections to members of the parliament should be absolutely free and fair, and not back to the old days, when the president said to me, in one conversation, "Yes, we have lots of political parties here. I started them all".'[16] The president's parties, as noted, have controlled the recruitment process, sifting elites and marginalizing other parties on the political spectrum. The Communist Party, for example, the only party with any form of meaningful institutionalization, was not registered until 1994.

Central authorities also ensured that there was no territorial representation at the regional level in national legislatures. The candidates who won the 1999 parliamentary round of elections were often handpicked by the central executives and brought to victory through the connivance of the provincial akimat (in charge of composition of the regional electoral commission), itself a representation of central power. Superficially, the Senat appears to represent territorial interests, as is the design for the US Senate. In practice, however, members were indirectly elected by the maslikhat, which is dependent on the akimat, and seven of the senators are directly nominated by the president. In addition, the Senat Chairman is appointed by the president. Once again, therefore, senators were not representing regional interests, but the interests of those who brought them to power. Parliamentarians were independent of the electorate, indeed of their party. They were dependent on the akim and on the president.

The centralized recruitment process was intended to ensure provincial support for the regime, especially prior to elections. Like Yeltsin in his early years, Nazarbaev adopted a policy that sought to maximise the power of the centre generally and the power of the presidency specifically. Like Yeltsin, Nazarbaev implemented a system of vertical integration through two main institutions: the use of the presidential inspector and the appointment of the provincial head. Again as in Russia, the provincial heads were initally called *glavi administratori*, but unlike Russian practice, their name was changed to akim in 1995. Unlike Yeltsin's regional representative, the role of inspectors in Kazakhstan was not codified, but like their Russian counterparts they enjoy less authority than provincial heads. On balance, they appear to have been rather ineffective, rarely being in the regions for sufficient time to exert any real impact.

Central power also falsified regional election results to ensure the maintenance of its own regime. The CEC reported the party list results as follows for the October 1999 parliamentary elections:

| | |
|---|---|
| Republican Party "Otan" | 30.89% |
| KPK (Kompartiia Kazakhstana) | 17.75% |
| Agrarian Party (Agrarnaia partiia) | 12.63% |
| Citizen Party (Grazhdanskaia partiia) | 11.23% |
| "Azamat" (Democratic Party) | 4.57% |
| People's Congress Party | 2.83% |
| "Alash" Nationalist Party | 2.76% |
| Rebirth Party (Partiia Vozrozhdeniia) | 1.97% |
| Political Labour Party (Partiia truda) | 1.38% |

While many indigenous observers claimed that the results of the two frontrunners had in fact been the reverse, with CPK gaining the majority vote. They based this conclusion on the evidence of polls and on the contention that there were blatant anomalies at provincial level, as seen in the preliminary results.[17]

Other than the Communist Party, Alash and Azamat, the movements were pro-executive. Although the *Grazhdanskaia Partiia* represented the interests of a foreign businessman, Aleksandr Mashkevich (noted as a 1995–1996 player by the Panel of Experts), at the time of election it was supported by President Nazarbaev. The unpopularity of the key executive party OTAN in the run-up to the elections was partly indicated by the number of OTAN candidates who opted to disguise their affiliation by registering as independents.

Manipulation by the centre of regional results would be considerably difficult were recruitment left solely to the regions. Cadre politics has been used to centralize power in a number of ways: the institution of the inspector; the appointment of the akim; the parachuting of central leaders to the provinces and the incoporation of provincial leaders in central institutions of power; and ethnic homogenization of provincial leadership, including forced ethnic Kazakh migration to areas dominated by non-Kazakhs.

The president reserved the right to appoint and dismiss the akim. This provision was justified by a transitional period which requires a high flexibility of public administration and operation of the principle of command. Unlike in Russia, election of the akim, other than in the occasional district, has been generally ruled out by the president. At what was to be the first of several meetings of regional heads in Almaty in April 1992, Nazarbaev announced that the 'penalties for non-fulfilment of my orders would be most severe'.[18] An akim that was deemed non-compliant, too influential or too popular could be removed (Chapter Two established the average longevity of the akim at two to three years). The centre's prerogative to appoint means that it could practise Soviet-era divide-and-rule. The non-election of the regional leadership placed limits on the types of working relationships and bargaining tools that the regions could develop with the centre. It constrained the development of ground-breaking treaties, as in the Russian Federation, as this assumes the operation of two separate tiers of government. Instead, it was in the interest of the akim to approach the Centre cautiously on reform.

The central authorities also sought to blur the distinction between centre and periphery by creating national-regional crossovers of elite recruitment, a trend shown in Chapter Two. The centre has stretched itself into the periphery since independence. It is possible to discern three phases, all of which served to centralize elite recruitment. In the early phase, the selectorate appeared to prefer continuity, choosing leaders from the regions. In seven out of 20 cases, therefore, former regional executive First Secretaries became akims. The preference was for 'home-grown' elites. During the second phase, under Kazhegeldin's government, there was a half-hearted attempt to introduce performance-related criteria to the longevity of the akim. Technocrats or former businessmen were sometimes selected. In the third phase since 1997, members of the national elite were parachuted into some regions, such as Imangali Tasmagambetov, Umirzak Shukeev, Vitalii Mette, Mazhit Esenbaev, Sarybai Kalmurzaev. Post-1995–1996, 12 central members of the elite were appointed to regional positions (compare that to 3 between 91 and 95) but only two travelled in the opposite direction i.e. from region to centre. The sort of mobility we saw from region to centre in the early years of independence has slowed.

Economically, the regime in its third phase of privatization (see Chapter One) sought to centralize policy. Explaining the privatization of Pavlodar's aluminium factory, one of Pavlodar's elite complained how they were presented with a contract that had already been signed by the Cabinet of Ministers and Central State Property Committee rather than its regional branches. 'We had no idea about the agreement, we were never consulted, ' he explained. 'Then I asked a friend to look up the address of the foreign management contract firm that had taken over the factory, White Swan. It turns out they are neither foreign nor English.' (Pavlodar, 3). The centre continued to make the final decision on foreign investment contracts but the regions expected to be consulted because they had been previously (Chapter 6).

In reality the de facto economic decentralization process (Chapter 6) delegitimized regional power in the population's eyes and President Nazarbaev was often therefore immune to the politics of blame because regional authorities, responsible for education and social welfare, acted as a buffer between central institutions and the population. Inadequate tax collection and constant per centage changes in central budget transfers to the regions ensure that the budget remains centralized. Formal powers are only a chimera if jurisdictional units are ill-equipped to back up their authority.

Centralization often stifled regional initiative, competition and chances for separatism and delegitimizing regional governments. Shortly after the January 1994 meeting of the Slav community in Ust-Kamenogorsk, the president issued a decree 'On Measures for Governing the Activity of the Free Economic Area', which abolished the free economic area. By so doing, writes *Focus Central Asia*, the president 'destroyed the economic ground for separatism'. Furthermore, writes *Focus Central Asia*, centralization allowed the president to play off members of his political elite against each other. For example, in the period of 1996 when Kazhegeldin and Nazarbaev began to disagree, Kazhegeldin criticized the poor performance of his birthplace, then Semipalatinsk oblast. Its akim, Kazhegeldin's long-time friend and Semipalatinsk business partner Galymzhan Zhakiianov, subsequently accepted an invitation by the president to head a new Agency for Strategic Resources in Almaty, a direct competitor to some of the functions originally entrusted to the Prime Minister's government.

# CADRE POLITICS: THE POLITICIAN'S DILEMMA

Finally, in terms of deliberate policy explanations for who has been recruited, we can explain their varied occupational backgrounds as a dual response to the need to recruit both allies and technocrats. This is what Barbara Geddes for Latin America termed 'the politician's dilemma' and many of the arguments she used for Latin America may be applied to the Kazakhstani case; we return to this later. The simultaneous recruitment of technocrats is the flip side of the politician's dilemma, namely that, on the one hand, recruitment has been about keeping the president's allies; on the other, about building up a compartmentalized economic elite sector which can act as a coherent team.

In addition to the centre-regional crossover just described, the regime was consolidated through the narrowing of the selectorate; *creation of* patron-client relations; frequent reshuffling and co-optation; and simultaneous and sequential recruitment through a policy of compartmentalization.

## Repression and Co-optation

To a far greater extent in the second half of the 1990s the elite resorted to repressive measures where previously it would have employed either legal or extra-legal ones. Particularly symptomatic was its treatment of the opposition, mass media and political parties. Cases in point included the former Prime Minister Akezhan Kazhegeldin, who was barred from standing for the 1999 presidential election. Overall, as noted in Chapter One, we have seen a strengthening of coercive organs of government, notably the National Security Committee (KNB).

Generally, however, the political elite has preferred the co-optation, rather than repression, of individuals considered by the selectorate as obstructionist or competitive to their power. These individuals may be either outside or inside government structures. Co-optation has been achieved by two principal methods: employment and policies. Pretenders have been co-opted or effectively banished as ambassadors: examples of the latter are Olzhas Suleimenov and Gaziz Aldamzharov, both of whom expressed their intention in 1994 to stand for the then scheduled 1995 presidential elections. Baltash Tursumbaev, a contender for the 1999 presidency, had been offered a post as Ambassador to Turkey, which he accepted. In November 1997, Murat Auezov, then co-chairman of the opposition movement Azamat, was offered a post as Head of the Department of Social Accord for the Almaty Regional Administration. The organizer of the World Congress of Kazakhs in 1992 was similarly ostracized, as was Kuanysh Sultanov, who was sent to become Ambassador to China on forming SNEK.

Co-optation was thus a frequent feature of the system. Members of the elite who had been sidelined, sometimes reappeared in (often higher) positions. An expert spoke of the president's fear of competitors:

Currently there is much talk about the ambitions of the Prime Minister [Akezhan Kazhegeldin] who has his eyes on the presidential position. (Expert, Group B); One further important point: Olzhas Suleimenov, representative of the Middle Zhuz, had been prepared to stand as a competitor to Nazarbaev for the Presidency. Nazarbaev was afraid of the a possible union between Suleimenov and [Gaziz]Aldamzharov (Middle and Junior Zhuz), and for this reason he held a referendum to prolong his rule. (Expert, Group B)

The elite also stayed ahead of its competitors by championing the agendas of those whom they viewed as oppositional or obstructionist, in particular when those agendas were perceived as populist. Partly for this reason, we find inconsistency in a number of policy areas in 1999–2001: while the regime has emphasized strong presidentialism, centralization and the prioritization of economics over politics, it has also promised democratization, the election of some regional officials and has incorporated the interests of regional players in the compilation of institutitional and electoral arrangements.[19] In the wake of increased repression in 1997, including a clampdown on the mass media which involved the state purchase of the country's most popular and until then independent newspaper, *Karavan*, Nazarbaev launched an informal election campaign in 1998 for the 2000 presidential elections. In his televised national address on 30 September 1998, he promised sweeping democratization measures, including the possible election of regional leaders, and ruled out early presidential elections. Meanwhile, he struck a deal with parliament to call early presidential elections for January 1999.[20] Nazarbaev was well-placed to win the presidential election but because parliament also arranged it, he would be free of accusations of back-tracking and of serving his own interests. In return for their support, both Houses of Parliament would see their next term of office extended by presidential decree by one more year each after the parliamentary elections of October 1999.

Another example of inconsistent policies and the co-optation of agendas came at the end of the 1990s when Nazarbaev and his government began a rhetoric on the need for an economic policy de-emphasizing foreign investment and taking into account the needs of domestic entrepreneurs by developing a policy of industrialization at home. As we shall see in the next chapter, a healthy economic record by the end of the 1990s and the prospect of an oil bonanza had raised the political stakes. By 2001 the development of domestic light industries had for the first time become more of a perceived possibility, empowering local business groups who had become increasingly dissatisfied with the support given to domestic industry by the regime. By also espousing this view, the president hoped to garner support both from the population at large, and, crucially, from key economic groupings.

## Patron-Client Relations

A second key recruitment means by which the elite kept itself in power was through patron-client relations, the retention of the Soviet patronage-client relations being perceived as an essential means of controlling access to the elite.

Chapter Two indicated that many individuals who had worked together and been socialized in the Soviet era continued to work together in the post-Soviet era. It established the importance of such socialization, and postulated that membership of the Soviet era elite facilitated membership in the post-Soviet elite. It is likely that this is not mere accident, but rather that past association created mutual obligation, friendship. Such reliance on informal power personalized the regime in the first decade and placed patronage at the centre of the regime's recruitment drive. Lemarchand and Legg write:

> Political clientelism may be viewed as a more or less personalized, affective and reciprocal relationship between actors, or sets of actors, commanding unequal resources and involving mutually beneficial transactions that have political ramifications beyond the immediate sphere of dyadic relationships.[21]

This definition of 'patron-client relations'[22] embodies three points: first, the development and use of personal relationships and mutual obligation; second, their purpose for the furthering of political ends; third, the unequal command of resources by 'patron' and 'client'.[23] A 'clientele' can therefore be distinguished from an interest group or an ideological movement; its leaders can be labelled 'patrons' and their followers 'clients'. Patrons are powerful, since they can gain access to and distribute tangibles – government contracts, jobs, loans – and, through the shrewd development of these resources, can build and maintain their personal clientele. In principle, the greater the resources controlled, the more powerful the patron.[24]

Patron-client relations underscore the deliberate nature of this action. Two broad senses of the word 'patronage' have thus been distinguished: the *creation* of patron-client bonds through personnel policy, and *drawing on* pre-existing bonds. Patronage remains, in a strict, irreducible sense, the kind of preferment or favouritism in which we suspect that obligations or reliance from past associations count for *more* than qualifications of any sort. Very few in the Kazakhstani political elite in this period entered the leadership as an unknown quantity and the younger members who rose meteorically to prominence at the end of the 1990s where often either relatives or close friends of the regime.

The second element of patron-client relations – 'their purpose for the furthering of political ends' – highlights another important aspect of this decade's recruitment policy: its strategic nature. The leadership's political ends, part of its overall aim of preserving its newly given sovereignty, were to exploit and manage its resources; to maintain interethnic stability; to keep good neighbourly relations, especially with Russia; and to keep itself in power.

Although patronage networks give an impression of security, they are, unlike kinship networks, far less secure in reality. They rely on the goodwill and the asymmetric power of the patron. Monocratic regimes are usually characterized by a selectorate of one; Kazakhstan's selectorate appears to have included more than the president, most notably a small circle of advisers that in the early years included the Head of the presidential Administration. Nevertheless, between 1991 and 2001, the selectorate became smaller and more homogeneous, comprising primarily the president's family relatives and close, sometimes working, colleagues. The selectorate appears to have narrowed and been consolidated since the relocation to Astana.

Elite theory suggests that the narrower the selectorate, the more that selectorate will try to promote 'its own'. 'Its own' here refers more to political loyalty than to specific social background criteria. By the end of the 1990s, the selectorate appeared to have narrowed and the core was increasingly picking 'its own'. The patron appeared able to exert an inordinate amount of influence on the system by virtue of his personality.

Many interviewed felt they could not refuse a job when offered one. Two top members of the political elite who had wanted to retire were forced to stay in politics 'because the president asked them to' (PE , 20, 33). Several members of the elite, when asked why they were in politics said that once in power it was very difficult to step out of it. Conscription had become a defining feature of this elite system: 'You cannot refuse the president' (Shymkent, PE 11).

Seligman suggests that systems with high-opportunity, low-risk eligibility structures, and with highly competitive and open selection procedures, will tend to have open decision-making structures. He also argues that the broader the range of elite sponsorship during recruitment, the more open the decision-making behaviours of elites will be.[25] In Kazakhstan's closed sytem, by contrast, regional actors felt excluded from shaping reform; explained one member of the Shymkent political elite, 'we do not affect the big questions of economic direction; these key questions are made by the government. We simply carry them out' (Shymkent, PE 12).

Third, patron-client relations demand that the selection process is simplified. To eliminate various channels of possible recruitment the selectorate must be small. To gain a place in political office, individuals did not have to go first through non-governmental political organizations such as political parties. In the early years, the selection of the national political elite took place largely within the structure of a dominant political party and consisted of a single act of choice. The president recruited allies from the past as political insurance in a deliberate process of bureaucratic ascent, where a person could rise to candidacy through long service, usually of a bureaucratic or administrative nature, in his or her political organization.

Fourth, patron-client relations imply that the patron has something to give to the client and this creates a conspiracy of sorts that is usually predicated on extensive corruption. Many argued that the nature of elite recruitment more generally was partly about controlling information of the extent of this corruption. Even if particular officials were not corrupt, the absence of elections meant they were perceived as such, since access to financial and other related resources was limited.

## Reshuffling and Institutional Overlap

Power was also maintained by excessive personnel reshuffling. While Chapter Two established that elites have essentially been circulated, and to a limited degree renewed, it also showed that circulation to have been relentless. Each of the four government changeovers was accompanied by changes in the occupants of certain posts in the presidential administration, government and regional administrations.

Further confusion arises from both elite and institutional changes. Elite changes did not necessarily correspond to institutional changes. As already noted, the status and influence of individuals identified in Chapter Two were not necessarily a function of institutional position. An expert commented: 'It can happen that a Deputy Minister has more influence on the president than the Minister himself' (Expert, Group B). Moreover, while changes in the presidency often prompted elite changes, changes have occurred just as frequently outside of governmental fluctuation.

This frequency of reshuffling suggests that recruitment was part strategic, part tactical. It was strategic in the sense that we hear how the president had both a clear conception of the type of institutional architecture he wanted and the desire to maintain access to the resources that would ensure the continued domination of that architecture. It was tactical in that it aimed to outmanoeuvre opponents and to manage conflict among individuals, groups and institutions.

By consistently employing loyal cadres to a post, Nazarbaev increased that post's institutionalization. This was a gamble; the resultant esprit de corps might indeed enable increased autonomy, but we should note how easily Nazarbaev could then reduce the functions and responsibilities of these units, either by diluting their responsibilities or by bringing the commissions, committees and agencies back into the fold of the presidential administration.

Institutions were often only as strong as the individuals that formed them. The Ministry of the Interior's influence was allegedly much diminished after the departure of its minister, Kairbek Suleimenov. The entire institution of government diminished in influence after the departure of Kazhegeldin, and the Ministry of Economics was deliberately kept weak by the appointment of symbolic figureheads in 1994.

The system, in sum, was highly personalized. In 1994, when people were voting according to single-mandate constituencies in the parliamentary elections, the primary factor was not a person's party affiliation, but a candidate's personality – according to Panorama, 16.4 per cent were interested in a candidate's job, 15.9 per cent in their profession, and only 7.15 per cent in their party political programme.[26] By the end of the 1990s the selectorate had also become more personalized. Serikbolsyn Abdildin, leader of the Communist Party, argued that the regime was taking clan and regional groupings into account in the selection process. Commenting on the appointment in January 2003 of Prime Minister Kasymzhomart Tokaev's successor, Imangaly Tasmagambetov, Gulzhan Ergalieva, Deputy Head of the 'People's Congress of Kazakhstan' reported that Tasmagambetov was a 'product of Nazarbaev', an expression borrowed from Tasmagambetov himself.[27] Presidential appointments seemed increasingly driven by whether the president could count, personally, on an individual.

Institutions often strengthened the authority of individuals by providing them with a legitimised setting. But by the same token institutions were often too weak to prevent groups from acquiring substantial personal and group power that even if not granting autonomy from the state, gave them considerable leverage within it. The leverage enjoyed by Nazarbaev's son-in-law Aliev, who had come to occupy the unique position of combining strong personal connections with substantial economic interests and a formal position in the republic's security services, was a case in point.

These events of November 2001 (Chapter One) in which Aliev's resignation prompted the formation of the republic's first counterelite illustrated a further feature of Kazakhstan's elite system: the tendency toward simultaneous incumbency. Increasingly in the period under review individuals held posts simultaneously, such as regionally and nationally, or in the executive and parliament. The intention seemed to be to concentrate and centralise power but the case of Aliev showed how the opposite could result, with a grouping becoming so powerful as to challenge the existing elite configuration. Simultaneity, moreover, did not necessarily amount to either subservience or effectiveness: the 1994–1995 parliament that included a list of presidential appointees to parliament (*gosspicok*) dramatically failed to provide the sort of institutional cross-cutting and interlocking anticipated; and appointed presidential inspectors carried little influence on regional politics.

Sequential overlap, the successive holding of top posts in diverse sectors, also increased in this period. C. Wright Mills was particularly impressed by such links among US business, government, and military elites:

The inner core of the power elite consists, first, of those who interchange commanding roles at the top of one dominant institutional order with those in another. By their very careers and activities, they lace the three types of milieux together.[28]

While until 1995 individuals tended to remain in the same branch of power, by 2001 more individuals had served sequentially in different institutions, perhaps moving from government, to a bank, to the presidential administration and then back into government.

## Strategy of Compartmentalization

Sequential overlap is part of a broader picture of co-optation. As Fleron uses the term, co-optation refers to a process in which persons in high-prestige *non-political* areas are co-opted by a political organization; in other words they would come from outwith the political sector. A criticism made of Tereshchenko and, later, of Tokaev, but not made of Kazhegeldin or Balgimbaev, was that neither had experience or understanding of the working of the post-Soviet economy. Under the premierships of Kazhegeldin and Balgimbaev, businessmen – either from the Gorbachev or early independence period – were co-opted into government. Nazarbaev expressed very clearly his intention that these younger recruits would work closely as a team with the existing economic specialists in the government, who might be younger or older technocrats: 'I tried to ensure that some new, competent officials would be brought into the government – people who understand business, the banking system and today's current reforms.'[29] Commenting on the team of his then newly appointed Prime Minister Akezhan Kazhegeldin: 'There have been cases of [government]failure for one simple reason – the team was not united by a common goal and it was not a team of like-minded people. We … cannot let his happen.'[30]

The younger technocrats, such as Uraz Dzhandosov and Grigorii Marchenko, had often gained their economics training in Moscow. Some aligned themselves with the figures who had been involved in economic planning in the Soviet era, notably, Daulet Sembaev, Marat Ospanov and Erzhan Urtembaev, and a team was created. In the early 1990s, the state sector had become saturated, even clogged, and this attracted new talent that had previously preferred the private sector. The inclusion of businessmen in government served the regime well in another sense: it delayed the need to offer businessmen concessions outside of government. Reporting on Mayor of Almaty, Shalmai Kulmakhanov's comment that he was finding the appointment of district administration chiefs 'a difficult job', the reporter continued that '[I]n this connection Mr Kulmakhanov is familiarizing himself with the personal files of successful young businessmen.'[31]

Various ministries and bodies, including the National Bank, worked in close alliance to create the discipline, cohesion and certainty germane to institutions. It was just this coherence that the technocrats who formed part of the movement DCK and later Ak Zhol wanted to restore in the period post November 2001, when their frustration at their inability to implement policy without politics was at its height.

This appointment of ethnic Kazakhs with economics training to key executive posts dealing with economic policy adds to the debate on the extent to which the ethnic factor was being emphasized over the technocratic one. One author argues that this remains disputed,[32] while another that 'the fundamental economic reorientation that began in 1994 suggested a need for radical restructuring of the state, and ethnicity remained a central operative principle of the actual organisation process.'[33] Chapter Three suggested that the demands of the state to formulate and implement an economic policy were being taken seriously and that the state could not afford to put ascriptive criteria of ethnicity before competence. Non-Kazakhs survived into the post-independence era in economic posts. The chapter further suggested that this dilemma by the close of the 1990s had often ceased to exist, as ethnicity and technocracy had often become mutually reinforcing.

Nazarbaev appears therefore to have recognized that the survival of the incumbent political regime in an independent Kazakhstan depended on its ability to keep competent people and attract new ones. The inclusion of these individuals became part of a wider government emphasis, especially in 1995–1996, on meritocracy and professionalism. The Ministry of Foreign Affairs, for example, was introducing its training of diplomats in a school openly modelled on the French *Ecoles d'Administrations Nationales*.

Kazhegeldin's government also made some attempt to introduce performance-related criteria to the longevity of the akim. A number of professional examinations were also introduced. The Agency for State Service, created in the late 1990s, was responsible for testing and recruiting these new officials. The 1999 Law on State Service[34] promised security of tenure. A 1997 survey indicated that a majority of the experts interviewed felt that meritocracy was becoming an increasingly important part of the recruitment process.[35]

This perceived tendency of employing individuals on the basis of merit was still occuring, however, in a system dominated by the patron-client relationship. Viewed in this light the appointment of an increased number of individuals on their merit in the economic sector may best be summarised by the term Barbara Geddes applied to Latin America, namely a 'compartmentalisation strategy', which 'entails that informal meritocratic appointments to positions be considered essential to programmatic success, while permitting the president to use other appointments for short-term support and the development of a loyal following.' By sponsoring such agencies, a regime is able to delay full-scale civil service reform.[36]

# CONCLUSIONS

Given this mix of mechanisms, then, what can we say of the links between power maintenance techniques and the wider political system? The typologies offered by Fleron are useful here.[37] He distinguishes between a monocratic, adaptive-monocratic, co-optive and pluralist type.[38] While Kazakhstan's elite system is not pluralist, it has displayed elements of the first three. In a monocratic system, groups do not represent independent centres of political power; access to the political elite is substantially controlled by the current occupants of elite positions, and is structured through the dominant political organization. It attempts to be self-perpetuating. The political elite is able to extract technical and managerial skills without having to offer any voice in the policy-making process in exchange. As society becomes more complex, the need for specialized elites increases. To maintain a monocratic order, the traditional political elite would have to be prepared to use co-ercion. There is no guarantee that this will succeed, so it might have to develop into an adaptive-monocratic type.

The adaptive-monocratic type develops when a monocratic elite does not itself have the skills necessary to make and carry out policy. Here the elite does *not* accept the transferring of segments of political power. Rather, it chooses to acquire these skills itself through the retraining of its own personnel and the specialized training of its already-accepted younger members. At the same time, it has to seek younger members outside of government structures. But, unlike Fleron's co-optative type, these nonpolitical elites do not have substantial bases of influence outside politics – only expertise. And while Fleron assumes that these individuals bring perspectives on the nature of political governance that are identifiably different from those of the traditional political elite, the findings in Chapter Two and Three suggest that this has not so far been the case, primarily because the existing Kazakhstani elite into which these newer recruits came was itself already considerably pragmatic. For the moment, the impact of this compartmentalized segment of the elite does, however, appear to have had an impact on decision-making in the economic sphere. Fleron had predicted this for the co-optative type more generally, including the institutionalization of policy roles for academics and the routinization of planning and decision procedures. The ostensible link between the elite system and the political system more generally is the subject of our next chapter.

# Chapter Six

# THE ENVIRONMENT AND ELITE BEHAVIOUR

While the previous chapter explored the techniques of power maintenance, this chapter looks at the environmental context that has shaped the elite system. The way society and the elite interact is shaped not only by the elite's attitudes and relations with it, but also by society's structure, attitudes and relations with the broader political system. These structural factors, as noted in the Introduction, both affect and are affected by the political elite and we do not claim to be able to separate both. But as Theda Skocpol has argued, context is left unexplained too often. She has outlined how context must be unpacked in both domestic and international terms, and that it should include culture, economy and the polity.[1] Here we aim to show how the elite behaviour we discussed in Chapter Four has altered the structural environment of opportunity, and also how this has blended with the pre-existing environment. Also, context is not just given exogenously but can be affected by policies: 'systemic outcomes (policies) must be analysed distinctly from attributes of the system.' The environment is therefore far from static, undergoing 'punctuated change'.[2] We shall see also that institutions may enable or disable elite autonomy, and in this context sub-ethnic identity is briefly revisited.

## INCONSISTENT POLICIES, MIXED REGIME

The power techniques analysed in the last chapter served to create a climate of suspicion and uncertainty. First, the personalization of recruitment created a system of dependency on one individual and personality both for an individual's tenure and for the morale of the state collective. 'Once Nazarbaev says something will happen', explained one member of the political elite, 'it will happen because Nazarbaev does not like to have to say something twice' (PE, Pavlodar, 3). Another described this trend: 'There was a brief moment when we seemed to be westernizing but now everything depends on the president. Thank goodness for this president, if it were anyone else it would be dreadful' (PE, Pavlodar, 5).

Regional leaders expressed how their career no longer merely depended on successfully implementing the goals set by central leaders. Several interviewed were filled with nostalgia for a time when their lives had actually been so simple. The concentration of power in key executive institutions, moreover, and the perception therefore that an office in government was associated with greater power, undermined the pull of alternative institutions, notably parliament. This also lowered the transaction costs of institutional transferral and partly explained the high degree of co-optation possible. Parliament did not produce benefits on the basis of co-operation and did not possess sufficient resources to impose heavy costs on its defectors.

Third, revisiting the five policy areas of Chapter One, the system was often perceived by the elite themselves and by observers as lacking a clear general direction. The panel of experts and members both of the opposition and regional administrations cited as a major systemic challenge the absence of a 'concrete strategy' on the part of the government to build a state; said one expert: 'All that the Kazakh elite is now concerned about is the repartition of property. They call it privatization' (Expert, Group B). The co-optation of other groups' agendas, also noted in the previous chapter, such as in the fields of regional elections, mass media and industrial policy, have led to policy inconsistencies. Exclaimed one Shymkent elite member: 'We must today define clearly our orientation, define ourselves and only then go further… We need to consolidate a state attitude' (PE, Shymkent, 5).

Furthermore, the early years of independence's relatively more liberal period, when Nazarbaev was still in the process of consolidating his power through some concessional tactics, meant that players had memories of alternative possibilities. This was particularly true of regional elites. Before privatization policy was centralized in the case-by-case phase, regional leaders and companies (see below) were allowed considerable freedom to participate in what soon became known as 'spontaneous privatization'. When case-by-case privatization became centralized, regional leaders still expected to be consulted and were deeply critical when they were not. Actors can then also become uncertain about the boundaries of the game, less likely to be the case for a stricter authoritarian regime with no history of liberal policies.

Importantly, a strong majority of the elite complained about the absence of elite cohesion, 'the constant need to gain agreement among different levels of power' and 'the lack of executive discipline'. They pointed to an underlying competition between and mutual suspicion of government departments. They perceived other institutions with deep mistrust, and a plurality interpreted the actions of other departments as initiated by extra-governmental forces. A majority were also deeply suspicious of third party interference, such as by another executive organ or state economic lobby group. A strong majority also referred frequently to internal lobbying by state interest groups.

The state, in many policy areas, appeared to have de-institutionalized. Unlike many post-colonial African states, like other Soviet successor states Kazakhstan inherited a vast bureaucracy and institutionalized power. Huntington writes that the 'level of institutionalization of any political system can be defined by the adaptability, complexity, autonomy and coherence of its organization and procedure.'[3] By concentrating institutional power in the presidential administration, the institutions have become less adaptable and complex. Political institutions, generally, have also become less autonomous: the presidential administration was increasingly inclined to promote the interests of one particular group. With the weakening of both parliament and government, the overall institutional coherence of the system declined. Institutional reshuffling weakened the institutional ethos. We posited in Chapter Two that institutions in Kazakhstan did not yet generally have 'personalities', that they did not have a collective ethos or standard operating procedures with which to socialize recruits.

We have noted how compartmentalization allowed for effective policy-making in the economic sphere, with many outside observers commenting on the competence of the economic reform team; this competence almost certainly played a role in the success of the economic reform programme. The economic sector seemed to be the exception rather than the rule, however, partly because in other areas the coincidence of individual and state interests was far weaker. For example, success in pension reform would have tangible benefits to those involved in the reform process but this could not be said of reform in all sectors. But, overall, neither the structure of the state nor that of the regime encouraged public service; instead, the abuse of public service for private gain had increased. If some institutionalization of economic reform had been achieved under Kazhegeldin, state reform in many other sectors had by the late 1990s stagnated.

## THE PSYCHOLOGY OF INDEPENDENCE AND THE INTERNATIONAL ENVIRONMENT

The political elite's relation to their new power container, independent Kazakhstan, underwent a significant transformation in the period under review. Many of those interviewed regretted the demise of the Soviet

Union and would have been content with 'the granting of sovereignty to each republic' (PE, 5) or with 'sovereignty but retaining economic links' (PE, Shymkent, 1). A significant number, however, already acknowledged that 'the main problem is getting used to working with Russia on the basis of a different relationship – as two independent states who should engage in mutually beneficial cooperation' (PE, 9). Leaders continued to watch closely developments in Russia, while acknowledging that their relations with that country 'no longer have that personal friendship, that personal understanding' (PE, Uralsk, 1).

The absence of a nationalist struggle or an elite settlement created a sense of initial unease among the leadership as to the purpose of its power and how it should best differentiate itself from Russia. Furthermore, as noted in the Introduction and Chapter One, it bequeathed a republic in which the titular nation was a minority outnumbered by the Slav population. The sense of insecurity was particularly stark in the northern and western regions, which had been strongly integrated into Soviet elite and economic networks and were now forced to look south to Almaty instead of north to Moscow for policy direction. Economic dependence was pointedly illustrated by the fact that, while an up-and-coming oil producer in its own right, Kazakhstan lacked the infrastructure to refine its own oil and, furthermore, all of its pipelines had to run through Russia.

By the end of the period under discussion here, however, this sense of relative insecurity had been transformed into a considerable confidence on the part of the Kazakhstani central political elite. If psychologically unsure at the outset, the Nazarbaev leadership did have the political economy in its favour. The elimination of major economic and ideological competitions from the system made it easier for Nazarbaev to consolidate his rule. In the absence of such structures, the technique of power maintenance by patronage (Chapter Five) would have been severely circumscribed. The 1999 nationwide census, furthermore, cited Kazakhs as the majority in their own state. The multivector foreign policy had enabled Kazakhstan to seek allies beyond Russia and become less dependent on its northern neighbour for the continuity of its rule. Economically, their republic was now often considered the success story of the entire post-Soviet region. By 1997, Kazakhstan had attracted the second largest amount of per capita foreign direct investment (FDI) of all post-communist states (after Hungary). This money was chiefly absorbed by the oil, gas and metallurgy sectors, which together accounted for eighty per cent of total FDI from 1997–1999. In 2000, an unprecedented surplus was recorded, partly as a result of higher tax revenues (especially corporate income tax). GDP growth rates in 2000 and 2001 were among the highest in the world at 9.6 and 13.2 per cent respectively. On 19 September 2002, the New York ratings agency, Moody's, upgraded Kazakhstan's sovereign foreign-currency bonds by two points to what is usually referred to as investment grade.[4]

However successful Kazakhstan's multivector foreign policy had been at diversifying investment and potential pipeline partners, Russia continued to be perceived by those interviewed as the single most important external influence on the republic. Russia remained the model for institutional change in Kazakhstan. As noted in Chapter Two, key posts demanding close relations with Russia continued to be staffed into the 1990s by individuals who had worked closely with Russia in the Soviet era. A majority of the panel of experts noted how institutional changes in Kazakhstan were often modelled on those in Russia, usually with a delay of roughly two years. The realization that in security terms Russia was still the primary partner has maintained Russia as primus inter pares. Kazakhstan's signing of a strategic partnership with the USA in Washington in 1997 was overridden in the wake of September 11 when Uzbekistan became the USA's strategic partner. Already in 1996 members of the elite interviewed were also doubtful that Central Asia could become a key partner for the USA because Uzbekistanis are 'our competitors, indeed sometimes they beat us' (PE, Shymkent, 4). This may partly explain the shift already in Spring 2001 from a 'multivector' to what might be termed a 'contiguous multivector' foreign policy.

These findings are again borne out by other surveys. A survey in 1999 found that despite its failure to bring about real integration, the CIS, 'was considered as the joint first option at 63.3 per cent in Kazakhstan, equal with the 'Eurasian bridge (neither Europe, nor Asia).'[5] A 1996 VIProblem survey found that 68 per cent felt that relations with Uzbekistan were 'not very promising' and 62 per cent felt the same about integration with Central Asia.[6] Some 74 per cent said the political situation in Russia had the single biggest effect on security in Kazakhstan. The next figure was China at 22 per cent. The majority viewed their security as guaranteed in a union with Russia.[7]

There is, however, no simple correlation between demographic or career origins and attitudes to foreign policy, as we hinted in Chapter Three. From the data, we cannot state with any firm conviction that ethnicity or gender or place of birth determined attitudes to Russia; only that for ethnic Kazakh members of the elite there was a weak correlation between age and pro-Russianness, with the older generation more pro-Russian than the younger. But even here there were important exceptions, which suggested that the difference lay instead in later socialization, education, or career experience. Those younger Russians with either educational or business experience in Russia tended to be more supportive of stronger relations with Russia. Those members of the central elite who had been highly ranked throughout the Soviet era continued to use these networks, as did high-ranking members of the Soviet regional elite. Elites of the North and West, who had been highly integrated into economic and social networks with Russia, were not always convinced of the necessity of erecting a border between the two countries. Ethnic Kazakh elite members in Uralsk referred to their Kazakh brethren across the border in Omsk; Russian elite members in Pavlodar referred to their relations and networks with Siberia.

## THE POLITICAL ECONOMY OF THE STATE

The regime's co-optation policy described in Chapter Five also contributed to the complexity of the environment. This was because in the 1995–1998 consolidation period, and to rally support in the upcoming presidential campaign, several different types of elite had been co-opted into power. This had made the management of disparate groups a key policy agenda. These groups were of four main kinds. A first group consisted of presidential family and friends. Key examples here were Nazarbaev's two son-in-laws. Second, an economic reform team that had been sheltered for these ten years, including, as we noted in Chapter Two, Uraz Dzhandosov, Zhannat Ertlesova, Grigorii Marchenko, Zeinulla Kakimzhanov and Erzhan Utembaev. Third, businessmen who had in the early 1990s operated outside, such as Galymzhan Zhakiianov, Mukhtar Abliazov and who in the 1995–7 consolidation phase had been invited into power. Fourth established heads of banks who had been protected by the elite, such as Nurlan Subkhanberdin, but whose loyalty to the incumbent regime was unpredictable.

The nature of economic reform, and the nature and speed of policies, without doubt affected the outcome of the race to power. Adam Przeworski argues that shock therapy economic reform tends to provoke a political backlash by those whom reform makes the losers. Shock therapy is generally associated with authoritarianism since 'the political process is reduced to elections, executive decrees, and sporadic outbursts of protest.'[8] Frye's findings, by contrast, suggest a negative correlation between radical economics and presidential power in which countries that have conducted a gradual economic reform have seen significant expansions of presidential power.[9] The evidence here was mixed because of the contradictory effects of that cornerstone of economic reform, mass privatization. 'Privatization is the main issue, ' explained Expert, Group A. ' The constitution is really not that important – it has no reality. The only thing it serves to do is to legitimize illegitimate actions by the government.'

As with political elites in the Middle East, the Kazakhstani elite exploited their position in the political sector to reinforce their social and economic position. To achieve this, the Middle Eastern political elites used as their major policy mechanism nationalization; the Kazakhstani political elite, by contrast, sold off state assets to foreign buyers to enrich themselves personally.

To recap, the chronology of privatization presented in Chapter One involved three phases: the first phase, begun already in the Gorbachev period, might be characterized as 'spontaneous, laissez-faire privatization'. Well-placed state officials and company managers were able to profit by spontaneously seizing state assets. This process was not regularized from the centre; the regions became key independent actors who were left to seize and distribute as they saw fit. In this early phase these regional actors were often able to dictate conditions of privatization to the State Property Committee (Goskomimushchestvo). It was precisely during this phase that the term *prikhvatizatsiia* (in the sense of 'to seize', 'to get') was coined. The second phase of mass privatization and IPFs was to prove a short-lived phase for the national bourgeioise because their IPFs (through little fault of their own) failed to capitalize. The national bourgeoisie was excluded from the third 'foreign management' stage, spearheaded by then Prime Minister Kazhegeldin.[10] The final, fourth phase of 'stagnation' (1998–2001), under Balgimbaev and Tokaev, saw privatization effectively halted and the rhetoric of import substitution and support for domestic entrepreneurs growing.

One of the major effects of these phases was to create at least three sets of relationships between the political and national business elites. One set, outside the political elite, remained considerably dependent on the elite for their prosperity and were politically loyal (amongst their ranks would be included the *plemianiki* or *krasnye direktora*). A second set, economically enriched mainly before having been co opted into power were not politically reliable and the numbers in this group were growing. The third set attempted to operate independently of politics, working for a normalization in the business environment so as to encourage the free flow of capital, civilized western society, transparency and regulation. The interests of this last group often conflicted with those of the middle and lower political elite. While advocates of varying economic relationships, all three sets generally supported the political status quo.[11] They all recognized, however, that the handing over of strategic companies to foreign management had slowed indigenous modernization and the formation of a national bourgeoisie.

The political elite had to strike a new relationship not only with its business leaders but also with foreign economic actors. Examples of key management contracts were: the Joint Stock Company (JSC) of Pavlodar's Aluminium Factory (managed by White Swan Ltd); the JSC of Zhezkazgan's copper concern, Zhezkazgantsvetmet (managed by Samsung Deutschland); JSC Dansk Mining Corporation (managed by Japan Chrome Corporation); and, the Sokolovsk-Sarbai Mining Facility (managed by Ivedon International Ltd).

As entire economic sectors were handed to foreign management and, in some cases, eventually to foreign ownership, the central state 'hollowed out'. Kazhegeldin's successor, Balgimbaev, was appointed partly because he was a well-known opponent of privatization policies. Under Balgimbaev, the stock-market flotation of Kazakhstan's blue-chip companies was temporarily halted. The centre tried to regain control over enterprises in the provinces, not least because it needed their export revenues to finance a gaping budget deficit. Attempts to renationalize provoked disputes with some foreign investors, with even well-known western oil companies being charged with tax evasion. In contrast to Kazhegeldin's privatization policy, Balgimbaev's industrial policy, sponsored and developed by his Trade and Industry Minister Mukhtar Abliazov, promised a statist approach to reform. Balgimbaev's successor and former Foreign Minister Kasymzhomart Tokaev replaced Abliazov with a former northern-based akim Danial Akhmetov. To some observers, this suggested a mere gesture toward including regional representatives in central policy.

As suggested by other surveys and media comment in Chapter Two, the privatization of assets led to the emergence of several economic interest groups within the central elite. As noted also, these groups were the subject of intense speculation.[12] By the end of the decade, indigenous analysts agreed on the existence of at least six, if not eight, of these groups, headed by the following individuals or organizations: Alexander Mashkevich, Oleg Li, Nurzhan Subkhanberdin, Abliazov, Nurlan Balgimbaev, Rakhat Aliev. The influence of groups reportedly varied; for example, while Mashkevich was supposedly strong in 1998, by 2002 his influence had declined considerably, as had the fortunes of the Aliev group.

The groups reportedly competed for the power to secure continued access to economic resources. Each group owned or partially owned various privatized companies, a bank for instance, and often sponsored a newspaper. Commodity interests were, broadly, infrastructure (electricity or telecommunications) or primary products (oil, minerals, metals, sugar). These commodity interests, and those who headed them, held varying degrees of influence within the political elite; some were very close (even related) to the president, others not. With regard to media ownership, after the political elite had succeeded in curtailing the role of the media in society, its members sought to establish their own media outlets. Key figures within this trend included Mukhtar Abliazov, whose interests include the newspaper *All Over the Globe*, published in English and Russian, *Delovoe Obozrenie-Respublika* and the *TAN* radio station. Kazhegeldin also financed various media outlets, including the Russian-language *21st Century*. Intra-elite relations and the fate of the media were directly related – the more intense the struggle between elite groups, the more intense the clampdown on the media. The clampdown affected their establishment as well as those of opposition outlets, with the former's key national casualties owned principally by the Aliev and Abliazov groups.

The emergence of these groups placed negotiation and bargaining at the core of the elite system. This made government a far harder task. November 2001, as we saw in Chapter Five, revealed the fragility of the balance, and led to the voluntary resignation of the vice-premier, minister, two deputy ministers, and the chair of the anti-monopoly committee. On this occasion it had been Aliev who had amassed disproportionate influence, particularly through his management and ownership of key security services. The jockeying for power intensified over the period partly in advance of expected oil income and possible political succession. The primary reason for the departure of Prime Minister Tokaev in 2002 was widely held to have been his inability to deal with the competing groups (*protivoborstvuiushchikh gruppirovok*) and the absence of a consolidating position. In Almaty, approximately 60 per cent of experts and, in Astana, one third, linked the Prime Minister's exit with 'the domination of the government by national companies' representatives and financial-industrial groups.'[13] The November events introduced a stage in Kazakhstani politics where elite interest fragmentations were likely to intensify, with implications for Nazarbaev as well as for the development of a counterelite.

Despite this muddier environment, these groupings did not, however, operate autonomously from the state. We did not witness in this period the separation of the political from the economic elite. The struggle remained one primarily over resources, scrambling to benefit from the opportunities that state privatization had created. Unlike Russia, Kazakhstan did not see elite groupings develop their own administrations, content in this first decade to have economic power without concomitant political and administrative power.

Nevertheless, by the end of the decade the groups did seem to exert some effect on economic policy direction. The regime had come under increasing pressure from business and public opinion, forced to take into account the views of these broad constituencies. A healthy economic record and the prospect of an oil bonanza raised the political stakes. By 2001, the development of domestic light industries had for the first time become more of a possibility and this empowered domestic technocrats and local businessmen. Local business representatives contended that the government should have actively supported the domestic companies over their foreign counterparts when the choice was available. Four principal factors explained popular, worker and government support for the development of indigenous light industry: the greater availability of domestic sources of income were perceived to create possibilities for developing indigenous production capacity; the new capital amnesty law promised to repatriate and bring into the formal economy more indigenous capital; lobbying by local businessmen strengthened; political power became dependent on good relations with domestic corporate groups. By supporting this view, the regime hoped to garner support both from the population at large and, crucially, from key economic groupings. In the absence of western-style elections, adopting a populist stance promised to strengthen the regime's authority. Granting economic concessions to domestic over foreign constituents might garner political loyalty from groups that had become increasingly important to the sustainability of the current regime.

November 2001 was significant, moreover, in that it openly questioned the direction of political reform to the extent that a grouping within the state felt it necessary to form a new movement to get its voice heard. In particular, some members of the business and technocratic members of the elite appeared to seek a normalization in relations between bureaucrat and politician, and an intensification of state reform which had in their perception ground to a halt by the end of the 1990s. Surveys in 2000–2001 indicated, moreover, that more members of both the central and regional elites were advocating substantial and immediate change, suggesting impatience with the current system and a sense that it had become dysfunctional. A VIProblem poll taken immediately after the November 2001 open elite fragmentation suggested that a considerably larger per centage than those polled in 1996 criticized the leadership and considered policy ineffective. Many felt that economic reform had simply ground to a halt.[14] Expert (Group A) explained:

> Probably the single main reason for the creation of the State Committee of Enquiry was so that it could reduce the powers of the Ministry of Interior and increase these powers directly under the president.

Dzhandosov and Ertlesova were prime examples of the technocratic group consolidated in government by the country's second post-independence prime minister, Akezhan Kazhegeldin, alongside entrepreneurs such as Zhakiianov (Chapter 4). After Kazhegeldin's ousting, pragmatism continued to dictate that Nazarbaev recruit technocrats into leading positions, but the latter have frequently been frustrated by the 'old guard, ' who they see as undermining their attempts to introduce the procedures and regulations necessary for effective state management. Uraz Dzhandosov has emphasized that this is a collective action problem: 'The Prime Minister does not need to be an economist but at the same it is important that he knows how to get a good team together and create a working discipline.'[15] This may have prompted them to become politically active, and the formation of the Democratic Choice of Kazakhstan expressed that need.

Unlike the top-down approach of the first half of the 1990s, by the dawn of the new century, recruitment decisions were therefore about finding candidates that could be mediators between the various parties to government: Nazarbaev in early 2002 spoke of the need to start a dialogue with the 'constructive opposition', and according to Azamat leader Petr Svoik, newly appinted Prime Minister Ismagambetov was 'probably the only figure in the presidential family that suits everyone'.[16]

We explained in Chapter Five how the political elite pursued a compartmentalized strategy on recruitment. On the one hand, the appointment of loyal individuals continued in the system as a whole, on the other, appointments according to professional and educational qualifications occurred primarily in the economic sector. Kazakhstan's first ten years demonstrated that the more established the president was among his followers, the more he was able to pursue a compartmentalization strategy. We noted in Chapters Two and Five an increased trend for the president to appoint more of 'his own' and this was a likely sign of decreased presidential autonomy and a challenge to the intentionality of the system, which could be attributed to the four sources outlined above: the declining popularity of the president; the need to manage disparate economic groups; the need to plan for succession; and the growing perceived incompatibility between appointing on the one hand technocrats and on the other loyals.

## DE FACTO ECONOMIC DECENTRALIZATION

The new international environment in turn transformed the relation between the central elite and its regions. With the diffusion of capital, patronage from the centre was no longer always readily forthcoming. Constitutionally Kazakhstan remained a unitary state in this first decade. Economically, however, the state underwent de facto decentralization. These contradictory tendencies not only made centre-regional relations increasingly tense, they also again altered the environment in which the central elite operated.

During the Soviet period, much of northern and eastern Kazakhstan had been closely integrated with neighbouring areas in Russia. Thus, for example, the provinces of Karaganda and Pavlodar formed part of the West-Siberian territorial production complex (TPK), and, to their south, Kostanai formed part of the Aral TPK. Moreover, provincial borders were conceived as economic units and coincided roughly with the layout of mineral resources. This integration involved economic production and dis-tribution; energy systems; transport infrastructure; and elite recruitment networks. The Soviet state and Communist Party ensured the maintenance of these ties.[17] With the collapse of these institutions, the regions bordering Russia became autonomous and no central institutions were readily available to replace those of the Soviet era. While during the Soviet era Moscow's relations with its republics had formed the essence of centre-periphery relations, these had now been supplanted by Almaty's relations with its own provinces.

The provincial administration was granted some responsibilities but without sufficient income to carry them out. In practice, it fell upon the provincial administrations, particularly the district level administrations, to handle most of those regional public services. District level administrations were handling more than 80 per cent of the country's expenditure on education, health, culture and transport, and the majority of this was funded out of general resources. The central budget, however, often financed only public salaries, and it was the province's responsibility to finance its own transport, communications, electricity, and the administration's services. The de facto economic decentralization resulted from two major forces: one, the infusion of international capital into regions as a result of the largest sell-offs of strategic assets in the post-Soviet region explained above, having provided regional leaders with alternative sources of income and therefore alternative patrons; and, two, the centre's own withdrawal from the regions.[18]

If Chapter Five suggested that the political elite deliberately centralized economic policy-making, economic withdrawal limited the ability of the centre to control the region and undermined the effectiveness of its key centralization tool, the appointment of the akim. Economic withdrawal forced regional elites to look elsewhere for funding, such as to international borrowing possibilities, and this was often a function of the degree of international investment in their region. Five main constellations occurred: the central elite continued to own regional resources with the regional, political, and economic interests subordinate to the centre; second, the central political elite was in partnership largely with foreign firms, which either managed or owned the resources and its activities in the region were driven largely by central decisions; third, the central and political elite were partnered with domestic owners, such as Kazakhstan's leading commercial bank, Kazkommertsbank; fourth, the alliance of domestic and foreign capital saturated the regional political elite; and fifth, the regional elite dominated, but was in alliance with, both the central elite and foreign firms.

The parachuting into regions of central leaders to take up akim positions may have come too late in this new context. The akim was able to appoint and dismiss his provincial administration. This happened almost wholesale when a new akim was appointed, for example, in Zhambyl in 1996. In the absence of a national civil service – and despite the 1996 Law on State Service – all government departments were staffed with locally recruited personnel, rather than national civil servants, whose first loyalty would naturally be to their own province. Moreover, the provincial akims began to request additional appointment powers; for example, they expressed the desire to appoint administration department heads without the approval of the corresponding ministries. The appointment of a centrally socialized elite, even one with a regional background, did not result in national coherence. This was because: individuals parachuted in from the centre did not command the loyalty of the regional administrations they were posted to; these regional administrations were composed on the basis of groupings that did not answer to the centre; and the regional heads and their administrations were linked to either local or foreign business interests.

Regional governors, in turn, were themselves constrained by their local environments. Zhakiianov, former akim of Semei and Pavlodar oblasts, described how large corporations escaped their regulation:

> We are afraid of the spectre of territorial autonomy, but ignore the reality of an already powerful regional autonomy in the form of oligarchies which, in my opinion, are dangerous for reform. The branch oligarchy is almost not controllable by the provinces and is not responsible for the performance of regional economies. As a result, we observe slow economic reform. In my mind one of the reasons for this is that local authorities are bound by hand and foot.[19]

Zhakiianov's 'branch oligarchy' referred to the considerable independent power exerted by the state or private companies.

The mounting frustration felt by regional leaders was reflected in interviews for this study. Their primary aim was, in the case of resource-rich areas, to gain greater autonomy over their finances, in the case of poorer regions, to be given the financial resources to carry out their policies. But we also noted in Chapter Five how the president relied on the support of the akim in elections and therefore rather than a simple patron-client relationship this is one of concessions, bargaining and agreement.

In other ways also this was not simply a top-down process. As already noted, the economies and infrastructure of the northern and eastern regions were locked into the south Siberian networks. This applied to elite recruitment networks also, and created cross-border ties at the elite level. Consequently, in the early years of independence, these regional elites continued to operate and conduct policy with the intention of maintaining these cross-border links, and there was little that the centre could do to stop them.[20] Indeed, considering the bankruptcy of the central state, it was not in the centre's interest to do so. These northern and eastern regions thus remained largely beyond the centre's control. They continued to regard Moscow as the centre and, in some districts, even after a year from the introduction of the new Kazakh national currency, the *tenge*, the rouble remained the local currency of transaction.

These mixed messages and the economic withdrawal of the centre from the regions provoked misunderstanding between centre and region, as well as substantial policy disagreements between the two. As noted in Chapter One, both the 1993 and 1995 Constitutions legalized Kazakhstan as a unitary state. The respondents, however, indicated a deep level of mistrust between the central and regional tiers of government. The central elites did not view the regional elites as central to decision-making in the republic and were sceptical about regional elites' capabilities. This was borne out by a May 1996 VIProblem survey in which 62 per cent thought that regional state capacity was low. The principal reasons given were: corruption of lower organs (48 per cent), 'serious slippage on cadre politics' (44), 'absence of a regional development concept'(36), 'stagnation' (32), 'weak control by society of their actions' (30), 'insufficient powers' (26), 'lack of coordination between central and regional organs of power' (24), and 'weak central control of regions' (10).[21] Even though 70 per cent of VIProblem respondents supported the election of the akim they did not see election as a panacea to these problems. In another study around this time, central elite members criticized the local elites for their lack of effectiveness: 62 per cent thought that problems in the effectiveness of regional state capacities were the major ones facing Kazakhstan (compared with only 22 per cent of the central elite questioned in Kyrgyzstan). (46 per cent felt that there were problems in the capacity also of central organs of power, compared to only 16 per cent in Kyrgyzstan).[22]

The regional elites interviewed felt abandoned by the centre; in response they were either indifferent, resentful or defiant:

> No-one in Almaty cares about us now. That era has gone. Today it lies at the level of the region. The problems of the people are our problems. We are allowed to do anything so long as it doesn't contradict our laws (PE, Uralsk, 5).

> I am the product of that system, not this one. I understand how that system worked. The planner would sit at the centre. They would decide that in 'x' region 'x' school would be built. And they gave money. Now the situation is quite different. Now we have to find the money to build these schools. I see a process of decentralization going on. Soon we will be depending on the taxes we raise ourselves and we will then be allocating that money to schools, hospitals (PE, Uralsk, 1).

> We don't need to go to Almaty, we resolve our own affairs. We don't receive any financial help, or any other help. So what's the point (PE, Shymkent, 3)?

Some regional differences nevertheless existed, with the southern elites giving the impression of being more confident of their relations with the centre than their northern or western counterparts.

Many were deeply critical of the policy of foreign management contracts. 'I think that our managers are no worse than foreign managers,' commented one member (PE, Uralsk, 5). Another elaborated: 'We should not have handed our major metals factories over to foreign management. Why did the government do this? Because we made a mistake (PE, Shymkent, 1). A third was adamant that 'the government is selling them [state companies] off at ridiculous prices. While I support small-scale privatization 100 per cent, I do not support a process which will impoverish the state at a time when it needs to be strengthened' (PE, Shymkent, 12)

# IDENTITY AND POLITICAL CULTURE

The previous chapters demonstrated the domination of power structures by ethnic Kazakhs, the persistence of a number of members of the political elite (Kazakh and Russian) born outside Kazakhstan, and the retention of a number of ethnic Russians in mid to high-level appointments, especially functionally specialist ones, though these were often not visible. We also noted that ethnic Kazakhs were increasingly occupying functionally specialist jobs by 2000. This final section of the chapter examines three main structural influences that have had an impact on the framework in which elites have risen: the legacy of a dual power system; the re-emergence of sub-national faultlines; and atomized civil and political society. These broader issues of national and social identity further reinforced the complexity of the environment.

The Soviet era bequeathed, in ethnic structural terms, two legacies. On the one hand, it had established a system of duality of power. On the other, different regions and different sectors had begun to strengthen the ethnic Kazakh cadre.

Martha Brill Olcott notes in *The Kazakhs* that a dual power system had emerged whereby the Slavic community dominated those areas of the economy and administration directly responsible to Moscow – for example, oblast level government and industrial production – while Kazakhs held sway over the livestock breeding economy and *raion* level party and state agencies.[23] Studies by Willerton, Cleary and Rywkin all demonstrate the duality of power.[24] Willerton notes how, in the 1950s, as a continuation of the policy of *korenizatsiia*, or nativization, a policy of dyarchy ensured that the first secretary was typically of the local nationality while the second secretary was Russian. The first secretary was thus able to 'enjoy the trust of the local nationality', while the second secretary, entrusted with recruitment decisions, exercized the real power. In the Soviet era, Russians were considered to have the know-how to run the managerial, technical and professional services while Kazakhs were employed in either political or administrative jobs.[25]

The duality of power institutionalized competition between Kazakhs and Russians. This competition was heightened geographically and demographically. While the south and east were primarily agricultural and a testing ground for nuclear weapons, the north was a centre of ferrous and nonferrous metallurgy industry, the west of oil. As Russians were mainly industrial labourers and technocrats, and Kazakhs unskilled labourers and agriculturalists, they were concentrated in the north/east and south/west respectively. Notes Pauline Jones Luong: 'The implementation of *korenizatsiia* is a case in point. Whereas in Kyrgzstan and Uzbekistan, the nativization of cadre was meant primarily for the titular nationality, in Kazakhstan it included Russians as well as Slavs.'[26]

We suggested that Nazarbaev was able to co-opt red directors in the early independence period. Nevertheless, this alone could not explain why key Russians at the level of directors of state enterprises, nomenklatura or state administrative and economic positions were also replaced so rapidly by Kazakhs. A key factor was emigration of these Soviet-era Slav elites, either involuntarily or voluntarily, either because of 'push' factors like loss of status in a newly independent state likely to be dominated by ethnic Kazakhs or because of 'pull' factors like attractive opportunities (a key example here being Oleg Soskovets or the significant number of former KaSSR Russian elites who obtained regional governorships in Russian regions bordering Kazakhstan), better economic conditions or close family ties in the parent states. Also, because Kazakhs generally made their career within the Socialist Republic of Kazakhstan, Slavs were able to profit from positions in Union-wide institutions.

Second, the appointment of ethnic Kazakhs to politico-administrative jobs was conducted, as noted in Chapter One, by Kazakh First Party Secretary Dinmukhamed Kunaev. Although he promoted the Kazakh republic (and therefore Russians also), Olcott contends that Kunaev 'deliberately used his position to give preferences to Kazakhs over Russians in the republic, and moved them into many key administrative positions.'[27] Olcott further observes that by 1981 Kazakhs constituted 51.9 per cent of the Central Committee in Alma-Ata. Kazakhs, she notes, 'also headed 47 per cent of the Central Committee department, although the key economic departments of heavy industry, agriculture, and construction continued to be run by Russians, as was the department of agitation and propaganda.'[28]

As elsewhere in the Soviet Union, elite building was given its own institutional network for the first time. Soviet institutional structures and policies suggested that the post-Soviet Kazakhization of the political elite was born of structure as well as intention. Preferential treatment of ethnic Kazakhs in some positions reinforced local political links, while at the same time creating widespread, broadly Kazakh patronage networks and thus providing the means for a smooth transfer of power. These networks matter because they had become deeply entrenched during the Soviet era. The regional differences in Soviet-era cadre policies also partly accounted for regional variations in the timing and extent of ethnic Kazakh appointments post-1991.

These differences were not only a function of regional difference in cadre policies but also broader differences in acculturation. Russification, as we saw in the Introduction and Chapter One, came unevenly to different parts of Kazakhstan. The Kazakhs of the Middle Zhuz had been longer under Russian rule than those of the Senior Zhuz, and their adoption of Russian practice was greater as a consequence.[29] The Junior and Inner Hordes, closest to European Russia, and the longest of all in close contact with the Russians, witnessed an even more marked degree of acculturation. The examination of varying political cultures is the subject of another study, however.

Degrees of acculturation bring us penultimately onto a brief discussion of political culture and sources of authoritarianism. Neil Melvin summaries some of the arguments that have been made in favour of cultural explanations for Central Asia generally.[30] He cites, for example, Karl Wittfogel who situated the source of despotism in the environmental and economic conditions of the region.[31] More recently, Melvin continues, it has been argued 'that while culture may not determine outcomes, it is hard to avoid the conclusion that it serves to shape and constrain the choices made by elites,'[32] and that: 'Central Asian traditions of patriarchy, popular submissiveness, deference to authority and to elders, and weak democratic institutions would seem to impel Central Asian societies toward an authoritarian future.'[33] We can only touch on these issues here.

To characterize the history of the Kazakh steppe as authoritarian would be erroneous. Chapter One demonstrated how the republic's history is not one of monolithic authoritarian rule but one where power has been competed for and fragmented, and in which society, far from being separate, has had a say in whether leaders were effective and indeed whether they even stayed around. This complexity appears to be reflected in contemporary elite political culture, where tradition and modernity coexist, with the culture of the territory absorbing, reshaping and reinventing itself.

The first decade of independence indicated low mobilization and participation rates and an absent vibrant civil society. The absence of organized society was partly a historical legacy of the Soviet period, during which civil society was tightly controlled by the state.[34] Elite respondents echoed this view: 'In Kazakhstan, the mentality of the average citizen is strongly influenced by the leadership' (PE, 21). This dovetails with a VIProblem 1995 survey which cited the main reason for the weakness in the party system as the political apathy of the population (54 per cent), followed by the absence of charismatic party leaders (26 per cent).[35] But this alone does not explain why other post-Soviet societies have been so much better at organizing themselves in the wake of Soviet collapse. One possible reason is the absence of a cohesive Kazakhstani identity.

The variations in political culture and attitudinal differences from below have been demonstrated by one of the few substantial surveys conducted on political culture by the National Endowment for Democracy under the directorship of historian Nurbulat Masanov.[36] It conducted three separate surveys in Autumn 1995, Winter 1995–1996 and Spring 1996 in five of Kazakhstan's cities: Almaty, Petropavlosk, Uralsk, Ust-Kamenogorsk and Shymkent.[37] The surveys revealed both fundamental differences between the way in which Russians and Kazakhs regard Kazakhstan's state-building policies and interesting provincial variations.

According to this study, ethnic Kazakh members appeared to view the state, consciously or unconsciously, as a primarily ethnic Kazakh construct, and believe firmly in the need for strong presidential power. The Russians interviewed, by contrast, identified either with the Soviet past or with Russia but only a few with the Kazakhstani state. Thus, for example when asked with what group the respondent most identifies, 51.1 per cent of Kazakhs said Kazakhstan compared to only 11.9 per cent of Russians. By contrast, the highest per centage of Russian respondents (41.8 per cent) said the family was their primary unit of allegiance (compared to 26.1 per cent of Kazakh respondents), followed by 24.6 per cent who associated themselves with the Soviet Union (compared to 5.9 per cent of Kazakhs) and 21.6 per cent with their own generation (21.6 per cent) (Kazakhs, 18.9 per cent). In reply to the question whether the respondent feels a citizen of Kazakhstan, 84.3 per cent of Kazakhs but only 24.2 per cent of Russians replied in the affirmative. And when asked, if given the possibility would the citizen emigrate immediately, 30 per cent of Russians said yes, compared to only 3.5 per cent of Kazakhs.

Even if studies such as these indicate varying political cultures, it is important to note, however, that Russian-dominated regions did not necessarily have greater expression of political activism than Kazakh-dominated regions. In Nancy Lubin's study Russians did not show more support for democratization than Kazakhs. In the context of Hirschman's choices of exit, voice and loyalty, the majority chose to exit and, of those who stayed, only a few have chosen to protest the loss of Russian status.[38]

Opinion polls on voting behaviour suggest that the population sought above all strong leaders and personalities, and often complained about the absence of both in regional administrations and political movements. While, already in 1995–1996, the regional elites wanted more autonomy and, by 2001, were at least unofficially keen to see regional elections, this was not reflected in the population, who saw their welfare and security in central not regional power.[39] Again this might change; if regional elites were given additional powers and resources, and are better able to deliver social services, populations may be more inclined to support regionalism.

Attitudes to the relationship between ethnicity and power are significant here, specifically the absence of active social protest against ethnic Kazakh elite monopolization. The sources and implications of ethnic Kazakh domination provoked mixed reactions. Furthermore, reports on voting behaviour indicated that ethnic groups did not necessarily vote for their own ethnic group, or that they regarded ethnicity as the key factor in their voting patterns. Similarly, for example, one Ukrainian maslikhat member explained:

When we meet with the Tatar-Bashkir cultural centre they say the Bashkirs only have five leaders in Pavlodar town, while we have 70.

We have it good, they say. And I reply. You know I would happily exchange your 7 Tatar-Bashkirs for our 70 Ukrainians because your Tatars help other Tatars (PE, Uralsk, 11).

Similarly, a Russian former member of parliament and now state executive explained that more ethnic Kazakhs than Russians voted for her because she was regarded as more impartial than an ethnic Kazakh, who might belong to another clan. In other words, intra-ethnic cleavages were in the mid-1990s running deeper than interethnic ones:

> During my electoral campaign many Kazakhs would approach me and say: we will vote for you, you will not be from any particular zhuz or clan which would put us under subjective pressure; at least we know with you it will be objective (PE, 13).

Such downplaying of ethnicity in attitudes and voting behaviour suggests that a civic understanding of Kazakhstani statehood might have been nurtured in the early independence years. Widespread popular disillusionment with the state instead set in. If all ethnic groups felt economically worse off in the wake of Soviet collapse, non-Kazakhs also felt psychologically disadvantaged as they came to perceive the state as an ethnic Kazakh construct, particularly because non-titular groups had been removed from top posts. Ethnic Kazakh members of the elite were themselves often unconvinced that Kazakhstani identification could be nurtured. This was reflected, consciously or unconsciously, in their own conflation of the terms Kazakh and Kazakhstani (Chapter Four).

Existing social ties that previously contributed to either interethnic or regional acculturation seemed to be breaking, and social identities appeared to be transforming into particularistic ones. Economic collapse, the absence of national cohesion, sub-ethnic differences between individuals, and the fact that these networks themselves are fluid, have all undermined the cohesion of even the informal networks. The result has been profound societal dislocation.[40]

## SUB-ETHNIC NETWORKS, THE STATE

In the preceding chapter we discussed the degree to which the regime has drawn on sub-ethnic identities in its recruitment decisions, and we concluded that the anecdotal evidence suggests the correlation is not definite. We demonstrated how Masanov's thesis in the early years of independence may have been partly accurate in legitimational terms, but how intentional criteria of recruitment then became far more complex and diverse. But is there a deeper, structural basis to tribalism than an instrumental one, one which leaders do not choose but are forced to use, consciously or unconsciously? And how best to conceive this structure – as enabling or constraining? Again, we can elaborate only briefly.

Traditional structures refer here primarily to the zhuz, tribe and clan. Clans and tribes together are summarized by the Russian '*rodoplemenaia struktura*' and the Kazakh '*ru*' (although *ru* can also often mean only clan, like *taipa*, as below).[41] Krader and Hudson noted the absence of precise terms relating to the tribal structure of Turkic peoples, adding to terminological confusion.[42] Evans-Pritchard has helped by giving us the delineation of tribe (Russian *plemya*, Kazakh *ru*), clan and lineage. By the nineteenth century, once the Kazakh steppe had been incorporated into the Russian empire, zhuz identification had been de-emphasized in favour of that of tribe and clan.

The genealogies of these structures were, however, often mythical. As explained by Talgat Ismagambetov, Tolybekov illustrates this fluidity vividly with his depiction of the aul of Elikei. Elikei's was one of eight auls united by the common ancestor Khodzhan. This Khodhzan group was part of the Tauke 'clan' (or *taipa*, to use Tolybekov's terminology, although the more general term 'ru' tends to be used colloquially). This clan, in turn, was a branch of the larger 'tribe' Alimul. Between the clan and the tribe there were three levels of belonging: the third (Diusek), the second (Suyon-Shomekei) and the first (Shomekei). In a simplified version by missing out the intermediary stages of belonging, Elikei's eighth generation ancestor was Khodzhan, who was in turn unilineally descended from the Tauke clan, and, further removed, from the Alimul tribe.[43]

Placing this aul in a broader context, the Kazakh nation and its subdivisions are regarded as parts of an extended family group. Nineteenth-century observers generally agreed that the primogenitor had three sons who branched off to form separate units which many deem were the precursors to the three 'hordes'.[44] Ethnographers have, however failed to pinpoint a common ancestor. Even the name of the primogenitor is disputed, although it is generally also believed to be Alash. Valikhanov confirms the name of the ancestor as Alash whom he sees as a real rather than mythical figure. Even the etymology of the word 'Kazakh' remains disputed.

Lineage is thus the vertical stratification of the horizontal formations of aul, clan, tribe. Talgat Ismagambetov shows that blood relations are the most important at the aul level while lineage at a higher level unites tribes and zhuzes. At the aul level, two to three generations, at most three to four generations, Ismagambetov writes, are remembered. The precise terms for these different lineages are: minimal (*minmal'nyii*) at two to three generations removed (this applied generally to Elikei and his relations);[45] small (*malii*) lineage at three to four (this applied to the Tauke clan);[46] large (*bol'shoi*) at four to five generations removed (named Diusek); and, maximum (*maksimal'nyi*) at five to seven generations removed. For those who recall their generations seven generations back the [illegible] ulu, or seven ancestors, is used. The most influential of all lineages was that furthest removed.[47]

The significance of 'seven' is seen by the term given to the eighth generation in Kazakh – *nemene*, which translates roughly as 'What (on earth) is that?' Hence, although remembering up to the seventh generation back is commended, already in traditional society it was held that at best nomads only remembered two to three generations removed. Fortes has demonstrated the role of genealogy as a kind of origin myth in a unilineal descent group, of which the Kazakhs and Kyrgyz are examples.[48] Myths can be forgotten, reshaped, invented and thus impart a considerable fluidity into nomadic political and social belonging.[49]

Not only were genealogies often mythical but, in reality, blood ties were often nothing of the kind. Thus, in Elikei's aul only four of the seven yurts housed his extended family: his own family; families of his first son; his second son and his poor relations; and his poor relations. The remainder consisted of one for his horse-herder and two for his shepherds.

Russian and Soviet colonization transformed these identities. With Russian colonization and the territorial administrative reforms in the late nineteenth century, several nomadic auls (*kochevoi aul*) were united into an administrative aul, which in turn answered to the larger territorial unit, the volost, then uezd, then oblast, then general-governor (*krai*). By fusing several extended families into one larger unit, Russian imperial rulers aimed to both divide clans and create new units of belonging that would be loyal to the empire. Tolybekov noted that several encampments could be united to form an administrative aul. The aul had a clear effect: it increased the sense of horizontal over vertical belonging. In short, as lineage (vertical stratification) decreased and clan allegiance (horizontal stratification) increased, tribal formations transformed from being three-dimensional (or vertical) to flat structures.

Lineage became even more fluid, genealogy more mythical. The more immediate ancestor was the most powerful in material affairs, and the most distant was the most powerful in ideational and affectional senses.

Bacon notes how under Russian rule, 'kolkhoz exogamy has replaced genealogical exogamy'.[50] *Kolkhoz* nomad brigades regularly consisted of a close family unit. A brigade tended a flock of sheep, a herd of horses, camels, or cattle, or cared for cultivated fields or cut hay from the meadows. Even if traditional auls always herded different types of animals separately, there was always close co-operation between different breeders, such as when horses were sent 'to teben' for sheep, and this practice continued between *kolkhozy*. The *kolkhoz* itself was made up of closely related families of a tribal kin segment. When these early *kolkhozy* were consolidated to form larger *kolkhozy*, such consolidation usually brought together kin groups that were related by virtue of their traditional sharing of a common territory. In some cases, where one small *kolkohz* kin group happened to be farther afield, it was nevertheless included in the *kolkohz* of its closest tribal kin segments rather than in that geographically nearest to it. Thus, the old tribal kin structure had not been destroyed. Bacon writes: 'Indeed, the formation of kolkhozes within the traditional territory has perhaps strengthened kinship ties.'[51] The *bii*, chief of the tribal kin groups, often reappeared as a district administrator. There were frequent newspaper complaints that administrators gave preference to members of their own tribal kin segment in making appointments and decisions. And the *aqsaqal* remained a person of importance – children within the extended family unit continued to be trained from earliest childhood to respect their elders. The influence of the kolkhoz has been more recently developed by Olivier Roy. Roy contends that 'the Soviet era created a new tribe: the kolkhoz' and 'a two-level political culture: on the one hand an appearance of conformity with the social project imposed by the authorities: on the other, a subversion of that project by practices of factionalism and clientelism.'[52] The kolkhoz refashioned these primordial ties and made them even stronger by sedentarizing them.

The status and importance of the zhuz increased in the Soviet period – at both the level of elite and society. Its status increased because this was the first time that the zhuzes were competing against each other for national-state posts. This was due both to Soviet practice of playing one zhuz off against the other, and also Kunaev's promotion of the Senior Zhuz, to which he belonged. The Senior Zhuz, moreover, suffered the least from the sedentarization campaign (having traditionally been part-agriculturalist), and was therefore in a better position to preserve its traditional social relations. This also brought prestige to the Senior Zhuz.[53] We can expect the identity of the Senior Zhuz to have been of particular signficance and a source of pride in the initial independence years and the willingness of the southern political elite to speak more openly about their sub-ethnic affiliations partly attest to this.

A number of conclusions may be drawn from this discussion. First, traditional structures, even if to a degree territorialized under Russian and Soviet rule, remained fluid and often mythical. They may be therefore less rigidly a constraining factor on the formation of the state than they might be in, for example, the Middle East or Africa. Furthermore, their often mythical nature and evolution pointed to the likely importance of social rather than blood relations in the selection of individuals to an elite post. This means that the word 'clan' is often used in reference to social rather than blood ties. 'Nazarbaev has deliberately put in place a growing number of clans from the Karaganda area,' noted Expert (Group )A. 'This is a good thing – they have industrial experience, and know Russian well. Nazarbaev grew up with these people. It is not just because of the move to Akmola.' Third, social and blood relations seemed to provide a strong sense of obligation on the part of the elite in the recruitment process, reflected here in elite replies: upwards, elite members felt obliged to accept jobs because the president has asked them to and downwards, elite members felt obliged to assist members of their own blood and social network once in power. Almaty's first post-independence mayor Zamanbek Nurkadilov from the Senior Zhuz in his autobiography stresses 'the sacred duty of relatives to look after their close ones who had come into misfortune'.[54]

Fourth, although sub-ethnic networks create this obligation and therefore partially constrain agency, they were also enabling in the context of power maintenance. Not only did a member of the political elite often have an automatic reserve of individuals on whom they can draw on the basis of loyalty criteria, but also, because of these structures' fluidity, they could expect to be able to co-opt members from other groups with less difficulty than would be the case in more highly structured tribal societies. That said, and finally, tribes of the Senior or Inner Zhuz could be expected to have boundaries that are less fluid because many of them were already at least partially sedentarized by the seventeenth century after the partial introduction of agriculture.

In conclusion, this chapter has demonstrated how the environmental context has also contributed to our understanding of elite behaviour. In particular we identified the following features of this environment: mixed regime type and inconsistent policies; the psychology of independence; the political economy of the state; de facto economic decentralization; the politics of identity; a weak cohesive Kazakhstani identity at the societal level and the nature of sub-ethnic identities in state formation. In the concluding chapter we shall assess how agency, structure and identity have interacted in shaping the elite and political systems.

# CONCLUSION

## ELITES, INSTITUTIONS AND REGIME TYPE

As noted in the previous chapter, scholars disagree on the sources of authoritarianism in Central Asia. This volume has offered reasons as to why and how the elite system is a compelling factor behind the emergence and maintenance of authoritarianism in Kazakhstan. The various features of the elite system that have propped up authoritarianism include: the strong control of institutions by the executive elite; obstacles to the emergence of oppositional movements through alternative institutional foci or incentives and also inhibiting the possibility of institutions playing an intermediary role; the associated absence of systemic cushions that would make it easier for oppositional members to exist outside the incumbent elite; a high degree of elite reshuffling preventing security of tenure; various attempts at the centralization of recruitment, including through centre/region crossovers; a general attitudinal elite consensus in favour of top-down central control; and, a strategy of compartmentalization which acts as a substitute for full-scale reform.

This authoritarianism, moreover, rather than resulting simply from top-down coercion, is the product of a high degree of negotiation, bargaining and co-optation by the incumbent elite. Initial decisions on formal constitutional and statutory provisions were only the framework in which leading political actors competed to shape the authority of specific institutions.

Where power is effectively centralized, or by contrast, well-diffused, patronage is correspondingly less common. When power is neither effectively centralized, nor well-diffused – as in Kazakhstan's case – patronage assumes added importance. This middle ground and the accompanying need to negotiate and bargain, to play to different elite constituencies, has often produced inconsistent policies and environments, has resulted in different degrees of authoritarianism in 1991–2001, and has blurred the distinctions between state and society, public and private.

The political elite's relationship to the state was therefore ambiguous. It was both reforming and rent-seeking. Reform included measures to rationalize decision-making and streamline government, and consultative mechanisms for groups outside the state. Under Kazakhstan's second prime minister, Akezhan Kazhegeldin (1994–1997), the government introduced a comprehensive economic reform programme which locked the state into the global economy. It also undertook several reform rounds in an attempt to improve the quality of governance, particularly the March 1997 decree that reduced the number of ministries from 20 to 14 and state committees from 12 to 2. Pockets of reliable business infrastructure, notably the banking sector, pension reform sector and foreign investment law emerged.

By the close of the 1990s, however, state-building initiatives had stagnated, and were often eclipsed by rent-seeking. Both mass privatization and the flow of oil revenues intensified rent seeking. As the political stakes from increased economic income were raised, so was the political influence of a narrower elite grouping as it attempted to strengthen the economic basis of its political power. In general, policy implementation, especially since the 1997 centralization, depended on a small number of individuals, thereby severely limiting the role of middle-ranking cadres.

We noted the symbiotic relationship between elites and institutions in Chapter Two. Institutions often provided the vehicle by which elites emerged, were protected and possibly strengthened. In turn, the political elite shaped this very institutional architecture, largely in an attempt to prevent the rise of competitors and maintain its rule. One way of stalling such reform has been for the elite to change the name of institutions without changing their functions, and repeated alterations to the institutional architecture have likewise hindered continuity in reform and recruitment.

The recruited elite was overwhelmingly associated with formal institutions of power, primarily in the executive branch of government. Nevertheless, some evolution had occurred over the period, with a few prominent members of the political elite cited by the panel of experts as being located outside executive government in the 1995–1996 period, such as leaders of political movements, foreign economic actors or certain high-profile members of parliament. Some of the informal power holders sought political office and were easily co-optable. By 2000, however, the political elite was nearly wholly affiliated to executive institutions.

The dominance of the executive was also seen at the regional level where the majority of the elite located in the three regions of Pavlodar, Shymkent and Uralsk was situated in the regional administrations (*akimats*). The centralization of power by the regional executive appears to have occurred earlier than at the central level, as very few actors, other than foreign economic actors (and sometimes local actors in partnership with foreign corporations), were cited as influential to their region. It did appear that the regional akim had acquired substantial influence over policy-making in their region. Centrally, the presidential administration strengthened in relation to the government, with many government agencies, particularly those involved in economic and security policy-making, having been brought under presidential control.

This executive is fused rather than interlocked, and does not contain a strong military (Chapter Two). Although, in the Gorbachev period, Nazarbaev had managed to consolidate the control of political institutions, in the early independence era up to around 1994, regional administrations and heads of large regional state companies enjoyed considerable independence and influence and were able to benefit considerably from 'spontaneous privatization' (see below). Under Kazhegeldin, the regime managed to co-opt major state corporations, centralize and invite representatives of major business groups into government. By 2001, this fused politico-economic-administrative elite had showed signs of fragmenting, but was still comprised of factions that enjoyed only limited independent economic power, rather than economic groups with autonomous sources of political and social power. We concluded that neither the pluralist nor the power models wholly captured the structure of the Kazakhstani elite but because of the elite's monopoly over economic and political resources the structure bore more resemblance to C. Wright Mills' power elite.

The predominance of the elite in formal executive, rather than, say, informal, parliamentary or judicial posts in part reflected the primacy of the executive in the Soviet era. Of Kazakhstan's 244 elite members identified in 1995–1996, nearly two thirds had served in either an executive or party post in the Soviet era. Those from the Soviet executive were drawn from a common field of two main occupational categories: senior administrative officials, and senior managers of economic enterprises.

Into the post-Soviet era, by contrast, five main former career categories were discernible: official, economic, professional, technocratic and business (Chapter Two). These are explained by a number of career trends in this first decade of independence. The first was an intense institutional and elite reshuffling, so that one individual might have served in several institutions either simultaneously or sequentially. This 'institution hopping' applied also to the interchangeability and crossovers between centre and region, region and centre. Second, although the number of individuals with engineering degrees declined, those with technical specializations, noticeably in finance and law, rose. Third, significantly fewer professionals worked in all major institutions of government, noticeably in parliament. Finally, several prominent businessmen (either those who had started their enterprises in the late Gorbachev period or in the early independence periods) were incorporated into various branches of government.

The core political elite identified in 1991–2001 thus comprised both 'old' and 'new'. On the one hand, those who remained in office after Soviet collapse provided a considerable degree of continuity between the Soviet and the post-Soviet elites. These Soviet-era members appeared to have been recruited for a variety of reasons – many of the core worked closely with Nazarbaev in the pre-1991 period; others seem to have been chosen because of the networks, knowledge and experience they amassed during that period, still others because of the status then conferred on them. The Introduction made no pretence to uncover the specific reason why any particular individual was recruited but the study has attempted to demonstrate the diversity of reasons as to why a Soviet past has mattered for membership in the contemporary elite. Many top elite members were still in power in 2001, indicating a high degree of elite retention and circulation (see below on Elite Recruitment).

On the other hand, we have seen the arrival of newcomers, some of whom enjoyed a meteoric rise in their career in their 20s and early 30s. This pool of newcomers consisted mainly of three types: relatives or friends of Nazarbaev and his selectorate; technocrats; and businessmen. The majority of these new arrivals were urban-born and ethnic Kazakh, and a majority had either worked or attended higher education in Almaty.

The technocratic class, formerly the preserve predominantly of Slavs, was thus gradually becoming associated with Kazakh ethnicity. The Soviet legacy had ensured that, while Kazakhs had tended to occupy politico-administrative posts, Slavs had technocratic training and in 1995–1996 in all three regional administrations visited, key members of financial and economic departments were Slavic. By 2001 this trend was already changing, with many of these departmental posts now occupied by younger ethnic Kazakhs, many of whom had been trained abroad, including in the USA, Europe and Turkey. They joined the ranks of the first group of young Kazakh technocrats who had been recruited at the beginning of independence, many of whom had received their specialized training in Russia.

This issue of the relationship between ethnicity and power may be compared with David Lane's discussion of the role of ethnicity and class in Stalinist Kazakhstan, where he argues that ethnicity, rather than being important in its own right, is a function of class i.e. certain classes tend to be dominated by certain ethnicities.[1] Chapter Three suggested that the transitional system functionally demanded a technocracy and that this technocracy was increasingly Kazakh. Kazakhization when viewed in this light is a structural 'push' feature from below as well as a 'pull' from above (see below).

If we were able to determine the social background of political elites, we, however, also contended that Kazakhstan has provided further evidence that the link between social background on the one hand, and attitudes, identity and behaviour is far from simple,[2] and would appear to support the statement that: 'We cannot infer the direction of policy merely from the social origins and careers of the policy makers'.[3] While we acknowledge that we could make only tentative links between social background and attitudes – because of sample size and the occasional understandable unwillingness of elite members to disclose policy disagreements – the answers given by the elite did not suggest the existence of group attitudes. There was not, for example, one female, ethnic Russian, or 'young' attitude on policies. Importantly also, the economic sub-elite who wanted to see a rule-based, transparent economy did not however see this necessarily as tantamount to democratization. Similarly, the regional elites were not always in favour of democratization or federalism. Promoters of civic nationhood were not necessarily democratizers; promoters of privatization did not necessarily wish to see the growth of participation. This picture of variegated attitudes suggests a cross-cutting rather than reinforcing attitudinal elite system.

This weakness in discernible group attitudes may partly reside in the high degree of elite and institutional reshuffling. This has weakened the possibility for institutions to play an intervening, moderating role. This contrasts with the Soviet era where institutional identity was stronger as career paths were clearly defined and individuals' associations with their institutions remained over a long period. As we noted in the discussion in Chapter Three, comparative examples have suggested that in those cases where institutions are strong, the link between social background and attitudes and even policy was likely to be stronger. Other scholars have emphasized the importance of institutional role or 'position'[4] and the influence of experience while 'working in a given field or institutional setting'.[5] As Putnam puts it: 'Role constraints may demand certain beliefs and behaviour... Where you get to sit depends on where you stand.'[6] Lodge, in his study of the Stalinist elite, explains attitudinal variations in terms of differences between the intervening variables – rather than the original variables we began with – of elite recruitment and socialization. This weakness of the intervening variables may be simply a function of maturity – the period reviewed is after all only a decade. But the trend may also have been exacerbated by the frequent institutional changes and elite reshuffling that characterized this period. As noted in Chapter Three, surveys of the elite conducted in 2001 nevertheless suggested that attitudinal divisions were growing and that these were primarily falling along a central/regional axis and an axis of economic groups. This may in turn suggest that for the moment attitudes are primarily being shaped by interest.

Nevertheless overall, rather than demonstrating that social background influences elite behaviour, attitudes and policy outcomes, elite composition and policy appear therefore more affected by wider socio-economic and political changes. This would suggest that, in the first years of independence, the political elite in Kazakhstan managed to remain more of an independent than a dependent variable, with the important caveat made in the Introduction that structure and agency are empirically inseparable.

Elite attitudes feed into the normative dimension of elite (dis)unity, which we partly addressed in Chapter Three and, in identity terms, in Chapter Four. This dimension refers to the extent of shared values and beliefs, as well as more specific norms, most of them informal and uncodified, of political access, competition, and restrained partisanship. In Higley et al.'s terms, elite unity or disunity has both a normative and interactive dimension.[7] In Chapters One and Five, we discussed the interactive dimension, the extent of the inclusive channels and networks through which elite persons and groups obtain relatively assured access to the key decision-making centres. We established that the elite has sought to exert control over these channels.

Elite differentiation, by contrast, is the extent to which the elite groups are socially heterogeneous, organizationally diverse, and relatively autonomous from the state and each other. It is manifested by functionally distinct elite sectors (political, economic, administrative, military, religious, educational, the media, the arts, and so on), each with its own boundaries, organizations, formal and informal rules of behaviour, and pecking order.[8] Differentiation may be slowed 'if a dominant elite requires that all functionally specialized, ostensibly autonomous elites nevertheless adhere to a single ideology, religious dogma, or ethnonationalist creed and to the party or movement that articulates it.'[9] We established the degree of the social heterogeneity of the political elite in Chapter One, and established the systemic absence of ideology in Chapters Two and Four. We noted, especially in Chapter Five, that the elite has attempted to slow differentiation by co-optation, particularly of the business elite. Overall, the evidence suggested a socially homogeneous group in the early years of independence, noting that this homogeneity had declined somewhat in the period concerned and, attitudinally, an elite who, although displaying some differences over issue orientations, also displayed elements of value congruence. Organizationally, the institutional mechanisms described in Chapter Five and the interest groups outlined in Chapter Six still pointed to organizations that operate within the state, rather than autonomously from it. The absence of acute polarization impeded division and collapse. When one group or faction within the elite was seen as having accrued too much control over political and economic resources, however, simmering discontent came into the open in November 2001.[10]

The characteristics of the political elite system appeared then closely related to the overall political order. We noted in the Introduction how Higley's model associated different national elite configurations with different regime types.[11] On this scale, Kazakhstan's elite resembled, but was not entirely congruent with, a fragmented one, suggesting a link, in the context of this model, between fragmentation and authoritarianism, with the relationship going in both directions.

Nor does Kazakhstan exactly fit one of the three types of elite systems suggested by Beck and Malloy, but again a comparison is useful. They identified three types of elite system according to two dimensions: *division/unity* and *permeability/impermeability*. They are: (1) the divided and permeable elite; (2) the unified and impermeable elite; and (3) the divided and impermeable elite.[12] Kazakhstan's system lay somewhere between (2) and (3). It began as (2) in the sense that its elite shared their political experiences and basic beliefs, as well as commitment to certain techniques of position maintenance, to a high degree. Recruitment was tightly controlled, and there were few independent bases of authority. Competition, including that in the parliament of 1994–5, was best characterized as factionalism, and it was very hard to change status from non-elite to elite. The elite was committed to explicit goals, in particular, that of interethnic harmony. By 2000, Kazakhstan showed some elements of (3), with the principle difference from (2) being that the elite group was becoming less economically cohesive – even if still politically dependent.

Welsh concludes that societies conforming to model (3) 'are frequently characterized by policy immobility, a failure to develop sufficient unity within the elite, or to mobilize sufficient support within the general population, to carry through coherent programs of governmental activity.'[13] This description may reflect the state of reform in 2001, the system having reached an impasse. The description also concords with another conclusion of Welsh's, that 'significant segments of the social order operate outside direct political control, lending a less highly structured flavour to the character of society.'[14] The absence of highly structured interests among society weakened the elite's social base but also lent the elite greater autonomy.

## ELITE RECRUITMENT

Even if, as suggested, newcomers have risen in the elite, they do not indicate that the elite system was an open one. This is because the primary method of selecting elites remained recruitment rather than election. Monocratic regimes, as the name suggests, are usually characterized by a selectorate of one. Many informal accounts of Nazarbaev describe a president who continued to be influenced by advice from an inner circle of advisers.[15] That inner circle, in line with the developments among the political elite, has undergone some changes. The number of political gatekeepers involved in the appointments process declined between 1991 and 2001. This narrowed selectorate became instead composed mainly of relatives and friends. Trends elsewhere have shown that a narrowing of the selectorate in turn leads to the gatekeepers tending to 'pick their own', a point that seems to be confirmed in this case.

The recruitment practiced by this selectorate takes on considerable importance in the absence of fair and free elections. The presidential (1991 and 1999) and parliamentary (1994, 1995 and 1999) elections were marred by irregularities, those irregularities becoming more serious in the latter part of the decade and, in the case of both 1999 elections particularly, results falsified. In the absence of accountable institutions, the study has attempted to show that recruitment of Kazakhstan's central political elite are a triple product of agency ('pull' and instrumental representativeness), structure ('push') and legitimation (symbolic representativeness). We take each of these in turn.

The instrumentality of recruitment was seen in various ways, of which the most important were the regime's use of both legal and illegal means to maintain itself in power; mass privatization, particularly the sale of strategic industries, which involved the centralization of policy making and the gaining of hard-needed finance; and the co-optation of people, ideas and institutions. Recruitment criteria were mutually reinforcing and served the elite's primary goal to keep itself in power. As Sabit Zhusupov has concluded: 'the emphasis on the strategic can in many ways explain the specifics of the way the Kazakhstani political system is functioning, indeed the sovereign state as a whole.'[16] Seen in this light the recruitment programme has been strategically grounded and tactically executed.

Co-optation was a central feature of the elite system of the 1990s. In the very early years, just upon collapse, communist-era directors and regional elites were co-opted in exchange for economic gains from privatization. In the 1994–5 period it was primarily parliamentarians who were co-opted into executive institutions, including key members of political parties. Some of these, such as Murat Auezov, have been re-co-opted; others, like opposition leader Petr Svoik, have been invited but refused. Towards the late 1990s businessmen were co-opted into the executive.

The use of co-optation partly depends on the perceived structure of political risk. Every society has a system of cushions that are used to 'break the fall' of those rejected by the operative selection mechanisms. Michels traced the roots of oligarchy in working-class movements in part to the very sharp drop in status and income that awaited ex-leaders, and a similar theory may fit some developing countries today.[17] These cushions may include the awarding of symbolic positions within political party organizations. Seligman demonstrates that there is great variation among societies in the extent to which cushions exist.[18]

Co-optation has been used by the elite as a power maintenance tool (Chapter Five). For most of this period it has minimized the possibilities for the development of alternative sources of authority and slowed differentiation. Co-optation has also lowered the transaction costs of institutional transfer. Rewards for the clients of one's competitors consolidated power and also signalled that factional politics had its limitations, that the struggle could not be conducted to extremes. Because the political elite was small enough, its best policy to maintain its rule was to enlist individuals from a different, non-elite background. There was good propaganda value in such a strategy, which included harder-working individuals and implied that they would be easily co-opted.

The elite also stayed ahead of its competitors by championing the agendas of those whom they viewed as oppositional or obstructionist, in particular when those agendas were perceived as populist, or as providing possible alternative sources of authority. One key example of the populist agenda was that of using indigenous companies and import substitution, one also increasingly being lobbied by economic groups within the state. Nazarbaev's rhetoric of internationalism and his creation of institutions symbolizing the rights of non-titular ethnic groups, such as the Assembly of Peoples' Deputies and National-Cultural Centres, seemed also to assist in reducing the possibility of nationalist agendas becoming institutionalized. This served to co-opt ethnic groups' agenda and also to neutralize the non-titular voting constituency. The electoral system also de-ethnicized politics by making loyalty rather than ethnicity endemic to the voting landscape. Nazarbaev's centrist position, epitomized in his autobiography strategically brought out in time for the 1991 presidential election, occupied the middle ground, as did many of the top-down parties he went on to create.

The regime has employed further institutional mechanisms to influence the nature and development of recruitment. Where it attempted to implement reform during 1991–3 through compromise and negotiation, by 1994 it had chosen the methods of decree, expansion of presidential personal power, and the exclusion of other political actors. The 1995 Constitution, in the preparation of which the president took an active role, gave the regime sufficient legal means to emaciate other branches of government, especially parliament and the judiciary. In both cases the president now had the right to appoint some of its members. He now also held powers to initiate legislation and to dissolve parliament. The 2000 powers additionally granted him immunity in office. The Constitution was also sufficiently ambiguous to allow for its manipulation; this enabled the regime to justify its actions in legal terms. When legal means were not available or sufficient, illegal remedies were often sought in their place. By the close of the 1990s the elite had increasingly used repressive measures in its treatment of political parties, the media and unloyal subjects.

Furthermore, the handing over of key strategic industries proved crucial for the elite in the 1995–1998 period when it sought support from key constituencies in what was to prove a pre-1999 electoral campaign. The sale supplied the government with badly needed finance to close the gaping budget deficit (only by 2000 had the government recorded its first budget surplus), to buy off key central and regional actors and to deliver quick returns to the population. By 1998, the first two had been achieved but the widespread discreditation of these contracts – not least their opaque nature – led to a stalling of privatization under Balgimbaev in 1998. The exclusion of the nascent national bourgeoisie from these mass sales – such as the exclusion of the Kazakhstani trading company Butya in the Karaganda Steel Mills negotiations – has slowed its formation and furthered group differentiation.

The mass privatization of key strategic industries was part of the regime's attempt to centralize policy-making and take back power from a regional elite that, along with regional state companies, had become increasingly influential. The increasing practice of Astana-region elite crossovers was part of this centralization. The continued dominance of executive power at the regional level meant that although the republic has a bicameral parliament, bargaining and lobbying occurred through executive institutions. Centralization further allowed the elite to narrow the selectorate and pick more of 'its own'.

The strategic nature of recruitment was further seen in the use of patron-client relations and the high degree of institutional reshuffling. The gatekeepers often appointed individuals who they regarded as loyal servants. This was most visibly seen in the drawing up of the *gosspicok* (candidate list) for the 1994–1995 parliament, in which the executive reserved a certain number of seats for presidential appointees. Similarly, by 2001, a significant number of regional governors appointed had become loyal members of the central elite not always with experience of that region (or any region for that matter). The intense elite reshufflements, a strong feature of Kazakhstan's political elite, was similarly explained by a fear on the part of the political leadership of competitors.

Importantly, a strong majority of the elite complained about the absence of elite cohesion and strategy and about the need to bargain for agreement to be reached at all levels of power. This pointed simultaneously to an underlying competition between and mutual suspicion of government departments, a drive to reach consensus, and the requirement of the central elite to bargain and negotiate.

Instrumentalism, as we have indicated, is however only part of the story. We have seen how Bob Jessop's strategic relational environment (Introduction) helps us also to understand the importance not only of systemic attributes but also how actors and their policies can affect the environment which in turn affects them.

Three main systemic outcomes that have fused with system attributes as a result of the power maintenance techniques briefly reviewed above are: an inconsistent policy environment that has led to a mixed regime type; a motley group of state actors that have become increasingly difficult for the selectorate to manage; and, what Barbara Geddes termed for Latin America 'the politician's dilemma' (Chapters Five and Six and below), which appeared to be leading increasingly to policy and institutional stagnation.

The mixed regime type is emphasized in Chapter One by different degrees of authoritarianism in the first ten years of independence. The chapter offered a quadruple division of the period into 1992–1994; 1995–1996; 1995–1998; and 1999–2001. During this period, the elite liberalized, then repressed. It politically centralized, but de facto economically decentralized. It placed special emphasis on a Kazakh national-cultural revival in the framework of a rhetoric of revival of all ethnic groups within the spirit of internationalism. Mass privatization involved the handing over to foreign management of key strategic industries, only for these to be neither 'foreign' nor without continued state ownership. Foreign policy was both multivector and Russia-dominated.

Not only policies but also processes have been mixed. Most importantly in the 1992–4 period non-central state actors, such as regional administrations and key state managers, were given considerable political freedom and did what they saw as their opportunity, including spontaneously privatize key economic objects. When the central elite subsequently attempted to centralize after 1995 it met significant opposition from regional elites and a rift in relations with several regions. Regional actors had also been consulted on institutional design,[19] and have been unwilling to renege on these powers and influence. In the post-1995 period the central elite was unsure of how best to manage this *bête noire*: for example, it attempted cadre central-elite crossovers, including the inviting of some of the prominent members of the regional elite to the centre and gave regional leaders greater economic powers without concomitant finance, delegitimizing regional elites both in the eyes of the central elite and the population more broadly and absolving the centre from the politics of blame.[20] Actors in this regime seem to have become accustomed to the system's middle ground and the flexibility it allows, and react when that flexibility is broken (November 2001 may be partly explained in these terms).

By the close of this period it was possible to propose with some certainty that recruitment was no longer the top-down process the term might suggest. The policy of co-optation had regrouped into the state a diverse set of actors with different economic interests that were increasingly difficult to control. Nurlan Balgimbaev, Kazakhstan's third Prime Minister (1997–1999), tried to some degree to address this by removing business representatives from visible posts of influence around 1998–1999, but November 2001 showed that this measure was insufficient. The events of

November 2001 were partly prompted by one group, led by Nazarbaev's son-in-law Rakhat Aliev, being given too much power and influence in both the economic and security sectors. Institutions did not provide a sufficient camouflage for these elite conflicts. The constant process of institutional changes and elite reshuffling deprived elites of institutional shields and made intra-elite, rather than intra-institutional, disagreements more likely. In a poll of independent experts and analysts in early 2002, the majority of those asked perceived the elite struggles not as struggles between political parties or between institutions of the state, but rather as between elite groupings.

The co-optation of groups reflects another dilemma that the selectorate has faced in its dual aim of enacting economic reform and building allies. Barbara Geddes has argued that a politician's dilemma is the product of a triple agenda: current survival, effective governance and the creation of a loyal machine. While Nazarbaev began with the creation of a loyal team and punctuated this with effective governance – in so far as the aim was to achieve economic reform, gain a macroeconomic stabilization programme from the IMF and encourage foreign investment – his appointments suggested that by the decade's close the creation of a loyal machine for regime survival had become a priority. These appointments were becoming increasingly difficult to reconcile. Those with single elite careers became the strongest supporters of presidential policy, those with multiple affiliations, less so. The data mirror Fleron's hypothesis for the Soviet era – that 'recruited' Party Officials differ from those who are 'co-opted' into Party positions after having first established careers in a specialist elite,[21] comparable to 'recruited' presidential political positions, to which individuals were co-opted after having first established careers in the economic specialist elite.

On the other hand, Geddes argues that a strategy of compartmental-ization in unreformed systems is the only way in which a technocratic sub-elite can be shielded from the onslaught of political actors who 'rely on access to state resources to build their support organization and administrative reform threatens such access'.[22] It may well be that by the end of the decade the selectorate was no longer able or willing to insulate the technocrats from pressure by officials who were benefiting from the status quo. Where previously these actors might have wished to remain isolated from politics, they were suddenly forced to take an open political stance in an attempt to seek control over the resources on which the organization depends. Differences in skill training and in orientation may produce fundamentally opposed views of the policy process.[23] Scholars such as Riggs, specializing in developing societies, point to the patterns of tension and conflict between elite sectors. Riggs sees the deterioration in bureaucratic autonomy and efficiency in the face of a power-expansionist set of party leaders to be the fundamental problem in such societies.[24] This, we indicated, may be beginning to occur along the axes of centre/region or economic groupings.

A further 'push' factor is the broader political system's legacy of Russian and Soviet rule. Russia had tangible effects on the role, behaviour, identity and self-categorization of the country's political elite. Russia has shown its support for the present Kazakhstani regime, overlooking the falsification practices of the 1999 elections. Many of the Russian members of the Pavlodar elite interviewed still saw their region as a part of Russia and found no practical reason for the border with Russia. The large-scale emigration of Slavs and Europeans in the wake of Soviet collapse also sharply reduced the availability of non-titular nationalities.

The rise to dominance of an ethnic Kazakh elite in predominantly executive institutions was also explained by broader domestic factors. The Soviet legacy led to the atomization of ethnic groups in society, in particular the Russian community,[25] and many were poorly organized, lacking leadership and finance. Non-titular group mobilization had also slowed because of a perception that actors in their parent states – governments or business – may be able to mobilize on their behalf (South Korean companies or the German government, for example). Opinion polls during this period also indicated that ethnicity did not appear the determining factor in the voting patterns of these groups; indeed sometimes individuals appeared to feel more protected by other nationalities. Weak leadership, poor organization and the absence of alternative ideologies also plagued the opposition. Very few outsiders have therefore been either willing or able to influence the agenda (second dimension of power), or indeed the other dimensions of power.

The incumbent core elite was also able to draw on the patronage networks inherited from the Soviet era. While these patronage networks differed in degree and form from region to region and from centre to region, they essentially comprised a mix of pre-existing and newly created patron-client relations. The pre-existing relations were a mix of social and blood relations, transformed from the traditional era through colonization and sedentarization. As sub-ethnicity is fluid, it is co-optable. Already in the traditional era identities were often, by necessity and habit, social rather than blood-based communities. We noted how the boundaries of horde (zhuz), tribe (taipa) and clan (uru) are fluid, particularly because of exogamy – indeed it was the fluidity and flexibility of these structures that gave the traditional system its strength. Communities based on social bonds grew stronger through the Soviet period with sedentarization and collectivization. Many of the networks established in this period incorporated both Russians and Kazakhs.

However fictional, these sub-ethnic identities appeared to play a role in the self-legitimation process at both central and regional elite levels. At the centre, the zhuz appeared of symbolic importance in the early recruitment process, although, as suggested, other factors had eclipsed its influence by the decade's close. By contrast, at the regional level, anecdotal evidence suggested that lower levels of belonging, clan and tribe, played a role in elite selection and self-legitimation, and continued to do so.

## ELITE IDENTITIES, LEGITIMATION AND INCONSISTENT KAZAKHIZATION

Symbolic representation feeds into a further argument of this study: the elite has often been as concerned about legitimating its behaviour and identification to itself as it has to the broader population. In this legitimation process alternative forms of identity have either been promoted or downplayed. Symbolic legitimation gains added importance in the absence of legitimation through the rule of law, such as through regular free and fair elections, or the possibility of multiple interests gaining multiple expression, such as through proportional representation, political parties or an effective parliament.

The key symbolic indication that the state now 'belongs' to ethnic Kazakhs is their domination of major institutions of power. The elite has Kazakhized itself, both relative to the Soviet period and *within* the period under review. Albeit to different degrees and at different speeds, Kazakhs have become the official face of power in regions and institutions.

Simultaneously, there have been some symbolic attempts to keep non-Kazakhs in power or to appoint them to visible positions, particularly in the Kazhegeldin era. The elite in its rhetoric has also sponsored 'internationalism' in the form of a civic Kazakhstani identity, and its institutional policies have deliberately been designed to de-ethnicize the political space, for Kazakhs and non-Kazakhs alike (Chapter Five). Foreign policy direction and content also compensated for internal cleavages. Nazarbaev's major foreign policy initiatives may be understood partly in this context, particularly towards the Eurasian Union. Nazarbaev's strongly confederal orientation, with his emphasis on Kazakhstan being in a wider unit that includes Russia, has sought to provide some psychological comfort to the Republic's large Russian community and is intended partly for their consumption.

This incomplete Kazakhization of appointments and policies was explained by three main factors: the absence of clear attitudinal categories on self-identification; the importance of region and sub-ethnicity as opposed to ethnicity to the elite's categorization process and the existence of a weak inner cultural core or 'negative identity' among the ruling elite.

First, Chapters Three and Four showed how neither institutional position, demographic/career background nor attitudinal variation can predict how an individual member of the elite categorizes him or herself vis-à-vis the state, nation or region. The overall impression from elite interviews, public statements and opinion polls was that elite identification did not offer any easy generalizations. Just as there were Russified Kazakhs whose attitudes were closer to Russian members of the elite, so there were substantial differences within the non-Kazakh group as to how they related to the nation and state. It was not possible to speak of a homogeneous non-Kazakh group. Within each of the regional elites, as within the central elite, there was not 'one' ethnic Kazakh or 'one' ethnic Russian viewpoint, only trends, suggesting that other factors beyond ethnicity were also important in determining how a member of the elite characterized his or her identity.

Second, region and sub-ethnicity were, in the (albeit not representative) sample here often as and sometimes more important to a person's self-categorization. Interviewees' answers also suggested that these multiple levels of identity can be mutually reinforcing. Sub-ethnic identities had undergone intense and rapid transformations since their assault by Russian colonization and Soviet sedentarization and collectivization. These identities survived partly because in traditional society they were already fluid entities, often more social than blood-based (Chapters One and Six). This fluidity has allowed them to incorporate new actors.

The state-led policy of national-cultural revival has, by contrast, attempted to suppress both sub-ethnic and regional identities. But by denying tribalism a place in official rhetoric, the state has both unwittingly encouraged its strengthening at the regional level[26] and denied itself a key legitimating tool in the construction of a state central identity.

Finally, the ultimately inconsistent policies on nation-building may partly be explained by the existence, in the period under review and within the aims of this volume, of a weak inner cultural core or 'negative identity' among the ruling elite. In many ways the Kazakhization of the elite and their policies does not always reflect the attitudes of self-categorization processes going on among the elite. The lack of commitment to a policy of Kazakhization, and its ultimately inconsistent implementation, is borne out by this volume's interviews with the elite, who were either uncomfortable at the speed of Kazakhization or perceived no benefits from, for example, the language changes. When we look beyond cadre politics to the wider cultural policies of the elite, the term 'Kazakhization' itself denotes a degree of intentionality and policy coherence that have not arisen in implementation.

In the initial years, the suggested 'negative identity' of ethnic Kazakhs may have encouraged ethnic Kazakhs to overcompensate, particularly in their monopolization of political and economic power. The stronger the national identification, the stronger the call to reject others, in terms of virulent nationalism. But the reverse might equally be true: The weaker the national identification, the stronger the call to reject others precisely because of this weakness. The process of Kazakhization and Kazakh assertiveness toward foreign investors could be partly explained in these terms.

Kazakhization of elite structures has therefore been part intentional, part structural. Kazakhization has been intentional insofar as that attempts to implement language and other cultural policies, were intentionally viewed as a means of securing their power. Kazakhization of appointments was viewed as essential to the legitimation of the new independent elite. Establishing an ethnic Kazakh face of power to the domestic and international audience was the most tangible display by Kazakhs of ownership of the new republic. Structurally, the Soviet era bequeathed an elite in which Kazakhs were already well-placed in politico-administrative positions, in part resulting from the recruitment policies of Kunaev. The Soviet era institutionalized a national elite both formally and informally. Formally, Soviet state policies encouraged the use of the vernacular language, the rewriting of history, and the production of state and national symbols. Informally, patronage networks ensured that the state penetrated society, and society the state. By the end of the 1990s, moreover, the new technocratic class had become largely ethnic Kazakh, reducing the possibility that the 'reds versus experts' debate could have become a 'Kazakhs versus non-Kazak experts' debate.

In all three spheres of Kazakhstan's elite system – institution-building, recruitment and legitimation  continuity and change therefore coexisted. Kazakhstan's pre-independence history has equally shown how systems and institutions break down, often tragically, by the deliberate intervention of actors, and that the country's territory has been subject to profound cultural and international transformations. Kazakhstani politics was, however, imbued with a strong sense of pragmatism which has managed to avoid ideological confrontation.

Certain cleavages throughout this work are the product of history and shape the environment within which elites operate, ethnicity and geopolitics being the most important. But to suggest that the development is culturally predetermined or historically instilled is erroneous. Kazakhstan's already varied regimes within the first ten years of its independence demonstrate that choice and strategy matter. While certain historical legacies may have contoured the decisions within which institutions and the state have been built, they have not determined them. They have resulted in unclear outcomes, partly because this state is still in flux and because balance has often encouraged pragmatism over ideology. The regime's short history suggests a polity open to innovation and change, and where decisions by a small number of individuals can have important consequences for political development. For the moment, Kazakhstan remains a complex political system comprising numerous cross-cutting forces.

# APPENDIX

## SOCIAL BACKGROUND CHARACTERISTICS OF POLITICAL ELITE INTERVIEWED

1. Central Elite: 34 Members of the identified 244 political elite (referred to in text by PE and Respondent Number)

| Respondent Number | Position at time of interview | Gender | Age Group | Birthplace: Oblast | Ethnicity | Date of Interview |
|---|---|---|---|---|---|---|
| 1 | Head of State Committee, Presidential Administration | Male | > 55 | South Kazakhstan | Kazakh | 15.01.96 |
| 2 | Head of State Organisation | Male | > 55 | Belarus | Belarusan | 4.11.95 |
| 3 | Almaty Regional Administration | Male | 46 - 55 | Zhambyl | Kazakh | 7.10.96 |
| 4 | State Company | Male | < 36 | Almaty | Kazakh | 21.11.95 |
| 5 | Minister | Male | 36 - 45 | Semei | Kazakh | 20.12.96 |
| 6 | Head of Key Parliamentary Committee | Female | 46 - 55 | Ukraine | Ukrainian | 31.09.96 |
| 7 | Prime Minister's Office | Male | 46 - 55 | Russia | Russian | 23.11.95 |
| 8 | Prime Minister's Office | Male | 36 - 45 | Semei | Kazakh | 23.02.96 |

| | Position | Gender | Age | Location | Ethnicity | Date |
|---|---|---|---|---|---|---|
| 9 | Minister | Male | 36 – 45 | Almaty | Kazakh | 10.01.96 |
| 10 | Head of Key Department, Presidential Administration | Male | > 55 | Atyrau | Kazakh | 09.09.96 |
| 11 | Minister | Male | 46 - 55 | East-Kazakhstan | Russian | 10.01.96 |
| 12 | State Company | Male | 46 - 55 | Russia | Russian | 9.09.96 |
| 13 | Head of Government Committee | Female | 46 - 55 | Almaty | Russian | 3.09.96. |
| 14 | Head of Presidential Administration Committee | Male | < 36 | Zhambyl | Kazakh | 1.12.95 |
| 15 | Almaty Regional Administration | Male | 46 - 55 | Almaty | Kazakh | 19.2.96 |
| 16 | Head, Committee, Parliament | Male | 46 - 55 | Atyrau | Kazakh | 09.09.96 |
| 17 | Prime Minister's Office | Male | 36 - 45 | Pavlodar | Russian | 2.12.95 |
| 18 | Presidential Assistant | Male | 36 - 45 | Caucasus | Russian | 12.09.96 |
| 19 | Minister | Male | < 36 | Almaty | Kazakh | 20.03.96 |
| 20 | Head, Committee, Parliament | Male | > 55 | Almaty | Kazakh | 6.09.96 |
| 21 | Minister | Male | 46 - 55 | Russia | Kazakh | 27.11.95 |
| 22 | Cultural Subgroup | Male | > 55 | Almaty | Kazakh | |
| 23 | Counterelite | Male | 46 - 55 | Russia | Russian | 4.10.96 |
| 24 | Head, Dept, Presidential Administration | Male | < 36 | Atyrau | Kazakh | 2.10.96 |
| 25 | Head, Dept, Presidential Administration | Male | 46 - 55 | Russia | Kazakh | 20.03.96 |
| 26 | State Company | Male | < 36 | Almaty | Kazakh | 18.03.96 |
| 27 | Minister | Male | 46 - 55 | South Kazakhstan | Kazakh | 17.01.96 |
| 28 | First Deputy Minister | Female | < 36 | Almaty | Kazakh | 12.02.96 |
| 29 | State Company | Female | < 36 | Russia | Russian | 20.02.96 |

| Respondent Number | Position at time of Interview* | Gender | Age Group | Birthplace: Oblast | Ethnicity | Date of interview |
|---|---|---|---|---|---|---|
| 30 | Prime Minister's Office | Male | 46 - 55 | Kyrgyzstan | Russia | 18.11.95 |
| 31 | Prime Minister's Office | Male | 36 – 45 | Atyrau | Kazakh | 16.01.96 |
| 32 | Minister | Male | 46 - 55 | Russia | Kazakh | 15.01.96 |
| 33 | Head, Dept, Pres Admin | Male | > 55 | Russia | Russian | 1.11.95 |
| 34 | First Deputy Minister | Male | 36 - 45 | Kostanai | Kazakh | 23.02.96 |

2. Regional Elite: Shymkent (referred to in text by PE, Shymkent and Respondent Number)

| Respondent Number | Position at time of Interview* | Gender | Age Group | Birthplace: Oblast | Ethnicity | Date of interview |
|---|---|---|---|---|---|---|
|  | Akim, Raion | Male | 46-55 | Shymkent | Kazakh | 27.02.96 |
|  | Akim, Raion | Female | 36-45 | Zhambyl | Kazakh | 27.02.96 |
|  | Akim's Office, Raion | Female | 36-45 | Shymkent | Kazakh | 28.02.96 |
|  | Akim's Office, Oblast | Male | 36-45 | Shymkent | Uzbek | 26.02.96 |
|  | Head, Dept, Oblast | Male | <36 | Shymkent | Kazakh | 27.02.96 |
|  | Dept, Oblast | Male | >55 | Shymkent | Uzbek | 26.02.96 |
|  | Maslikhat | Male | 36-45 | Shymkent | Uzbek | 1.03.96 |
|  | Akim's Office, Oblast | Male | 46-55 | Zhambyl | Ukrainian | 28.02.96 |
|  | Head, Dept, Oblast | Male | 36-45 | Shymkent | Korean | 27.02.96 |
|  | Akim's Office Oblast | Male | 46-55 | Shymkent | Kazakh | 29.02.96 |
|  | Akim's Office Oblast | Male | 46-55 | Shymkent | Kazakh | 26.02.96 |
|  | Akim's Office Oblast | Male | <36 | Shymkent | Kazakh | 1.03.96 |
|  | Head, Dept, Oblast | Male | >55 | East Kazakhstan | Russian | 29.02.96 |
|  | Akim's Office, Raion | Male | 46-55 | Shymkent | Kazakh | 27.02.96 |
|  | Head, Dept, Oblast | Male | 36-45 | Shymkent | Kazakh | 28.02.96 |
|  | Akim's Office, Oblast | Male | 36-45 | Shymkent | Kazakh | 28.02.96 |

| 17 | Akim's Office, Town | Male | 36-45 | Uzbekistan | Kazakh | 27.02.96 |

* Unless otherwise stated, raion (district) and oblast (region) refer to the level of administration in the region.

3. Regional Elite: Pavlodar(referred to in text by PE, Pavlodar and Respondent Number)

| Respondent Number | Position at time of interview | Gender | Age Group | Birthplace: Oblast | Ethnicity | Date of Interview |
|---|---|---|---|---|---|---|
| 1 | Akim's Office | Male | 36-45 | Pavlodar | Kazakh | 6.11.95 |
| 2 | Head, Dept, Oblast | Female | 36-45 | Pavlodar | Kazakh | 9.11.95 |
| 3 | Akim's Office, Raion | Female | 46-55 | Semei | Kazakh | 10.11.95 |
| 4 | Head, Dept, Oblast | Male | >55 | Russia | Russian | 9.11.95 |
| 5 | Head, Dept, Oblast | Male | 46-55 | Russia | Russian | 7.11.95 |
| 6 | Business | Male | <36 | Pavlodar | Kazakh | 7.11.95 |
| 7 | Apparat, Oblast | Male | 46-55 | Pavlodar | Tatar | 8.11.95 |
| 8 | State Company | Male | 36-45 | Ukraine | Ukrainian | 7.11.95 |
| 9 | Mayor's Office | Male | 36-45 | Pavlodar | Russian | 8.11.95 |
| 10 | Maslikhat | Male | >55 | Ukraine | Ukrainian | 10.11.95 |
| 11 | Maslikhat | Male | 46-55 | Ukraine | Ukrainian | 9.11.95 |
| 12 | Political Party | Male | 46-55 | Russia | Russian | 8.11.95 |
| 13 | Head, Dept, Oblast | Male | 46-55 | Russia | Russian | 8.11.95 |
| 14 | Head, Dept, Oblast | Male | <36 | Pavlodar | Russian | 8.11.95 |
| 15 | Business | Male | <36 | Pavlodar | Russian | 7.11.85 |
| 16 | Political Party | Male | 36-45 | Pavlodar | Russian | 8.11.95 |
| 17 | Maslikhat | Male | 46-55 | Pavlodar | Russian | 7/11/95 |

4. Regional Elite: Uralsk(referred to in text by PE, Uralsk and Respondent Number)

| Respondent Number | Position at time of interview | Gender | Age Group | Birthplace: Oblast | Ethnicity | Date of Interview |
|---|---|---|---|---|---|---|
| 1 | Akim's Office | Male | >55 | Uralsk | Kazakh | 30.09.96 |
| 2 | Political Party | Male | 36–45 | Uralsk | Kazakh | 28.09.96 |
| 3 | Mayor's Office | Male | 36–45 | Uralsk | Kazakh | 28.09.96 |
| 4 | Political Party | Male | >55 | Uralsk | Cossack | 27.09.96 |
| 5 | Head, Dept, Oblast | Male | >55 | Russia | Russian | 27.09.96 |
| 6 | Head, Dept, Oblast | Female | 36–45 | Uralsk | Kazakh | 27.09.96 |
| 7 | Cultural Leader | Male | 36–45 | Uralsk | Russian | 28.09.96 |
| 3 | Political Party | Male | 36–45 | Uralsk | Kazakh | 30.09.96 |

# NOTES

## Introduction

1. Mattei Dogan and John Higley (eds.), *Elites, Crises, and the Origins of Regimes* (Lanham, Boulder, New York and Oxford: Rowman and Littlefield Publishers, Inc., 1998), p. 9.

2. *Itogi perepisi naseleniia 1999 goda v Respublike Kazakhstana.* Vol. 1. *Natsional'nyi sostav naseleniia RK.* 2000, Almaty: Agenstvo RK po statistike, 21–22. The 1999 Census slightly amended the Kazakh and Russian figures from the 1989 census stated figures of 39.7 per cent and 37.9 per cent respectively.

3. Donald Carlisle, 'Islam Karimov and Uzbekistan: Back to the Future?', in Timothy J. Colton and Robert C. Tucker (eds.), *Patterns in Post-Soviet Leadership* (Boulder: Westview Press, 1995), p. 211.

4. Sally N. Cummings, 'Eurasian Bridge or Murky Waters between East and West?: Ideas, Identity and Output in Kazakhstan's Foreign Policy', *Journal of Communist Studies and Transition Politics*, Vol. 19, No. 3 (2003), pp. 139–55.

5. For an overview of China's relations with Central Asia, see K. Syroezhkin, 'Vzaimnootnosheniia Kitaia s gosudarstvami Tsentralnoi Azii', *Kazakhstan-Spektr*, No. 1 (2000), pp. 77–8.

6. Shireen Hunter, *Central Asia Since Independence* (Washington, DC: Center for Strategic and International Studies, Praeger Press, 1996), pp. 124–5.

7. For an analysis of the relations between the major powers and Kazakhstan, see Robert Levgold (ed.), *Thinking Strategically: The Major Powers, Kazakhstan, and the Central Asian Nexus* (Cambridge, MA: MIT Press, 2003).

8. Sally N. Cummings, 'Central Asian States: Renegotiating US Presence', in Mary Buckley and Rick Fawn (eds.), *Global Responses to Terrorism: 9/11, Afghanistan and Beyond* (London: Routledge, 2003), pp. 239–51.

9. *Kazakhstan Today*, 3 March 2001.

10. *Statististicheskoe Obozrenie Kazakhstana* (Almaty: National Statistics Agency, 1997), p. 21, cites 1997 foreign direct investment as US$1633, 2 million. Japan at 28.7 per cent tops the list of foreign direct investors, followed by South Korea at 27.6, UK at 15.7, USA at 11.1 and Germany, Italy and Turkey roughly at 4 per cent each. The largest sector of foreign direct investment is the metallurgical sector, followed by the oil and then energy sectors. See also *Interfax-Kazakhstan*, 12 January 1998; and the local Kazakhstani newspaper *Panorama*, 31 July 1998.

11. Martha Brill Olcott provides a useful summary of the industrial legacy. See her *The Kazakhs* (2nd edn., Stanford: Hoover Institution Press, 1995), p. 272.

12.    The President also claimed at the Almaty Investment Summit that Kazakhstan ranked first worldwide with respect to estimated reserves of uranium, and seventh worldwide for gold. See *Panorama*, 4 June 1998; and *Interfax-Kazakhstan*, 4 June 1998.

13.    Oil reserves estimated for the Caucasus and Central Asia as a whole vary greatly and range from 30bn to 200bn barrels. These estimates include proven and possible reserves. Industry analysts often use a middle-range figure of 90bn barrels. See the analysis by Rosemarie Forsythe, *The Politics of Oil and The Caucasus and Central Asia* (London: International Institute for Strategic Studies, Adelphi Paper 300, 1996). She cites Robert O'Connor, Richard Castle and David Nelson, 'Future Oil and Gas Potential in the Southern Caspian Basin', *Oil and Gas Journal*, 3 May 1993, pp. 117–26; Michael J. Strauss, 'Caspian Sea May Offer Wealth of Oil and Gas, Geologists Say', *Journal of Commerce*, 16 September 1991, p. 6B; Khartukov and Vinogradova, 'Former Soviet Union: Another Poor Year', *World Oil*, Vol. 215, No. 8 (August 1994), p. 69. See also John Roberts, *Caspian Pipelines*, (London: Royal Institute of International Affairs, 1996). Kazakhstan and Azerbaijan have the largest oil deposits of the region. Forsythe cites geophysical estimates of 10bn barrels; she also points out that industry analysts cite Kazakhstan as the richest of the former Soviet republics in oil and gas, with more than 60bn barrels.

14.    Some estimate a potential to produce up to 2m barrels of light crude a day once the field is fully developed. See Gawdat Bahgat, 'Pipeline Diplomacy: The Geopolitics of the Caspian Sea Region', *International Studies Perspectives*, Vol. 3 (2002), p. 313.

15.    See Forsythe, *The Politics of Oil*.

16.    R. B. Collier and D. Collier, *Shaping the Political Arena: Critical Junctures, the Labour Movement and Regime Dynamics in Latin America* (Princeton, NJ: Princeton University Press, 1991).

17.    Colin Hay, 'Crisis and the Structural Transformation of the State: Interrogating the Process of Change', *British Journal of Politics and International Relations*, Vol. 1, No. 3, pp. 317–44; S. Skowronek, *Building a New American State: The Expansion of National Administrative Capacities, 1877–1920* (Cambridge: Cambridge University Press, 1982).

18.    F. R. Baumgartner and B. D. Jones, *Agendas and Instability in American Politics* (Chicago, Il: University of Chicago Press, 1993).

19.    *Statisticheskii Biulletin* (National Statistics Agency: Almaty, 1997).

20.    Samuel J. Elderveld, Jan Kooiman and Theo van der Tak, *Elite Images of Dutch Politics: Accommodation and Conflict* (Ann Arbor, MI: University of Michigan Press, 1983), p. 3.

21.    For indigenous writings on the Kazakhstani elite, see, for example: Al'-Khalel Karpyk, *Belaia Kost' Proshlogo. Nashi sovremenniki* (Almaty: Deuir, 1994); V. N. Khliupin, *Bol'shaia Sem'ia' Nursultana Nazarbaeva: Politicheskaia Elita Sovremennogo Kazakhstana* (Moscow: Institute Aktual'nykh Politicheskikh Issledovanii Moskva, 1998); A. Nysanbaev, M. Mashan, Zh Murzalin and A. Tulegulov, *Evolutsiia Politicheskoi Sistemy Kazakhstana* (Almaty: Qazaq Entsiklopediiasy, 2001), Vols.1 and 2, especially Vol. 2, Chapter 5; D. A Satpaev, *Lobbizm: Tainye Rygachi Vlasti* (Almaty, 1999); Tsentral'noaziatskoe Agentstvo Politicheskikh Issledovanii (APR), *Reitingi politicheskikh I gosudarstvennykh deiatelei Respubliki Kazakhstan (v period s marta 2000 po iiun' 2001 goda* (Almaty: 2001); and Tsentral'noaziatskoe Agentstvo Politicheskikh Issledovanii (APR), *Politicheskie Elity Tsentral'noi Azii* (Tel-Aviv, 2001).

22.    For an introduction to transition literature, see G. O'Donnell and P. C. Schmitter, *Transitions from Authoritarian Rule: Tentative Conclusions* (Baltimore and London: Johns Hopkins University Press, 1986).

23.    The focus on national elites in transition is often associated with the work of Dankwart Rustow, 'Transitions to Democracy: Toward a Dynamic Model', *Comparative Politics*, Vol. 2, No. 3 (1970), pp. 337–63. See also his 'The Study of Elites: Who's Who, When and How', *World Politics*, Vol. 18, No. 3 (July 1966), pp. 690–717. On the role of elites in transition, see John Higley and Michael G. Burton, 'The Elite Variable in Democratic Transitions and Breakdowns', *American Sociological Review*, Vol. 54, No. 1 (1989), pp. 17–32; Thomas A. Baylis, 'Plus ça Change? Transformation and

Continuity Amongst East European Elites', *Communist and Post-Communist Studies*, Vol. 27, No. 3 (September 1994), pp. 315–28; 'Circulation vs Reproduction of Elites during the Postcommunist Transformation of Eastern Europe', special issue of *Theory and Society*, Vol. 24, No. 5 (October 1995); 'Regime Transitions, Elites, and Bureaucracies in Eastern Europe', special issue of *Governance: An International Journal of Policy and Administration*, Vol. 6, No. 3 (July 1993); John Higley, Judith Kullbert and Jan Pakulski, 'The Persistence of Postcommunist Elites', *Journal of Democracy*, Vol. 7, No. 2 (April 1996), pp. 133–47; John Higley and Jan Pakulski, 'Revolution and Elite Transformation in Eastern Europe', *Australian Journal of Political Science*, Vol. 27 (1992), pp. 104–19; and Heinrich Best and Ulrike Becker (eds.), *Elites in Transition: Elite Research in Central and Eastern Europe* (Opladen: Leske + Budrich, 1997).

24.   Alan Knight, 'Historical and Theoretical Considerations' in Dogan and Higley (eds.), *Elites, Crises and Regimes*, p. 41.

25.   An excellent introduction to the study of comparative elites is Robert Putnam, *The Comparative Study of Political Elites* (Englewood Cliffs, NJ: Prentice-Hall, 1976). See also Gerraint Parry, *Political Elites* (New York: Praeger, 1969).

26.   Important relationships between regimes and elites have also been made by John Higley and David Lane. See David Lane (ed.), *The Legacy of State Socialism and the Future of Transformation* (Lanham MD, Oxford: Rowman and Littlefield, 2002); 'What Kind of Capitalism for Russia? A Comparative Analysis', *Communist and Post-Communist Studies*, Vol. 33, No. 4 (December 2000), pp. 485–504; David Lane and Cameron Ross, 'Russian Political Elites, 1991–1995: Recruitment and Renewal', *International Politics*, Vol. 34, No. 2 (June 1997), pp. 169–92; David Lane, 'Transition under Eltsin: the Nomenklatura and Political Elite Circulation', *Political Studies*, Vol. 45, No. 5 (December 1997), pp. 855–74; David Lane, 'The Gorbachev Revolution: The Role of the Political Elite in Regime Disintegration', *Political Studies*, Vol. XLIV, No. 1 (March 1996), pp. 4–23; David Lane, 'The Transformation of Russia: The Role of the Political Elite', *Europe-Asia Studies*, Vol. 48, No. 4 (June 1996), pp. 535–50; David Lane, 'The CPSU Ruling Elite 1981–1991: Commonalities and Divisions', *Communist and Post-Communist Studies*, Vol. 28, No. 3 (September 1995), pp. 339–60; David Lane, 'Gorbachev's Political Elite in the Terminal Stage of the USSR: A Reputational Analysis', *Journal of Communist Studies and Transition Politics*, Vol. 10, No. 1 (March 1994), pp. 104–16; David Lane (ed.), *Elites and Political Power in the USSR* (Aldershot: Elgar, 1988); David Lane, 'Ethnic and Class Stratification in Soviet Kazakhstan 1917–39', *Comparative Studies in Society and History*, Vol. 17, No. 2 (1975), pp. 165–89.

27.   John Higley, Jan Pakulski and Wlodzimierz Wesolowksi (eds.), *Postcommunist Elites and Democracy in Eastern Europe* (Basingstoke: Macmillan Press, 1998). Prospects for such consensual elites are judged to be best in Poland and Hungary, less good in Czechoslovakia, poor in Romania, Bulgaria and Albania, and virtually non-existent in the Yugoslav republics.

28.   See Higley et al., *Postcommunist Elites and Democracy in Eastern Europe*, Chapter 1. As the authors point out, for 'transitologists' and 'consolidologists', 'the achievement of democratic consensus and power sharing among divided elites through pacts is regarded as decisive.'

29.   See especially Frederic J. Fleron Jr., 'System Attributes and Career Attributes: The Soviet Political Leadership System, 1952–1965', in Carl Beck, Frederic J. Fleron Jr., Milton Lodge, Derek J. Waller, William A. Welsh and M. George Zaninovich, *Comparative Communist Political Leadership* (New York: David McKay Company, Inc., 1973), pp. 43–85; and Lester G. Seligman, *Recruiting Political Elites* (New York: General Learning Press, 1971).

30.   For an excellent analysis of elite integration in the USA, see Gwen Moore, 'The Structure of a National Elite Network', in Marvin E. Olsen and Martin N. Marger (eds.), *Power in Modern Societies*, (Boulder: Westview Press, 1993), pp. 183–95.

31.   William A. Welsh, 'Introduction: The Comparative Study of Political Leadership in Communist Systems', in Carl Beck et al., *Comparative Communist Political Leadership* (New York: David McKay Company, Inc., 1973), pp. 1–42.

32.    David Easton, 'An Approach to the Analysis of Political Systems', *World Politics*, Vol. 9, No. 3 (April 1957), pp. 383–400; David E. Apter, 'A Comparative Method for the Study of Politics', *American Journal of Sociology*, Vol. 64 (November 1958), pp. 221–37; Karl W. Deutsch, *The Nerves of Government: Models of Political Communication and Control* (New York: Free Press, 1963), and 'Social Mobilization and Political Development,' *American Political Science Review*, Vol. 55, No. 3 (September 1961), pp. 493–514; Gabriel Almond and G. Bingham Powell, *Comparative Politics: A Developmental Approach* (Boston: Little, Brown and Co., 1966); Herbert J. Spiro, 'Comparative Politics: A Comprehensive Approach', *American Political Science Review*, Vol. 56, No. 3 (September 1962), pp. 577–95.

33.    William A. Welsh, 'Communist Political Leadership: Conclusions and Overview', in Carl Beck et al., *Comparative Communist Political Leadership*, p. 17.

34.    For notions of elite cohesion, see John Higley and Jan Pakulski, 'Revolution and Elite Transformation in Eastern Europe', *Australian Journal of Political Science*, Vol. 27, No. 1 (March 1992), pp. 104–19.

35.    See Daniel Lerner, Harold D. Lasswell and C. Easton Rothwell, *The Comparative Study of Elites: An Introduction and Bibliography* (Stanford, CA: Stanford University Press, 1951). See also Lasswell and Lerner, *World Revolutionary Elites* (Cambridge, MA: MIT Press, 1965).

36.    Reinhard Bendix, 'Social Stratification and Political Power', *American Political Science Review*, Vol. 46 (June 1953), p. 596.

37.    Lewis J. Edinger and Donald D. Searing, 'Social Background in Elite Analysis: A Methodological Inquiry', *American Political Science Review*, Vol. 61, No. 2 (June 1967), p. 430. See also D. D. Searing, 'The Comparative Study of Elite Socialization', *Comparative Political* Studies, Vol. 1 (January 1969), pp. 471–500.

38.    See Milton Lodge, 'Attitudinal Cleavages Within the Soviet Political Leadership', in Carl Beck et al., *Comparative Communist Political Leadership*, pp. 202–25. Also his *Soviet Elite Attitudes Since Stalin* (Columbus, Ohio: Charles E. Merrill Publishing Co, 1969).

39.    William A. Welsh, *Leaders and Elites* (New York: Holt, Rinehart and Winston, 1979), p. 29.

40.    For example, K. Jowitt, *New World Disorder: The Leninist Extinction* (Berkeley: University of California Press, 1992).

41.    Peter A. Hall and Rosemary C. R. Taylor, 'Political Science and the Three New Institutionalisms', *Political Studies*, Vol. 44 (1996), pp. 936–57; Kathleen Thelen, 'Historical Institutionalism in Comparative Politics', *Annual Review of Political Science*, Vol. 2 (June 1999), pp. 369–404; Kathleen Thelen and Sven Steinmo, 'Historical Institutionalism in Comparative Analysis', in Sven Steinmo, Kathleen Thelen and Frank Longstreth (eds.), *Structuring Politics: Historical Institutionalism in Comparative Analysis* (Cambridge: Cambridge University Press, 1992), pp. 7–9.

42.    Carl Beck and James M. Malloy, *Political Elites: A Mode of Analysis* (Pittsburgh: University Center for International Studies, University of Pittsburgh, October 1971).

43.    Colin Hay, *Political Analysis: A Critical Introduction* (Basingstoke, Hampshire: Palgrave, 2002), p. 94.

44.    Hay, *Political Analysis*.

45.    Peter A. Hall and Rosemary C. R. Taylor, 'Political Science and the Three New Institutionalisms', *Political Studies*, Vol. XLIV (1996), p. 939.

46.    Bob Jessop, *State Theory: Putting Capitalist States in their Place* (Cambridge: Polity, 1990).

47.    Tony Bilton, *Introductory Sociology* (London: Macmillan, 1987), p. 197.

48.    Hay, *Political Analysis*, Chapter 5.

49.    Principal examples of pluralists are: Robert A. Dahl, *A Preface to Democratic Theory* (Chicago, IL: University of Chicago Press, 1956); Robert A. Dahl, *Who Governs? Democracy and Power in an American City* (New Haven, CT: Yale University Press, 1961); R. A. Dahl and C. Lindblom, *Politics, Economics and Welfare* (New York: Harper and Brothers, 1953); and elite theorists include: Robert Staughton Lynd and Helen Merrell Lynd, *Middletown in Transition* (London: Constable, 1937 and 1964); Floyd Hunter, *Community Power Structure* (Chapel Hill, NC: University of North Caroline Press, 1953); Harold Lasswell, *Who Gets What, When, How?* (New York: p. Smith, 1936 and 1950)· C

Wright Mills, *The Power Elite* (Oxford: Oxford University Press, 1956).

50.   Steven Lukes, *Power: A Radical View* (Basingstoke: Macmillan, 1990), p. 24.

51.   Alan Zuckerman, 'The Concept "Political Elite": Lessons from Mosca and Pareto', *The Journal of Politics*, Vol. 39, No. 2 (May 1977), pp. 324–44.

52.   Robert Dahl, 'A Critique of the Ruling Elite Model', reprinted in Edward Laumann, Paul Siegel and Robert Hodge (eds.), *The Logic of Social Hierarchies* (Chicago: Markham, 1970), p. 269.

53.   Mills, *The Power Elite*, pp. 3–4.

54.   Meisel explains the three C's: all the members of the elite are alert to their group interests; that this alertness is in turn caused or affected by a sense, implicit or explicit, of group or class solidarity; and last, that this solidarity is expressed in a common will to action'. James Meisel, *The Myth of the Ruling Class: Gaetano Mosca and the Elite* (Ann Arbor: University of Michigan Press, 1962), p. 4.

55.   Geoffrey Roberts, *A Dictionary of Political Analysis* (New York: St Martin's Press, 1971), p. 79.

56.   Harold Lasswell, 'Agenda for the Study of Political Elites', in Dwaine Marvick (ed.), *Political Decision-Makers* (Glencoe, IL: Free Press, 1961), p. 66.

57.   Various authors have discussed the problems of finding the powerful. See Frederick Frey, 'The Determination and Location of Elites: A Critical Analysis', paper read at the Sixty-sixth Annual Meeting of the American Political Science Association, Los Angeles, September 1970, cited by Robert Putnam, *The Comparative Study of Political Elites* (Englewood Cliffs, NJ: Prentice-Hall, 1976); and Jerry Hough, 'The Soviet Experience and the Measurement of Power', *Journal of Politics*, Vol. 37 (August 1975), pp. 685–710.

58.   Leading contributors on the methodology of elite studies include Edinger and Searing, 'Social Background in Elite Analysis'; Wahlke et al., *The Legislative System*; C. Beck and J. M. Malloy, *Political Elites: A Mode of Analysis* (Pittsburgh: University of Pittsburgh, Archive on Political Elites in Eastern Europe, 1966); C. Beck, *A Survey of Elite Studies* (Washington, DC: American University, 1965); J. Dennis, 'Major Problems of Political Socialisation Research', *Midwest Journal of Political Science*, Vol. 12 (February 1968), pp. 85–144; and R. S. Robins, 'Elite Career Patterns as a Differential: A Use of Correlation Techniques and the Construction of Uniform Strata', *Behavioral Science*, Vol. 14 (May 1969), pp. 232–8. Briefer methodological discussions are included in a number of other publications, including S.E. Finer et al., *Backbench Opinion in the House of Commons* (London: Penguin, 1961); Frederick Frey, *The Turkish Political Elite* (Cambridge, MA.: MIT Press, 1965); and William B. Quandt, *The Comparative Study of Political Elites* (Berkeley, CA: Sage, 1969). See also Samuel J. Eldersveld, *Political Elites in Modern Societies: Empirical Research and Democratic Theory* (Ann Arbor: University of Michigan Press, 1989).

59.   Mills, *The Power Elite*, pp. 10–11.

60.   Floyd Hunter, *Top Leadership, U.S.A.* (Chapel Hill: University of North Carolina Press, 1959), pp. 16, 195.

61.   Robert A. Dahl, *Who Governs?*, pp. 104–62.

62.   Theodore J. Lowi, *At the Pleasure of the Mayor: Patronage and Power in New York City, 1898–1958* (New York: Free Press,1964).

63.   Peter Bachrach and Morton S. Baratz, 'Two Faces of Power', *American Political Science Review*, Vol. 56 (December 1962), pp. 947–52.

64.   Allen H. Barton et al., *Opinion-Making Elites in Yugoslavia* (New York: Praeger, 1973).

65.   See, for example, Charles Kadushin, 'Social Structure of Yugoslavia's Opinion-Makers: Part I, Informal Leadership', in Allen H. Barton et al., *Opinion-Making Elites in Yugoslavia, pp.* 155–219.

66.   I used a combination of sources on the political elite: my panel of experts, informal data (inevitably speculative and subjective); newspapers; biographical data; government directories. Russian-language newspapers primarily were used: *Kazakhstanskaia Pravda, Sovety Kazakhstana, Delovaia Nedelia, Panorama, Karavan*; on occasion, *Egemen Qazaqstan* and *Ana Tili* were consulted. The key sources of biographical data were: A. Z. Asylbekov, V. N. Voloshin and V. N. Khliupin, *Kto Est' Kto v Respublike Kazakhstan* (Almaty: Evraziya-Polis, 1995); D. R. Ashimbaev, *Kto Est' Kto v Kazakhstane*

(Almaty: Credo, 2001); individual biographies were also sourced from *Kazakhstanskaya Pravda*. The key government directories used were: *Spisok Telefonov Rukovoditelei Oblastei*, 1995 and 1996; *Spisok Telefonov Rukovodiashchikh Rabotnikov Organov Gosudarstvennogo Upravleniia, Partiinykh, Obshchestvennykh i Drugikh Organizatsii Kazakhskoi SSR*, July 1991 and January 1995; *Spisok Telefonov Rabotnikov Administratsii Prezidenta Respubliki Kazakhstan*, October 1992 and April 1996; and *Spisok Deputatov Verkhovnogo Soveta Respubliki Kazakhstan* (12th Parliament, 1993).

67.     One of the most useful sources for both rankings and elite attitudes are the often monthly elite opinion polls published in the local *Panorama* newspapers, called VIProblem surveys. In the text I refer to two compilations of these monthly articles: Zhusupov, S., Zhusupov, B., and Ezhenova, K., *Dinamika Obshchestvennykh Protsessov v Kazakhstane (Dinamika 1)* (Almaty: Kazakhstan Institute of Strategic Research under the President of Kazakhstan, Newspaper 'Panorama', Republican Centre of Public Opinion, 1997). S. Zhusupov, B. Zhusupov and K Ezhenova, *Dinamika Obshchestvennykh Protsessov v Kazakhstane (Dinamika 2)*(Almaty: Panorama and Gruppa VIProblem, 2002).

68.     Time did not permit a panel of experts to be interviewed at the regional levels but various heads of political movements, associations and companies were asked for their input. Those interviewed included: Akim, (First) Deputy Akims, Heads of Department (generally Socioeconomic, Interior Affairs, Finance and Economics), Mayor of City, Heads of Districts, 'party' leaders, business elite and cultural leaders.

69.     The 1989 census recorded the following percentages for the main nationalities: Pavlodar – 45.4 Russians, 28.5 Kazakhs, 10.1 Germans, 9.2 per cent Ukrainians; Southern Kazakhstan – 55.7 Kazakhs, 15.3 Russians, 2.4 per cent Germans which by the mid 1990s had been surpassed by the growing Uzbek population in the region; Western Kazakhstan – 55.8 Kazakhs, 34.4 Russians, 4.5 Ukrainains, 2 per cent Tatars. The 1999 census put the ethnic Kazakhs at 38.2, 67.6 and 64.8 per cent respectively. 'Predvaritel'nye itogi pervoi Natsional'noi perepisi naseleniya 1999 goda v Respublike Kazakhstan', National Statistics Agency, Press Release No. 10 (1999). See also Foreign and Commonwealth Office, *Research and Analysis Note: Kazakhstan's regions*, Eastern Research Group, July 1998 and Sally N. Cummings, *Kazakhstan: Centre-Periphery Relations* (Washington, D.C.: Brookings Institution and London: Royal Institute of International Affairs, 2000).

70.     An anonymised list of the central and regional elites interviewed may be found in the Appendix.

# Chapter 1

1.      Olcott, *The Kazakhs* (2nd edn., Stanford, CA: Hoover Institution Press, 1995), p. 26.

2.      Olcott, *The Kazakhs*, p. 31.

3.      The Steppe Commission was formed in 1865 and its report, considerably amended, became the basis of the *Statute on the Administration of Turkestan* (including the *Provisional Statute on the Administration of the Semirech'e and Syr Darya Oblasts*) (1867), and the *Provisional Statute on the Administration of the Turgai, Akmolinsk, Uralsk, and Semipalatinsk Oblasts* (1868; called the Steppe Statute). See Olcott, *The Kazakhs*.

4.      See Shirin Akiner, *The Formation of Kazakh Identity: From Tribe to Nation-State* (London: Royal Institute of International Affairs, 1995), p. 24.

5.      See Akiner, *The Formation of Kazakh Identity*.

6.      Akiner, *The Formation of Kazakh Identity*, p. 36.

7.      Iu. A. Poliakov (ed.), *Vsesoiuznaia perepis naseleniia 1937 g. – kratkie itgoi* (Moscow: Akademiia Nauk SSSR, 1991).

8.      Olcott, *Kazakhstan: Unfulfilled Promise* (Carnegie Endowment for International Peace, Washington DC, 2002), p. 13.

9.      Of the Kazakh Communist Party First Secretaries between 1920 and 1991, 10 were ethnic Russians, 1 Pole, 1 Georgian, 1 Jew, 1 Armenian, 1 Uighur and 4 Kazakhs. These last four were Murzagaliev, Shaiakhmetov, Kunaev and Nazarbaev.

10.     The other two were Mukashev and Kamalidenov.

11.  For an excellent analysis of Nursultan Nazarbaev, see Olcott, 'Kazakstan: Nursultan Nazarbaev as Strong President' in Ray Taras (ed.), *Postcommunist Presidents* (Cambridge: Cambridge University Press, 1997), pp. 106–29.

12.  Olcott, 'Nursultan Nazarbaev and the Balancing Act of State-Building in Kazakhstan' in Colton and Tucker (eds.), *Patterns in Post-Soviet Leadership*, pp. 169–90.

13.  The data for 1959 may be found in the 1970 census. *Itogi vsesoiuznoi perepisi naseleniia 1970 goda.* Vol. IV. (Moscow: Statistika, 1973).

14.  Two of four groups underscored by Akiner are, on the one hand, the new small secular elite, consisting of three particularly influential individuals: Chokan Valikhkhanov (1835–1865), Ibrahim Altynsarin (1841–1889), and Abai Kunanbaev (1845–1904); and, on the other, the 'bourgeois nationalists' consisting largely of professionals who had grown through their contacts with Russia. See Akiner, *The Formation of Kazakh Identity*, pp. 29–33.

15.  Lawrence Krader, *Social Organization of the Mongol-Turkic Pastoral Nomads*, Indiana University Publications, Uralic and Altaic Series, Vol. 20 (The Hague: Mouton and Co, 1963), p. 237.

16.  Olcott, *The Kazakhs*, p. 102.

17.  For this tripartite division, see Eric R. Wolf, *Europe and the People Without History* (Berkeley, CA: University of California Press, 1982); G.E. Markov, *Kochevnichestvo: Istoricheskaia Entsiklopediia* (Sovetskaya Entsiklopediya, 1965); and, Nurbulat Masanov, *Kochevaia Tsivilizatsiia Kazakhov* (Moscow: Gorizont, 1995).

18.  Akiner, *The Formation of Kazakh Identity*, p. 15.

19.  As Grodekov maintains, in Kazakh tradition marriage was forbidden between patrilineally related kinsmen up to the seventh generation. See N. I. Grodekov, *Kirgizy i Karakirgiz Syr-Dar'inskoi oblasti* (Taskhent, 1889).

20.  See Anatoly M. Khazanov, *Nomads and the Outside World* (Madison, WI: University of Wisconsin Press, 1973), p. 146.

21.  See Elizabeth E. Bacon, *Obok: A Study of Social Structure in Eurasia* (New York: Wenner-Gren Foundation for Anthropological Research, Inc., 1958); and see also Edward Evans-Prichard, *The Comparative Method in Social Anthropology*, (London: Athlone Press, 1963). The classic example was Evans-Pritchard's work among the Nuer of the Sudan: E. E. Evans-Pritchard, *The Nuer: A Description of the Modes of Livelihood and and Political Institutions of a Nilotic People* (Oxford: Clarendon Press, first edition 1940).

22.  See Irina V. Erofeeva, 'Kazakhskie Khany XVIII – Serediny XIXv', *Vostok*, No. 3 (1997), pp. 5–32 for an excellent analysis of khans, according to their origins, dates of rule, territorial responsibility and political biographies.

23.  Irina Erofeeva, 'Titul i Vlast: K Probleme Tipologii Instituta Khanskoi Vlasti V Kazakhstane V XVII-Nachale XIX VV', *Saiasat* (Almaty, 1997), pp. 37–46, 44.

24.  Irina Erofeeva, 'Titul i Vlast', p. 44.

25.  Writes Olcott: 'Within the larger Kazakh community, the clan leaders and elders had far more influence than the khan.' See *The Kazakhs*, p. 15.

26.  Pauline Jones Luong, *Institutional Change and Political Continuity in Post-Soviet Central Asia: Power, Perceptions and Pacts* (Cambridge: Cambridge University Press, 2002), p. 93.

27.  For an excellent overview of Soviet legacies, see Teresa Rakowska-Harmstone, 'Soviet Legacies', *Central Asia Monitor*, Vol. 3 (1994), pp. 1–23.

28.  S. D. Asfendiarov, *Istoriia Kazakhstana (s drevneishikh vremen)* (Alma-Ata: Kazakhstanskoe Kraevoe Izd-vo, 1935); Kh. A. Argynbaev, *Etnograficheskie Ocherki po Skotovodstvu Kazakhov* (Alma-Ata, Nauka, 1973); and, Nurbulat Masanov, *Kochevaia*, 1995.

29.  There is also a fourth, the Inner or *Bukei* Zhuz. For an excellent account of the Inner Horde at the end of the last century, see A. N. Kharuzin, *Kirgizy Bukeevskoi Ordy: Antropologo-etnologicheskii Ocherk*. ('Izvestiia Obshchestva Liubitelei Estestvosnaniia, Antropologii i Etnografii pri Moskovskoe Universitets', Vol. LXIII., Moscow, 1989).

168 Kazakhstan

30. Elizabeth E. Bacon, *Central Asians under Russian Rule: A Study in Culture Change* (Ithaca, NY: Cornell University Press, 1966); Krader, *Social Organization of The Mongol-Turkic Pastoral Nomads*.

31. According to an ancient Kazakh proverb: 'Please give whips to the hands of the Great Horde so that they can herd our sheep, lances to the Junior Horde so they can defends us from our enemies, but let the Middle Horde carry pens so they can act as judges for our affairs.'

32. V. V. Vostrov and M. S. Mukanov, *Rodoplemennyi sostav i rasselenie kazakhov*, (Alma-Ata, 1968), pp. 9–15.

33. Mukhtar Auezov, *Abai*, 2 vols. (Alma-Ata, 1980) has attributed the formation of the Kazakh nation to the fifteenth century.

34. On the origins of the Kazakhs, see, for example, Zeki Velidi Togan, 'The Origins of the Kazaks and the Oezbeks' in H. B. Paksoy (ed.), *Central Asian Reader* (Armonk, NY: M. E. Sharpe, 1994).

35. Olcott, in *The Kazakhs*, p. 4 writes: 'The term Kazakh came into use by the residents of the area possibly as early as the end of the fifteenth century and certainly by the mid-sixteenth century', citing V. V. Barthol'd, *Four Studies on the History of Central Asia*, Vol. 3, trans. V. and T. Minorsky (Leiden: E. J. Brill, 1962), p. 129.

36. Olcott, *The Kazakhs*, p. 4, citing N. I. Grodekov, *Kirgizy i Karakirgizy Syr'darinskoi oblasti*, Vol. 1, *Iuridicheskii byt'* (Tashkent, 1889), p. 1.

37. See Alexis Levshin, *Description des hordes et des steppes des Kirghiz-Kazaks ou Kirghiz-Kaisaks*, trans. Ferry de Pigny (Paris: Imprimerie Royale, 1840) and S. S. Krivtsov (ed.), *Kazakhstan i Kirgiziia* (Moscow: Moskovskoi Oblastnoe Otdelenie Gosizdat RSFSR, 1930).

38. Akiner, *The Formation of Kazakh Identity*, p. 34.

39. There were two script changes to the Kazakh language: from the Arabic to the Latin in 1929, then from the Latin to the Cyrillic in 1940.

40. Akiner, *The Formation of Kazakh Identity*, p. 55.

41. Olcott, *The Kazakhs*.

42. For an excellent analysis of the independence period, see Martha Brill Olcott, *Kazakhstan: Unfulfilled Promise* (Washington, DC: Carnegie Endowment for International Peace, 2002).

43. Ivo D. Duchacek, *Power Maps: Comparative Politics of Constitutions* (Santa Barbara: ABC Clio, 1973).

44. See the interview with Zinaida Fetodova, *Kazakhstanskaia Pravda*, 10 April 1992

45. Cited by Vitalii Voronov and Alexander Peregrin in *Kazakhstanskaia Pravda*, 13 July 1995.

46. The text of the draft constitution was published in the press on 11 June and then subjected to four months of extensive debate during which one survey reported the improbable statistic that 47.6 per cent of those polled claimed to have read the draft. *Kazakhstanskaia Pravda*, 29 August 1998. Elsewhere it was claimed that over 3 million people took part in the discussion with more than 18,000 proposals being received by the constitutional commission. In late October the draft went for revision to the constitutional commission before being forwarded to the Supreme Soviet for discussion by deputies in early December. Here, extensive discussion led to yet further amendment before the document was passed by an overwhelming majority at the ninth session of the Supreme Soviet of the twelfth Convocation on 28 January 1993. See Sally N. Cummings, 'Politics in Kazakhstan: The Constitutional Crisis of March 1995', *FSS Briefing No. 3* (London: Royal Institute of International Affairs, August 1995), pp. 1–6.

47. *Ogni Alatau*, 19 May 1992.

48. *Kazakhstanskaia Pravda*, 2 June 1992.

49. *Qazaqstan Respublikasynyn konstitutsiiasy* (Almaty: Edilet, 1993).

50. Cummings, 'Politics in Kazakhstan', p. 1.

51. *Trud*, 14 May 1992.

52. Informal conversations with local journalists. The author was present at the voting of parliamentary dissolution.

53. 'Law On the Temporary Delegation of Additional Powers to the President of the Republic of Kazakhstan and the Local Chiefs of Administration', *Sovety Kazakhstana*, 10 December 1993.

54.  The president was given the right to exercise certain other powers of the Supreme Soviet (appointing and removing judges, the Prosecutor General, and the Chairman of the National Bank, ratifying and denouncing international treaties, etc.) and to exercise independent powers which, according to the Constitution, the president could only exercise with the consent of the Supreme Soviet (appointing the Chairman of the Council of Ministers and certain other ministers).

55.  For further legislative detail, see Rinat Shamsutdinov, 'The Legislative History of Presidential Government in Kazakhstan', The Jamestown Foundation, *Prism*, No. 16, Part 4, 7 August 1998.

56.  *Kazakhstanskaia Pravda*, 13 July 1995.

57.  This prompted Olzhas Suleimenov, poet, writer, politician and former leader of the anti-nuclear movement 'Nevada-Semipalatinsk' to state in March 1995: 'In Yeltsin's Russia, to dissolve parliament you need tanks; in Nazarbaev's Kazakhstan to dissolve parliament you only need one tank: Tatyana Kvyatkovskaya'.

58.  Presidential Decree, 'On Measures for Public Administration Restructuring in the Republic of Kazakhstan', 4 March 1997, *Sovety Kazakhstana*, 5 March 1997.

59.  *Republic of Kazakhstan: Transition of the State*: Volume 1, p. i, World Bank, Country Operations Division I, 15 July 1996.

60.  Khabar television channel, 22 April 1997.

61.  EIU, *Kazakhstan Country Profile*, 1998–1999, p. 19.

62.  *Vremya po grinvichy*, 3 July 1998.

63.  Khabar television channel, 22 April, 1997.

64.  See *The Jamestown Monitor*, 1 October 1998.

65.  *Interfax*, 7, 8 and 9 October 1998.

66.  *Konstitutsionnyi zakon Respubliki Kazakhstan*, 8 May 1998, Astana 'O vnesenii izmenenii i dopolnenii v ukaz prezidenta respubliki Kazakhstan, imeiushchii silu konstitutsionnogo zakona, 'O vyborakh v Respublike Kazakhstan', published in *Kazakhstanskaia Pravda*, 9 May 1998.

67.  RFE/RL Newsline, Part I, 20 January 1999. Nevertheless, this refusal was shrouded in ambiguity; moreover, only a few weeks later the European Union granted Kazakhstan another substantial aid package.

68.  *Financial Times*, 2 February 1999.

69.  Olcott, *Kazakhstan*, p. 123.

70.  *Delovaia Nedelia*, No. 1, 1998.

71.  *Delovaia Nedelia*, No. 1, 1998.

72.  Olcott, *Kazakhstan*, p. 138.

73.  29 October 1994, as cited in *Delovaia Nedelia*, No. 3, 1998.

74.  *Delovaia Nedelia*, No. 1, 1998.

75.  E. K. Dosmukhametov, *Foreign Direct Investment in Kazakhstan: Politico-Legal Aspects of Post-Communist Transition* (St. Antony's Series, Palgrave Macmillan, 2002).

76.  For individual accounts of provinces' varying histories, economies, geographies and polities, see Eastern Research Group, *Kazakhstan's Regions: Research and Analysis Note*, July 1998.

77.  The provincial structure of the USSR dates from the 1930s. By 1944, Kazakhstan had 16 provinces. In 1957, the republic was granted the right to restructure its territorial-administrative divisions and opted to expand the number to 19. In 1991, the new post-independence capital of Almaty was granted provincial status. A. K. Kotov 'Konstitutsionnye Osnovy Mestnogo Gosudarstvennogo Upravleniia', *O Mestnom Samoupravlenii: Realii, Problemy, Perspektivy (Almaty, 1997) pp.* 43–9.

78.  'O merakh po optimizatsii administrativno-territorial'nogo ustroistva Respubliki Kazakhstan', *Ukaz Prezidenta Respubliki Kazakhstan* (No.3466), 22 April 1997.

79.  'Ob izmeneniiakh v administrativno-territorial'nom ustroistve Akmolinskoi i Severo-Kazakhstanskoi oblastei', *Ukaz Prezidenta Respubliki Kazakhstan* (No.114), 8 April 1999.

80.  John Roberts, 'Caspian Oil and Gas: How Far Have We Come and Where Are We Going?', in Sally N. Cummings (ed.), *Oil, Transition and Security in Central Asia* (London and New York: Routledge

Curzon, 2003), pp. 143–60.

81.     See Sally N. Cummings, *Understanding Politics in Kazakhstan* (DEMSTAR, 2002).

# Chapter 2

1.      Robert Dahl, *Who Governs? Democracy and Power in an American City* (New Haven, CT: Yale University Press, 1961).

2.      Suzanne Keller, *Beyond The Ruling Class: Strategic Elites in Modern Society* (New York: Random House, 1963), p. 23.

3.      The next chapter outlines elite structure in demographic terms (some authors have chosen to categorize careers as demographic as they form part of a person's background, and this is not contested here; but the two are placed together here with the aim to compare changes in career paths with changes in regimes).

4.      Ronald J. Hill, *Soviet Union: Politics, Economics and Society* (2nd edn., London: Pinter Publishers Ltd, 1990), p. 92.

5.      See Frederick Frey, *The Turkish Political Elite* (Cambridge, MA.: MIT Press, 1965).

6.      Informal evidence given by my chosen 'panel of experts', July 1996.

7.      The panel of experts was given a list of possible 'power institutions' as well as a list of possible top elite members and were asked to rank these. They were also asked to make further suggestions of top-ranking elites and institutions.

8.      Like its Russian counterpart, the administration changed its name from *apparat* to *administratsiia* in 1995.

9.      Robert Putnam, *The Comparative Study of Political Elites* (Englewood Cliffs, N.J.: Prentice-Hall, 1976).

10.     Dahl, *Who Governs?*

11.     C. Wright Mills, *The Power Elite* (New York: Oxford University Press, 1959), p. 4.

12.     Mills, *The Power Elite*, p. 6.

13.     Mills, *The Power Elite*, p. 9.

14.     See *Dinamika* 2, p. 138.

15.     'Dinamika Reitingov Politikov', August 1996 in *Dinamika Obshchestvennykh Protsessov v Kazakhstane (Dinamika 1)* (Almaty: Kazakhstan Institute of Strategic Research under the President of Kazakhstan, Newspaper 'Panorama', Republican Centre of Public Opinion, 1997), pp. 50–1 and 'Reiting Perspektivnosti Politikov', October 2001 in S. Zhusupov, B. Zhusupov, K. Ezhenova, *Dinamika Obshchestvennykh Protsessov v Kazakhstane (Dinamika 2)* (Almaty: Panorama and Gruppa VIProblem, 2002), p. 29.

16.     See, for example, Anton Steen, *Between Past and Future: Elites, Democracy and the State in Post-Communist Countries – A Comparison of Estonia, Latvia, and Lithuania* (Andover: Ashgate Publishers, 1997) and Olga Kryshtanovskaya and Stephen White, 'From Soviet Nomenklatura to Russian Elite', *Europe-Asia Studies*, Vol. 48, No. 5 (July 1996), pp. 711–34. For an excellent study of regional deputies, see James Hughes, 'Sub-National Elites and Post-communist Transformation in Russia: A Reply to Kryshtanovskaya and White', *Europe-Asia Studies*, Vol. 49, No. 6 (1997), pp. 1017–36.

17.     David Lane (ed.), *Elites and Political Power in the USSR* (Aldershot: Elgar, 1988).

18.     Hughes, 'Sub-National Elites', pp. 1017–36.

19.     See the two excellent analyses by Reef Altoma, *Deputies Elected to the Supreme Soviet of the Republic of Kazakhstan on 7 March 1994*, American Legal Consortium under USAID's Rule of Law Program, Chemonics International (Almaty, 31 March 1994) and *The 13ᵗʰ Convention of the Supreme Soviet of the Republic Kazakhstan: Spring Session Results*, American Legal Consortium under USAID's Rule of Law Program, Chemonics International (Almaty, 1 August 1994).

20.     Tajikistan joined in 1999.

21.     This career pattern is starkly reminiscent of the old Tsarist pattern.

22.     Interview with the author.

23.  The key sources in this section are: A. Z. Asylbekov, V. N. Voloshin and V. N. Khliupin, *Kto Est' Kto v Respublike Kazakhstan* (Almaty: Evraziia-Polis, 1995); D. R. Ashimbaev, *Kto Est' Kto v Kazakhstane* (Almaty: Credo, 2001); individual biographies were also sourced from *Kazakhstanskaia Pravda*; *Spisok Telefonov Rukovoditelei Oblastei*, 1995 and 1996; *Spisok Telefonov Rukovodiashchikh Rabotnikov Organov Gosudarstvennogo Upravleniia, Partiinykh, Obshchestvennykh i Drugikh Organizatsii Kazakhskoi SSR*, July 1991 and January 1995; *Spisok Telefonov Rabotnikov Administratsii Prezidenta Respubliki Kazakhstan*, October 1992 and April 1996.

24.  Frey, *The Turkish Political Elite*, identified three categories: 'professional', 'official' and 'economic'.

25.  Interviewees who originated from business liked to make a distinction between those who had made it under Gorbachev and those who cam into business after 1991.

26.  Shukeev was Minister of Economics between 1995 and 1997.

27.  This occurred under Zhaksylyk Kulekeev.

28.  John Higley, Judith Kullberg and Jan Pakulski, 'The Persistence of Postcommunist Elites', *Journal of Democracy*, Vol. 7, No. 2 (April 1996), pp. 133–47.

29.  The 50 per cent of parliamentarians who were formerly state officials is broken down as follows: of the 28 in the Senate, 16 had served in regional administrations and regional parliaments; nine in the presidential administration and ministries; three in the police, procuracy, and other security organs; of the 29 in the Mazhilis 19 had worked in regional administrations, seven in the presidential administration and ministries; two in the police, procuracy and other security organs and one in the military. Part of this information may be found at www.election.kz.

30.  See Altoma, *Deputies Elected to the Supreme Soviet of the Republic of Kazakhstan on 7 March 1994*; and Sally N. Cummings, 'Kazakhstan's Parliamentary Elections and After', *Former Soviet South Briefing Paper No. 5* (London: Royal Institute of International Affairs, February 1996).

31.  'Kakie iz sotsialnykh grupp, po Vashemy mneniiu, igraiut znachitel'nuiu rol' v formirovanii kazakhstanskogo gosudarstva…', April 2000, in S. Zhusupov et al., (Dinamika 2), p. 128

32.  The six cited by Satpaev are headed by: Kazkommertsbank (Uraz Dzhandosov, Nurzhan Sukhanberdin, Saut Mynbaev, Evgenii Feld', Nurlan Bizakov, Erzhan Utembaev, Zeinulla Kakimzhanov, Kasymzhomart Tokaev, Zhannat Ertlesova, Danial Akhmetov, Daulet Sembaev); Mukhtar Abliazov (plus Nurlan Smagulov); Timur Kulibaev – Nurlan Kapparov (plus Ulan Ksembaev of Aktsept); Rakhat Aliev (plus Dariga Nazarbaeva, Al'nur Musaev, Marat Tazhin, Galimzhan Zhakiianov); Aleksandr Mashkevich (plus A. Ibragimov, T.Shodiev, D. Duisenov, A. Perushev). See, D. A. Satpaev, *Lobbizm: Tainye Rygachi Vlasti* (Almaty: 1999), pp. 80–1.

33.  See Thomas A. Baylis, 'Elites, Institutions, and Political Change in East Central Europe: Germany, the Czech Republic, and Slovakia', in Dogan and Higley, *Elites, Crises, and the Origins of Regimes*, pp. 107–30.

34.  K. Banting and R. Simeon, 'Introduction: The Politics of Constitutional Change', in K. Banting and R. Simeon (eds.), *The Politics of Constitutional Change in Industrial Nations: Redesigning the State* (London: Macmillan, 1985), pp. 10–13.

35.  *Konstitutsiia Respubliki Kazakhstan* (Almaty: Jety Jargy, 1998). Kazakhstan has introduced two constitutions since independence. Since 1995 there has been one major constitutional amendment to the institutional framework of the Republic in 'O vnesenii izmenenii i dopolnenii v Konstitutsiyou Respubliki Kazakhstan', *Zakon Respubliki Kazakhstan*, 7 October 1998. Of note also are the amendments to the election law,'O vyborakh v Respublike Kazakhstan' of 6 May and 28 June 1999 which concerned parliamentary elections.

36.  See Cummings, 'Kazakhstan's Parliamentary Elections', p. 3.

37.  'Politicheskie Partii Kazakhstana: Vozmozhnaia Transformatsiia Ustanovok', December 1995, in *Dinamika 1*, pp. 40–2.

38.  'Deesposobnost' Mestnykh Organov Upravleniia – Indikator Obshchestvennogo Razvitiia', May 1996, in *Dinamika 1*, pp. 43–5.

39.  'Perelom v obshchestvennom soznanii: ustalost' ot deklaratsii', April 1996, in *Dinamika 1*, pp. 33–9.

40.   'Noiabr'skie sobytiia v RK: shag k demokratii?', 27–28 November in in S. Zhusupov, B. Zhusupov, K. Ezhenova, *Dinamika* 2 (Almaty: Panorama and Gruppa VIProblem, 2002), pp. 30–41.

41.   'Deesposobnost' Mestnykh Organov'.

## Chapter 3

1.    David Lane, 'Russia: The Oil Elite's Evolution, Divisions, and Outlooks', in John and Gyorgy Lengyel (eds.), *Elites After State Socialism: Theories and Analysis* (Rowman and Littlefield Publishers, Inc, 2000), p. 187.

2.    'O Traibalizme, Koroliakh i 'Kapuste'', September 2002, pp. 15–17.

3.    Cf. Anton Steen, *Between Past and Future.*

4.    UNDP, *Human Development Report: Kazakstan 1997* (Almaty, Kazakhstan), p. 27.

5.    Putnam, *The Comparative Study of Political Elites.*

6.    Elizabeth E. Bacon, *Central Asians under Russian Rule: A Study in Culture Change* (Ithaca, NY: Cornell University Press, 1966), p. 41.

7.    David Lane, 'Ethnic and Class Stratification in Soviet Kazakhstan, 1917–1939', *Comparative Studies in Society and History*, Vol. 17, No. 2 (1975), p. 184.

8.    See Michael Rywkin, *Moscow's Muslim Challenge*, Chapter 8.

9.    UNDP, *Human Development Report: Kazakstan 1997*, p. 46.

10.   Putnam, *The Comparative Study of Political Elites.*

11.   Suzanne Keller, *Beyond the Ruling Class: Strategic Elites in Modern Society* (Transaction Publishers: 1963, reprinted 1991), p. 121.

12.   Frey, *The Turkish Political Elite* (Cambridge, MA: MIT Press, 1965).

13.   *Itogi vsesoiuznoy perepisi naseleniia 1959 goda, SSSR* (M. 1962), pp. 88–9, cited by Lane, 'Ethnic and Class Stratification', p. 178.

14.   Frey, *The Turkish Political Elite*, p. 63.

15.   Frey, *The Turkish Political Elite*, p. 63.

16.   Rywkin, *Moscow's Muslim Challenge*, p. 104.

17.   Frey, *The Turkish Political Elite.*

18.   Putnam, *The Comparative Study of Political Elites*, p. 23.

19.   Bohdan Harasymiw, *Political Elite Recruitment in the Soviet Union* (Basingstoke: Macmillan, 1984), p. 34.

20.   Zbigniew Brzezinski and Samuel p. Huntington, *Political Power: USA/USSR* (New York: Viking Press, 1964), p. 135; Allen H. Barton et al., *Opinion-Making Elites in Yugoslavia* (New York: Praeger, 1973), p. 125.

21.   Of the 244 members here considered, we have data on father's occupation for around 101 individuals.

22.   Nursultan Nazarbaev, *Without Right and Left* (London: Class Publishing, 1992), p. 2.

23.   Marvin Zonis, *Political Elite of Iran* (Princeton Studies on the Near East) (Princeton: Princeton University Press, 1971).

24.   Putnam, *The Comparative Study of Political Elites*, pp. 24–6.

25.   Cynthia Werner places the overall population data as follows: Middle Zhuz, 41.24 per cent, Junior Zhuz, 33.96 per cent and Senior Zhuz, 24.63 per cent. Cynthia Werner, 'The Significance of Tribal Identities in the Daily Life of Rural Kazakhs in South Kazakhstan', paper presented at annual conference of Association for the Study of Nationalities, Columbia University, 24–26 April, 1997.

26.   Edward Aaron Schatz, '"Tribes" and "Clans" in Modern Power: The State-Led Production of Sub-Ethnic Politics in Kazakhstan', unpublished Ph.D. dissertation (University of Wisconsin-Madison, August 2000).

27.   Schatz, '"Tribes" and "Clans" in Modern Power'.

28.   Putnam, *The Comparative Study of Political Elites*, p. 32.

29.   'Predvaritel'nye itogi pervoi Natsional'noi perepisi naseleniia 1999 goda v Respublike Kazakhstan'

*National Statistics Agency*, Press Release No. 10, 1999.

30.   Frey, *The Turkish Political Elite*.

31.   V. D. Kurganskaia, V. Yu. Dunaev, *Kazakhstanskaia Model' Mezhetnicheskoi Integratsii* (Almaty 2002), p. 84.

32.   Spisok Telefonov Rukovodiashchikh Rabotnikov Organov Gosudarstvennogo Upravleniia, Partiinykh, Obshchestvennykh i Drugikh Organizatsii Kazakhskoi SSR, July 1991.

33.   Kurganskaia and Dunaev, *Kazakhstanskaia Model' Mezhetnicheskoi Integratsii*, p. 86.

34.   *Itogi vsesoiuznoi perepisi naseleniia 1970 goda*, Vol. IV, Natsional'nyi sostav naseleniia SSSR. Moscow: Statistika, 1973. *Itogi perepisi naseleniia 1999 goda v Respublike Kazakhstan*. 1999. Almaty: Agenstvo respubliki Kazakhstana po statistike.

35.   *Itogi perepisi naseleniia 1999 goda.*

36.   See, for example, Turkey: Frey, F.W., *The Turkish Political Elite* (Cambridge: MA: MIT Press, 1965).

37.   Harold D. Lasswell, *World Revolutionary Elites: Studies in Coercive Ideological Movements* (Cambridge, MA: MIT Press, 1965), p. 9.

38.   S. J. Eldersveld, Political Elites in Modern Societies. Empirical Research and Democratic Theory (Ann Arbor, MI: University of Michigan Press, 1989).

39.   See Klaus von Beyme, *Die Politische Elite in der Bundesrepublik Deutschland* (Munich: R. Piper, 1971).

40.   Daniel Lerner and Morten Gorden, *Euratlantica: Changing Perspectives of the European Elites* (Cambridge,A: MITPress).

41.   Fred I. Greenstein, *Personality and Politics* (Chicago: Markham,1969)

## Chapter 4

1.   See Clifford Geertz, 'The Integrative Revolution: Primordial Sentiments and Civil Politics in the New States', in Clifford Geertz (ed.), *Old Societies and New States: The Quest for Modernity in Asia and Africa* (New York: The Free Press, 1967), pp. 100-10 and 128.

2.   See Paul R. Brass, 'Elite Groups, Symbol Manipulation, and Ethnic Identity among the Muslims of South Asia', in D. Taylor and M. Yapp (eds.), *Political Identity in South Asia*, (London: Curzon Press, 1979), pp. 35–43.

3.   Rodney Barker, *Legitimating Identities: The Self-Presentations of Rulers and Subjects* (Cambridge: Cambridge University Press, 2001), p. 28.

4.   Stephen Reicher and Nick Hopkins, *Self and Nation: Categorization, Contestation and Mobilization* (London : Sage Publications, 2001).

5.   Reicher and Hopkins, *Self and Nation*, pp. 43–4.

6.   Fredrik Barth (ed.), *Ethnic Groups and Boundaries* (Boston: Little, Brown and Co., 1969).

7.   Edward Schatz, 'Framing Strategies and Non-Conflict in Multi-Ethnic Kazakhstan', *Nationalism and Ethnic Politics*, Vol. 6, No. 2 (Summer 2000), pp. 70–92.

8.   See Nursultan Nazarbaev, Idei'naia Konsolidatsiia Obshchestva – kak uslovie progressa Kazakhstana, Kazakhstan – XXI Vek, Almaty 1993; K Obnovlennomy Kazakhstany – cherez iglublenie reform, obshchenatsional'noe soglasie, Kazakhstan, Almaty, 1994; Kontseptsiia Gumanitarnogo Obrazovaniia v Respublike Kazakhstan, Almaty 1994; and Za mir i soglacie v nashem obshchem dome, Almaty, 1995. See also, Paul Kolstoe, 'Anticipating Demographic Superiority: Kazakh Thinking on Integration and Nation Building', *Europe-Asia Studies*, Vol. 50, No. 1 (1998), pp. 51–69.

9.   *Kazakhstanskaia Pravda*, 12 January, 1992. For other major statements by Nazarbaev concerning Kazakhstan's secularism, see *Egemen Qazaqstan*, 10 November 1992; *Panorama*, 13 July 1993; *Ana tili*, 14 August, 1994; *Express-K*, 12 December 1994; *Zaman Qazaqstan*, 1 December 1995; *Turkestan*, 2 June, 1996; and *Panorama*, 15 June, 1997.

10.  Bhavna Dave, 'Kazaks Struggle to Revive Their "Language of Folklore"', *Transition*, 29 November 1996, pp. 23–5. See also her, 'National Revival in Kazakhstan: Language Shift and Identity Change', *Post-Soviet Affairs*, Vol. 12, No. 1, 1996, pp. 51–72.

11. For discussion of the 'Turkish model', see *Jas Alash*, 14 March, 1992; *Kazakhstanskaia Pravda*, 22 February 1992; and *Zaman Qazaqstan*, 24 July and 1 August, 1992. Also, Paul Kubicek, *Nation, State and Economy in Central Asia: Does Ataturk Provide a Model?* (Henry M. Jackson School of International Studies, University of Washington, Donald Treadgold Papers, No. 14, August 1997).

12. *Inside Central Asia*, Issue 444, 16–22 September 2002.

13. All Central Asian states barring Kazakhstan have joined the Economic Cooperation Organization (ECO), which was initially established by Iran, Turkey and Pakistan in 1964, and now also includes Azerbaijan and Afghanistan.

14. Kasenov, *Institutions and Conduct*, p. 282.

15. Kasenov, *Institutions and Conduct*, p. 265–6.

16. See *Jas Alash*, 10 October 1995; and *Kazakhstanskaia Pravda*, 9 November 1995.

17. For an analysis of the law see *Kazakhstanskaia pravda*, 25 March, 1993 and *Panorama*, 24 August, 1993.

18. The Russian Embassy would, understandably, only supply an approximation.

19. BBC, 'Summary of World Broadcasts', 2 June 1994.

20. Eventually, the two sides reached a compromise elaborated by the Kazaks called the 'Simple Exchange of Citizenship Agreement' (Uproshchennyi' poryadok priobretenie grazhdanstva). See *Kazakhstanskaia Pravda*, 21 January, 1995.

21. The elite's state policy was outlined at a roundtable conference in Moscow in mid-November 1995. See Karlygash Ezhenova, 'Put' k resheniiu problem grazhdanstva – v konstruktivnom poiske integratsionnykh resheni'i real'noi' podderzhke so storony Rossii svoikh sootechestvennikov', *Panorama*, 28 October 1995.

22. *Aziia*, 13 April 1994.

23. Kasenov, *Institutions and Conduct*, p. 265.

24. Nursultan Nazarbaev, *Kazakhstan-2030. Prosperity, Security and Ever Growing Welfare of all the Kazakhstanis* (Almaty, 1997), p. 17.

25. Nazarbaev, *Kazakhstan-2030*, p. 17.

26. Nazarbaev, *Kazakhstan-2030*, pp. 26–7.

27. President Nursultan Nazarbaev, 'A Strategy for the Development of Kazakhstan as a Sovereign State', *Kazakhstanskaia Pravda*, 16 May 1992.

28. M. Titarenko, 'Aziatskiy aspekt evraziystva, *Etnopoliticheskiy vestnik*, No. 5, 1995, pp. 114–15, cited by Mikhail Alexandrov, *Uneasy Alliance: Relations Between Russia and Kazakhstan in the Post-Soviet Era, 1992–7* (Westport, CT and London: Greenwood Press, 1999), p. 185.

29. *Nezavisimaia Gazeta*, 11 November 1996.

30. Kasenov, *The Institutions and Conduct*, p. 284.

31. Nursultan Nazarbaev, *Without Right and Left* (London: Class Publishing, 1992), p. 127. Kasenov writes: 'The Kazakhs and other Central Asian people have common historical ties with the people of these countries [Turkey, Iran, Pakistan and India] that had been interrupted by the Russian and then Soviet empires.' Kasenov, *The Institutions and Conduct*, p. 280.

32. Nursultan A. Nazarbaev, *Evraziiskii Soiuz: idei, praktika, perspektivy 1994–1997* (Moscow: Fond Sodeistviia Razvitiiu Sotsial'nykh Politicheskikh Nauk, 1997), p. 67.

33. Tsentr monitoringa mezhetnicheskikh otnoshenii v Kazakhstane, *Etnopoliticheskii Monitoring v Kazakhstane* (Almaty: Arkor, 1995), p. 20. The monitoring, organized by Nurbulat Masanov under the auspices of the Friedrich Ebert Stiftung, was conducted over three time periods: *Etnopoliticheskii monitoring v Kazakhstane*, Vols. 1–3, Autumn 1995, Winter 1995/6 and Spring 1996, Almaty.

34. Suverennomu Kazakhstanu – 10 let, 1992.

35. Anthony Cohen, 'Owning the Nation, and the Personal Nature of Nationalism: Locality and the Rhetoric of Nationhood in Scotland', in Vered Amit-Talai and Caroline Knowles (eds), *Re-Situating Identities: The Politics of Race, Ethnicity and Culture* (Ontario, Canada: Broadview Press, 1996), p. 157.

36.     Masanov et al, *The Nationalities Question in Post-Soviet Kazakhstan*.

37.     Karin and Chebotarev, 'Policy of Kazakhization', p. 80.

38.     Karin and Chebotarev, 'Policy of Kazakhization', p. 80

39.     Edward A. D. Schatz, 'The politics of multiple identities', pp. 489–506.

40.     For a more detailed discussion of these issues, see Sally N. Cummings, 'The Kazakhs: Diasporas, Demographics and the Kazakhstani State', in Charles King and Neil Melvin (eds.), *Nations Abroad: Diaspora Politics and International Relations in the Former Soviet Union* (Boulder: Westview Press, 1998), pp. 133–52.

41.     *ITAR-TASS News Agency*, Moscow, 28 April 1997.

42.     *Panorama Shimkenta*, 22 September 1996.

43.     See *The Jamestown Monitor*, 30 January, 1998.

44.     For a detailed analysis of the revised language law, see the excellent piece by William Fierman, 'Language and Identity in Kazakhstan: Formulations in Policy Documents 1987–1997', *Communist and Post-Communist Studies*, Vol. 31. No. 2 (June 1998), pp. 171–86. See also 'Zakon Respubliki Kazakhstan. O iazykakh v Respublike Kazakhstan,' *Mysl*, Vol. 9 (1997), pp. 2–7.

45.     See the excellent article by William Fierman, 'Language and Identity in Kazakhstan: Formulations in policy documents 1987–1997', *Communist and Post-Communist Studies*, Vol. 31. No. 2 (June 1998), pp. 171–86.

46.     Kazakh Television First Channel, Almaty, 17 April 1997.

47.     *Kazazkhstanskaia Pravda*, 2 June 1990.

48.     *Karavan*, 5 February 1994; *Delovaia nedelia*, 8 December, 1994.

49.     Almaty's only Soviet-era mosque, deserted for decades, completed its face-lift with Saudi Arabian money, in 1996.

50.     Foreign donors have also ensured the wide distribution of Kazakh-language Korans.

51.     *Delovaia Nedelia*, 18 December 1997; and *Panorama*, 19 December 1999.

52.     See Eric Hobsbawm's account of the creation of the French Third Republic in his, 'Introduction: Inventing Traditions', and 'Mass-Producing Traditions: Europe, 1870–1914', in Eric Hobsbawn and Terence Ranger (eds.), *The Invention of Tradition* (Cambridge: Cambridge University Press, 1983), pp. 13–14, 264–5, 271–8.

53.     See M. Agulhon, 'La Statumanie et l'Histoire', *Ethnologie Francaise*, 1978, pp. 3–4.

54.     *Panorama*, 25 August 1996.

55.     The Supreme Kenges (Parliament) passed a decree on 14 May 1993.

56.     *Express-Kazakhstan*, 12 June 1996.

57.     Benjamin Akzin, *State and Nation* (London: Hutchinson University Library, 1964).

58.     Reicher and Hopkins, *Self and Nation*, p. 39.

59.     Billig, Michael, *Banal Nationalism* (London: Sage, 1995).

60.     Bhavna Dave, 'National Revival in Kazakhstan'.

61.     See *Karavan*, 25 October 1994; and *Karavan*, 15 July 1996.

62.     See also, 'Mirovozzrencheskie orientatsii studentov: otnoshenie k religii', *Saiasat*, Vol. 8 (September 1997), pp. 46–50.

63.     Mark Beissinger, 'Elites and Ethnic Identities in Soviet and Post-Soviet Politics', in Alexander J. Motyl (ed.), *The Post-Soviet Nations: Perspectives on the Demise of the USSR* (New York: Columbia University Press, 1992), p. 149.

64.     Olcott, *The Kazakhs* (Stanford, CA.: Hoover Institution Press, 1987, 1995).

65.     Schatz, 'The Politics of Multiple Identities', pp. 489–506.

66.     Anthony D. Smith. *The Ethnic Origins of Nations* (Oxford : Basil Blackwell, 1986), p. 31.

67.     Nazarbaev, *Kazakhstan-2030*.

# Chapter 5

1.      Robert Putnam, *The Comparative Study of Political Elites* (Englewood Cliffs, N.J.: Prentice-Hall, 1976),

p. 171.

2. Putnam, *Comparative Study*, p. 172.

3. William A. Welsh, 'Introduction: The Comparative Study of Political Leadership in Communist Systems' in Carl Beck, *Comparative Communist Political Leadership* (New York: David McKay Company, Inc, 1973), p. 29.

4. Erlan Karin and Andrei Chebotarev, 'The Policy of Kazakhisation and Government Institutions in Kazakhstan', in Nurbulat Masanov, Erlan Karin, Andrei Chebotarev and Natsuko Oka, *The Nationalities Question in Post-Soviet Kazakhstan* (Tokyo: Institute of Developing Economies, Jetro, 2002), p. 69.

5. A. Chubar, 'Oshibka prezidenta. Poidet li Nazarbaev na dosrochnoe preizbranie?', *Obshchaia gazeta*, 15–21 October 1998.

6. V. N. Khliupin, *Bol'shaia sem'ia Nursultan Nazarbaeva* (Moscow: Institute of Contemporary Political Research, 1998), p. 52.

7. Cited by Timothy Edmonds, 'Power and Powerlessness in Kazakhstani Society', *Central Asian Survey*, Vol. 17, No. 3 (September 1998), p. 467.

8. See especially Frederick J. Fleron, Jr., 'System Attributes and Career Attributes: The Soviet Political Leadership System, 1952–1965', in Carl Beck et al., *Comparative Communist Political Leadership*, pp. 43–85.

9. Talgat Ismagambetov, *Electoral Systems in Kazakhstan* (Almaty, 2001).

10. Juan J. Linz and Alfred Stepan, *Problems of Democratic Transition and Consolidation* (Baltimore: Johns Hopkins University Press, 1996).

11. Pauline Jones Luong, *Institutional Change and Political Continuity in Post-Soviet Central Asia: Power, Perceptions and Pacts* (Cambridge: Cambridge University Press, 2002).

12. Sally N. Cummings, 'Parliamentary Elections in Kazakhstan', *Former Soviet South Briefing Paper*, Royal Institute of International Affairs, No. 5 (February 1996). See also 'Politics in Kazakhstan: The Constitutional Crisis of March 1995', *Former Soviet South Briefing Paper*, Royal Institute of International Affairs, No. 3, August 1995.

13. *Konstitutsionnyi zakon Respubliki Kazakhstan*, 8 May 1998, Astana; 'O vnesenii izmenenii i dopolnenii v ukaz prezidenta respubliki Kazakhstan, imeiushchii silu konstitutsionnogo zakona', 'O vyborakh v Respublike Kazakhstan', published in *Kazakhstanskaia Pravda*, 9 May 1998.

14. While the average participation rate of the Kazakhstani electorate in previous elections and referenda had been between 35 and 40 per cent, the Central Electoral Commission claimed a participation percentage of 62.56 per cent.

15. See Sally N. Cummings, *Kazakhstan: Centre-Periphery Relations* (London and Washington DC: Brookings Institute and Royal Institute of International Affairs, 2000).

16. http://usinfo.state.gov/topical/pol/terror02021110.htm.

17. For example, in the Medeu district of Almaty, the clear leader in the opinion polls had been Lira Baisitova; the eventual winner, Sharip Omarov, who represented the pro-executive party of Otan, had stood only fourth in the pre-election polls. In the Alatau district of Almaty, Seidakhmet Kuttykadam received only 34.7 per cent of the vote, followed by Valentin Makalkin with 14.7 per cent. According to election rules, this result should have led to a second round. Instead, the CEC claimed that Kuttykadam had received 51.2 per cent. Dyachenko similarly won in the Industrial constituency of Almaty with allegedly only 27.5 per cent of the votes. In the Kurmangazy constituency of Atyrau, Gaziz Aldamzharov, one of the key potential opponents to Nazarbaev back in 1995, apparently won outright, but the election went to a second round. In the second round, the elections, along with those of districts in the Zhambyl and South Kazakhstan provinces, were declared null and void because of alleged electoral mispractice. The Senat elections the month previously had already strengthened executive central rule. Of the 16 candidates, 13 were Kazakhs, five were re-elected from the previous Senat and seven were handpicked from executive institutions.

18. *Egemen Qazaqstan*, 15 January 1992.

19.  Jones Luong, *Institutional Change and Political Continuity in Post-Soviet Central Asia*.

20.  See *Jamestown Monitor*, 1 October 1998.

21.  R. Lemarchand and K. Legg, 'Political Clientelism and Development: A Preliminary Analysis', *Comparative Politics*, Vol. IV (January 1972), pp. 51–2. See also, John H. Miller, 'Putting Clients in Place: the Role of Patronage in Cooption into the Soviet Leadership', in Archie Brown (ed.), *Political Leadership in the Soviet Union* (Bloomington and Indianapolis: Indiana University Press, 1989), pp. 54–95.

22.  Typologies have been developed of all 'dependency relations in traditional Africa' in which the 'type of clientelism' is seen as characterising the overall system of domination. See R. Lemarchand, 'Political Clientelism and Ethnicity in Tropical Africa: Competing Solidarities in Nation-Building', *American Political Science Review*, Vol. LXVI (March 1972), pp. 68–90.

23.  See also T.H. Rigby and Bohdan Harasymiw (eds.), *Leadership Selection and Patron-Client Relations in the USSR and Yugoslavia* (London: Allen and Unwin, 1983).

24.  See Gellner and Waterbury, *Patrons and Clients*, especially Alex Weingrod, 'Patronage and Power', pp. 41–51. Also, G. Roth, 'Personal Rulership, Patrimonialism and Empire-Building: The New States', in Reinhard Bendix and Gunther Roth (eds.), *Scholarship and Partisanship: Essays on Max Weber* (Berkeley: University of California Press, 1971).

25.  Seligman, *Recruiting Political Elites*.

26.  *Panorama*, 23 September 1995

27.  *Panorama*, No. 4, February 2002.

28.  C. Wright Mills, *The Power Elite* (Oxford: Oxford University Press, 1956), pp. 288–9.

29.  Kazakh Radio, Alma-Ata, in Kazakh, 22 June 1994 in SWB 25 June 1995.

30.  Kazakh TV, in Russian, 14 October 1994 in SWB 18 October 1995.

31.  Almaty Kazakh Radio in Russian, 21 June 1994, in FBIS-SOV 22 June 1994.

32.  Gregory Gleason, as cited by Edward A. D. Schatz, 'The Politics of Multiple Identities. Lineage and Ethnicity in Kazakhstan', *Europe-Asia Studies* Vol. 52, No. 3 (2000), pp. 489–506.

33.  Schatz, 'The Politics of Multiple Identities', p. 495.

34.  See Article 7, 'Zakon o Gosudarstvennaia Sluzhba', 23 July 1999 in *Ofitsial'nye Teksty Zakondatel'nykh Aktov na* 1.10.2001, Almaty, Yourist, 2001, p. 6.

35.  VIProblem Survey, 'Politicheskaia elita Kazakhstana. Mify i deistvitel'nost'', *Panorama*, 14 March 1997.

36.  Barbara Geddes, *Politicians' Dilemma* (Berkeley CA, University of California, 1994), p. 146.

37.  See especially Frederic J. Fleron, Jr., 'System Attributes and Career Attributes: The Soviet Political Leadership System, 1952–1965,' in Beck et al., *Comparative Communist Political Leadership*, pp. 43–85.

38.  Fleron, Jr., 'System Attributes and Career Attributes'.

## Chapter 6

1.  Peter Evans, Dietrich Rueschemeyer and Theda Skocpol, *Bringing the State Back In* (Cambridge: Cambridge University Press, 1985).

2.  Colin Hay, *Political Analysis: A Critical Introduction* (Basingstoke, Hampshire: Palgrave, 2002).

3.  Samuel P. Huntington, 'Political Development and Decay', *World Politics*, Vol. 17, No. 3 (April 1965), p. 394.

4.  www.moodys.com website, 19 September 2002.

5.  Rafis Abazov, *The Formation of Post-Soviet International Politics in Kazakhstan, Kyrgyzstan, and Uzbekistan* (Henry M. Jackson School of International Studies, University of Washington, Donald W. Treadgold Papers, No. 21, June 1999).

6.  'Prezidentskie Vybory', *Dinamika 1*, March 1996.

7.  This was based on 27 experts from four Central Asian countries minus Turkmenistan, together with Russia and Germany. 'Aktual'nye Problemy Bezopasnosti Tsentral'no-Aziatskogo Regiona', December 1995 in *Dinamika 1*, pp. 5–13.

8.    Adam Przeworski, *Democracy and the Market: Political and Economic Reforms in Latin America and Europe* (New York: Cambridge University Press), p. 186.

9.    Sally N. Cummings (ed.), *Power and Change in Central Asia* (London and New York: Routledge, 2002).

10.   *Delovaia Nedelia*, 28 February 1998.

11.   *Delovaia Nedelia*, 13 March 1998.

12.   V. N. Khliupin,'*Bol'shaia Sem'ia' Nursultana Nazarbaeva: Politicheskaia Elita Sovremennogo Kazakhstana* (Moscow: Institute Aktual'nykh Politicheskikh Issledovanii Moskva, 1998); D. A. Satpaev, *Lobbizm: Tainye Rygachi Vlasti* (Almaty, 1999); 'Razdelennaia Elita – narod dolzhen znat' svoikh 'geroev', *Soldat*, 11 April 2000.

13.   *Panorama*, No. 8, 2002.

14.   'Noiabr'skie sobytiia v RK: shag k demokratii?', 27–28 November in in S. Zhusupov, B. Zhusupov, K. Ezhenova, *Dinamika Obshchestvennykh Protsessov v Kazakhstane (Dinamika 2)*(Almaty: Panorama and Gruppa VIProblem, 2002), pp. 30–41.

15.   *Panorama*, No. 4, February 2002.

16.   *Panorama*, No. 4, February 2002.

17.   Neil J. Melvin, 'Russian Kazakhstani Cross-Border Relations' For the conference 'Central Asia in a New Security Context', Swedish Institute of International Affairs info@ui.se, Stockholm, 2–3 September 1999.

18.   Sally N. Cummings, *Kazakhstan: Centre-Periphery Relations* (London and Washington DC: Brookings Institution and the Royal Institute of International Affairs, 2000).

19.   'The Former Capital is Doomed for Financial Dead-Lock', *Focus Central Asia Annual Report*, 1998, p. 114.

20.   See Neil J. Melvin, 'Russian-Kazakhstani Cross-Border Relations'.

21.   'Detsupozobnost Mestnykh Urganov Upravleniia – Indikator Obshchestvennogo Razvitiia', May 1996, in *Dinamika Obshchestvennykh Protsessov v Kazakhstane (Dinamika 1)* (Almaty: Kazakhstan Institute of Strategic Research under the President of Kazakhstan, Newspaper 'Panorama', Republican Centre of Public Opinion, 1997), pp. 43–5.

22.   'Perelom v obshchestvennom soznanii: ustalost' ot deklaratsii', April 1996, in *Dinamika 1*, pp. 33–9.

23.   Olcott, *The Kazakhs* (Stanford, CA: Hoover Institution Press, 1987, 1995), pp. 242–3.

24.   John P. Willerton, *Patronage and Politics in the USSR* (Cambridge and New York: Cambridge University Press, 1992); J. W. Cleary, 'Elite Career Patterns in Kazakhstan', *British Journal of Political Science*, No. 4, 1974, pp. 323–44; and 'Politics and Administration in Soviet Kazakhstan, 1955–1964' (Ph.D. dissertation, Australian National University, 1967); also, Michael Rywkin, *Moscow's Muslim Challenge* (London: C. Hurst, 1982).

25.   The basis of this was already being established in the Stalinist era. See David Lane, 'Ethnic and Class Stratification in Soviet Kazakhstan, 1917–1939', *Comparative Studies in Society and History*, Vol. 17, No. 2 (1975), pp. 165–89.

26.   Pauline Jones Luong, *Institutional Change and Political Continuity in Post-Soviet Central Asia*, p. 96.

27.   Olcott, *The Kazakhs*, 240ff as cited by Jones Luong, p. 97.

28.   Olcott, *The Kazakhs*, p. 244.

29.   Krader, *Social Organization of the Mongol-Turkic Pastoral Nomads*, p. 237.

30.   See Neil Melvin, 'Authoritarian Pathways in Central Asia: A Comparison of Kazakhstan, the Kyrgyz Republic and Uzbekistan', presented at the European Consortium for Political Research, April 2001.

31.   Karl Wittfogel, *Oriental Despotism: A Comparative Study of Total Power* (New Haven: Yale University Press, 1957), cited in Melvin, 'Authoritarian Pathways in Central Asia'.

32.   John Anderson, 'Elections and Political Development in Central Asia', *Journal of Communist and Transition Politics*, Vol. 13, No. 4 (December 1997), p. 47, cited in Melvin, 'Authoritarian Pathways'.

33.   Gregory Gleason, *The Central Asian States: Discovering Independence* (Boulder, CO: Westview, 1997), p. 38, cited in Melvin, 'Authoritarian Pathways in Central Asia'.

34.  See Neil Melvin, *Russians beyond Russia: The Politics of National Identity* (London: Pinter, 1995).

35.  'Politicheskie Partii Kazakhstana: Vozmozhnaia Transformatsiia Ustanovok', December 1995, in *Dinamika 1*, pp. 40–2.

36.  *Etnopoliticheskii monitoring v Kazakhstane*, Vols. 1–3, Autumn 1995, Winter 1995/6 and Spring 1996, Almaty.

37.  Three periods were chosen to demonstrate the validity of the findings, each with different respondents. The findings showed little significant variations, and here the middle period of 1995–1996 is used to illustrate the findings.

38.  Albert O. Hirschman, *Exit, Voice and Loyalty; Responses to Decline in Firms, Organizations and States* (Cambridge, MA: Harvard University Press, 1970).

39.  USIA Opinion Polls, 1995–1999.

40.  See, Joma Nazpary, *Post-Soviet Chaos: Violence and Dispossession in Kazakhstan* (London: Pluto Press, 2001).

41.  Note also that *taipa* refers more strictly to clan only. Ru is more akin to taipa than to tribe more generally.

42.  Krader, *Social Organization of the Mongol-Turkic Pastoral Nomads*.

43.  See the excellent article by Talgat Ismagambetov, 'Geneaologicheskoe Rodtsvo i Etnicheskaia Konsolidatsiia: Opyt Proshlogo', *Megapolis*, No. 8 (2002).The total number of yurts was determined by factors such as geography and the number of animals e.g. wide, flat spaces permitted larger settlements than narrow, uneven ones.

44.  Bacon, *Central Asians Under Russian Rule*, p. 36.

45.  Ismagambetov, 'Geneaologicheskoe Rodtsvo'. See also Nurbulat Masanov, *Kochevaia Tsivilizatsiia*, pp. 138, 141.

46.  Note that up to four generations back could also be living in one aul, minimalnaya obshchina.

47.  Ismagambetov, 'Geneaologicheskoe Rodtsvo', 2002.

48.  Meyer Fortes, 'The Structure of Unilineal Descent Groups', *American Anthropologist*, No. 55 (1953), p. 25.

49.  Ismagambetov, 'Geneaologicheskoe Rodtsvo', 2002.

50.  Bacon, *Central Asians Under Russian Rule*, p. 136.

51.  Bacon, *Central Asians Under Russian Rule*, p. 234.

52.  Olivier Roy, *The New Central Asia: The Creation of Nations* (London and New York: I.B.Tauris, 2000), p. 85.

53.  See Ismagambetov, 'Razvitie Kazakhskogo Isteblishmenta', pp. 7–22.

54.  Zamanbek Nurkadilov, *Ne Tol'ko O Sebe* (Almaty: Shartarap, 1996), p. 11.

## Conclusion

1.   David Lane, 'Ethnic and Class Stratification in Soviet Kazakhstan, 1917–1939', *Comparative Studies in Society and History*, Vol. 17, No. 2 (1975), pp. 165–89.

2.   Fred I. Greenstein, *Personality and Politics* (Chicago: Markham, 1969).

3.   C. Wright Mills, *The Power Elite* (Oxford: Oxford University Press, 1956), pp. 279–80.

4.   Ezra Suleiman, *Politics, Power, and Bureaucracy in France: The Administrative Elite* (Princeton, NJ: Princeton University Press, 1974).

5.   Allen H. Barton, 'Determinants of Leadership Attitudes in a Socialist Society,' in Allen H. Barton et al. (eds.), *Opinion Making Elites in Yugoslavia*, (New York: Praeger, 1973), p. 242.

6.   Putnam, *The Comparative Study of Political Elites*, p. 97.

7.   John Higley and Gyorgy Lengyel, *Elites after State Socialism: Theories and Analysis* (Boston Way, Maryland: Rowman and Littlefield, 2000), p. 2.

8.   Suzanne Infeld Keller, *Beyond the Ruling Class: Strategic Elites in Modern Society*, (Transaction Publishers, 1963, reprinted 1991).

9.   Higley and Lengyel, *Elites after State Socialism*, p. 2.

10. On elite consensus and conflict, see Samuel J. Elderveld, Jan Kooiman and Theo van der Tak, *Elite Images of Dutch Politics: Accommodation and Conflict* (Ann Arbor, MI: The University of Michigan Press, 1983).

11. John Higley, Jan Pakulski and Wlodzimierz Wesolowksi (eds.), *Postcommunist Elites and Democracy in Eastern Europe* (Basingstoke: Macmillan Press, 1998), especially Chapter One.

12. The fourth logically possible elite type – unified and permeable – is considered empirically unlikely by Beck and Malloy.

13. William A. Welsh, 'Introduction: The Comparative Study of Political Leadership in Communist Systems', in Carl Beck et al., *Comparative Communist Political Leadership* (New York: David McKay Company, Inc, 1973), p. 33.

14. Welsh, 'Introduction', p. 33.

15. Informal evidence given by my chosen 'panel of experts', July 1996.

16. Sabit Zhusupov, 'Politicheskaia Elita Kazakhstana: mekhanizmy konsolidatsii i rekrutirovaniia', paper presented at the Carnegie Foundation, Moscow, Spring 1998, p. 5.

17. Seligman, *Recruiting Political Elites*, pp. 9–12.

18. Seligman, *Recruiting Political Elites*.

19. See Jones Luong, *Institutional Change and Political Continuity in Post-Soviet Central Asia*.

20. See Cummings, *Centre-Periphery Relations* (Brookings Institution and Royal Institute of International Affairs, 2000).

21. Frederic J. Fleron, Jr., 'Representation of Career Types in Soviet Political Leadership', in R. Barry Farrell (ed.), *Political Leadership in Eastern Europe and the Soviet Union* (Chicago: Aldine Publishing Co., 1970), pp. 108–39.

22. Barbara Geddes, *Politicians' Dilemma* (Berkeley CA: University of California Press, 1994), p. 46.

23. Henri Comte de Saint Simon, *Selected Writings*, ed. F. M. H. Markham (Oxford: Basil Blackwell, 1952); James Burnham, *The Managerial Revolution* (New York: John Day, 1941); Daniel Bell, *The Coming of Post-Industrial Society: A Venture in Social Forecasting* (New York: Basic Books, 1973); John Kenneth Galbraith, *The New Industrial State* (Harmondsworth: Penguin Books, first published 1967).

24. Fred W. Riggs, *Administration in Developing Countries* (Boston: Houghton Mifflin, 1964).

25. On this, see Neil Melvin, *Russians Beyond Russia* (London: Pinter 1995).

26. Edward A. D. Schatz, 'The Politics of Multiple Identities: Lineage and Ethnicity in Kazakhstan', *Europe-Asia Studies*, Vol. 52, No. 3 (2000), pp. 489–506.

# BIBLIOGRAPHY

## Pre-Soviet and General Central Asian History

Adshead, S.A.M., *Central Asia in World History* (Basingstoke: Macmillan, 1993).

Allworth, Edward (ed.), *Central Asia: 130 Years of Russian Dominance: A Historical Overview* (Durham, NC: Duke University Press, 1994).

Atkinson, Thomas Witlam, *Oriental and Western Siberia: A Narrative of Seven Years' Explorations and Adventures in Siberia, Mongolia, the Kirghis Steppes, Chinese Tartary, and Part of Central Asia* (London: Hurst and Blackett, 1858).

Auezov, Mukhtar, *Abai*, 2 Vols (Alma-Ata, 1980).

Bacon, Elizabeth E., *Obok: A Study of Social Structure in Eurasia* (New York: Wenner-Gren Foundation for Anthropological Research, Inc, 1958).

Bacon, Elizabeth E., *Central Asians under Russian Rule: A Study in Culture Change* (Ithaca, NY: Cornell University Press, 1966).

Bartold, V. V. 1869–1930, *Four Studies on the History of Central Asia* (Four Volumes, E.J. Brill, 1958–1962) .

Becker, Seymour *Russia's Protectorates in Central Asia: Bukhara and Khiva,1865–1924* (Cambridge, MA: Harvard University Press, 1968).

Bonvalot, Gabriel 1853–1933, *En Asie centrale: de Moscou en Bactriane* (Paris: E. Plon, Nourrit, 1884).

Bruce, Clarence Dalrymple, *In the footsteps of Marco Polo: Being the Account of a Journey Overland from Simla to Pekin* (Ch'eng Wen, 1971).

DeWeese, Devin A., *Islamization and Native religion in the Golden Horde: Baba Tukles and Conversion to Islam in Historical and Epic Tradition* (Pittsburg: Pennsylvania State University Press, 1994).

Franz, H.G., *Kunst und Kultur entlang der Seidenstrasse* (Akademische Druck-u. Verlagsanstalt, 1987).

Geyer, Dietrich, *Russian Imperialism: The Interaction of Domestic and Foreign Policy, 1860–1914* (Leamington Spa: Berg, 1987).

Grodekov, N.I., *Kirgizy i Karakirgiz Syr-Dar'inskoi oblasti* (Taskhent, 1889).

Gumilev, L. N., *Searches for an Imaginary Kingdom: The Legend of the Kingdom of Prester John* (Cambridge: Cambridge University Press, 1987).

Hedin, Sven 1865–1952 *Die geographisch-wissenschaftlichen ergebnisse meiner reisen in Zentralasien, 1894–1897* (J. Perthes, 1900).

Holdsworth, Mary, *Turkestan in the Nineteenth Century: A Brief History of the Khanates of Bukhara, Kokand and Khiva* (Oxford: St. Antony's College Soviet Affairs Study Group, 1959).

Hopkirk, Peter, *The Great Game: On Secret Service in High Asia* (Oxford: OUP Paperbacks, 1990).

Hopkirk, Peter, *Setting the East Ablaze: Lenin's Dream of an Empire in Asia* (Oxford: Oxford University Press, 1986).

Khazanov, Anatoly M., *Nomads and the Outside World* (Madison, WI: The University of Wisconsin Press, 1973).

Krader, Lawrence, *Social Organization of the Mongol–Turkic Pastoral Nomads*, Indiana University Publications, Uralic and Altaic Series, Vol. 20 (The Hague: Mouton & Co, 1963).

Krivtsov S.S. (ed.), *Kazakhstan i Kirgiziia* (Moscow: Moskovskoi Oblastnoe Otdelenie Gosizdat RSFSR, 1930).

Lattimore, Owen, *Inner Asian frontiers of China* (Oxford: Oxford University Press, 1940).

Levshin, Alexis, *Description des hordes et des steppes des Kirghiz–Kazaks ou Kirghiz–Kaisaks*, trans. Ferry de Pigny (Paris: Imprimerie Royale, 1840).

Maclean, Fitzroy, *A Person from England and other travellers [to Turkestan]* (London: J. Cape, 1958).

Marvin, Charles Thomas, *The Russians at Merv and Herat, and their Power of Invading India* (W.H. Allen & Co., 1883).

Pahlen, Konstantin Konstantinovich, *Count Mission to Turkestan: Being the Memoirs of Count K.K. Pahlen, 1908–1909* (Oxford: Oxford University Press, 1964).

Park, Alexander Garland, *Bolshevism in Turkestan, 1917–1927* (New York: Columbia University Press, 1957).

Pierce, Richard A., *Russian Central Asia, 1867–1917: A Study in Colonial Rule* (Berkeley: University of California Press, 1960).

Schuyler, Eugene, *1840–1890 Turkistan: Notes of a Journey in Russian Turkistan, Khokand, Bukhara, and Kuldja* (Sampson Low, Marston, Searle, & Rivington, 1877).

Sinor, Denis, *Cambridge History of Early Inner Asia* (Cambridge: Cambridge University Press, 1990).

Sokol, Edward Dennis, *The Revolt of 1916 in Russian Central Asia* (Baltimore: Johns Hopkins University Press, 1954).

Tolybekov, S.E., *Obshchestvenno-ekonomicheskii stroi Kazakhov v XVII-XIX vv* (Alma-Ata: AN Kaz SSR, 1959).

Valikhanov, Chokan, *Izbrannye proizvedeniia* (Almaty: Nauka,1986).

## Central Asia in the Soviet period

Akiner, Shirin, *Islamic Peoples of the Soviet Union (with an Appendix on the non-Muslim Turkic peoples of the Soviet Union): An Historical and Statistical Handbook* (London: KPI, 1986).

Akiner, Shirin (ed.), *Cultural Change and Continuity in Central Asia* (London, and New York: Kegan Paul International, 1991).

Allworth, Edward (ed.), *Soviet Nationality Problems* (New York: Columbia University Press, 1971).

Aslund, Anders, *Gorbachev's Struggle for Economic Reform* (London: Pinter, 1991).

Balzer, Marjorie Mandelstam, *Shamanism: Soviet Studies of Traditional Religion in Siberia and Central Asia* (Armonk, NY: M.E. Sharpe, 1990).

Barfield, Thomas J., *The Central Asian Arabs: Pastoral Nomadism in Transition* (Austin: University of Texas Press, 1980).

Bennigsen, Alexandre and Lemercier-Quelquejay, Chantal, *Islam in the Soviet Union* (London: Pall Mall Press, 1967).

Bennigsen, Alexandre and Wimbush, S. Enders, *Muslims of the Soviet Empire: A Guide* (Bloomington, IN: Indiana University Press, 1986).

Buckley, Mary, *Redefining Russian Society and Polity* (Boulder: Westview Press, 1993).

Caroe, Sir Olaf Kirkpatrick, *Soviet Empire: The Turks of Central Asia and Stalinism* (London: Macmillan, 1953).

Carrere d'Encausse Helene, *The End of the Soviet Empire: The Triumph of the Nations* (New York: Basic Books, 1993).

Castagne, Joseph, *Le Bolchevisme et l'Islam* (Paris: E. Leroux, 1922).

Coates, William, *Soviets in Central Asia* (London: Lawrence & Wishart, 1951).

Edmondson, Linda, *Women and Society in Russia and the Soviet Union* (Cambridge: Cambridge University Press, 1992).

Fierman, William, *Soviet Central Asia: The Failed Transformation* (Boulder: Westview Press, 1991).

Hambly, Gavin, et al., *Central Asia* (London: Weidenfeld and Nicolson, 1969)

Rakowska-Harmstone, Teresa, 'Soviet Legacies', *Central Asia Monitor*, Vol. 3, 1994, pp. 23–34.

Hauner, Milan and Canfield, Robert L., *Afghanistan and the Soviet Union: Collision and Transformation* (Boulder: Westview Press, 1989).

Hauner, Milan, *What Is Asia to Us?* (London and New York: Routledge, 1992).

Hill, Ronald J., *The Soviet Union: Politics, Economics and Society*. 2nd edn (London: Pinter Publishers Ltd, 1989).

Hosking, Geoffrey, *A History of the Soviet Union* (London: Fontana Press, 1992).

Hosking, Geoffrey, Aves, Jonathan and Duncan, Peter J. S., *The Road to Post-Communism: Independent Political Movements in the Soviet Union, 1985–1991* (London and New York: Pinter Publishers, 1992).

Irons, William, *The Yomut Turkmen: A Study of Social Organization among a Central Asian Turkic Speaking Population*, University of Michigan Museum of Anthopology Papers, No. 58 (Ann Arbor, MI: University of Michigan, 1975).

Lewis, Robert A., *Geographic Perspectives on Soviet Central Asia* (London & New York: Routledge, 1992).

Lubin, Nancy, *Labour and Nationality in Soviet Central Asia: An Uneasy Compromise* (London: Macmillan in association with St. Antony's College, 1984).

Massell, Gregory J., *The Surrogate Proletariat: Moslem Women and Revolutionary Strategies in Soviet Central Asia, 1919–1929* (Princeton: Princeton University Press, 1974).

Nove, Alec, *An Economic History of the U.S.S.R.* (Harmondsworth: Penguin, 1972).

Pipes, Richard, *The Formation of the Soviet Union: Communism and Nationalism, 1917–1923* (Cambridge, MA: Harvard University Press, 1964).

Ro'i, Yaacov (ed.), *Muslim Eurasia: Conflicting Legacies* (London: Frank Cass, 1995).

Rumer, Boris Z., *Soviet Central Asia: 'A Tragic Experiment'* (London: Unwin Hyman, 1989).

Rywkin Michael, *Moscow's Muslim Challenge: Soviet Central Asia* (Armonk, NY: ME Sharpe, 1990).

Sakwa, Richard, *Soviet Politics: An Introduction* (London and New York: Routledge, 1989).

Shahrani, M. Nazif Mohib, *The Kirghiz and Wakhi of Afghanistan* (Seattle: University of Washington Press, 1980).

Shalinksy, Audrey, 'Central Asian Emigres in Afghanistan: Social Dynamics of Identity Creation' (Ph.D. diss., Harvard University, 1979).

Slobin, Mark, *Music in the Culture of Northern Afghanistan* (Tucson: University of Arizona Press, 1976).

Skosyrev, Petr Georgievich, *Turkmenistan* ( Molodaia gvardiia, 1955).

Tolstova, S.P., *Arkheologicheskie i etnograficheskie raboty Khorezmskoi ekspeditsii, 1945–1948* (Izd-vo Akademii nauk SSSR, 1952).

Tuzmukhamedov, Rais Abdulkhakovich, *How the National Question Was Solved in Soviet Central Asia (A Reply to Falsifiers)* (Moscow: Progress Publishers, 1973).

Wheeler, Geoffrey, *The Modern History of Soviet Central Asia* (London: Weidenfeld and Nicolson, 1964).

Wheeler, Geoffrey, *Racial Problems in Soviet Muslim Asia* (Oxford University Press, 1962).

White, Stephen and Nelson, Daniel (eds.), *Communist Politics: A Reader* (London: Macmillan, 1986).

White, Stephen, *Gorbachev and After* (Cambridge: Cambridge University Press, 1991).

## General Post-Soviet Central Asia

Akbarzadeh, Shaharam, 'Nation-building in Uzbekistan', *Central Asian Survey*, Vol. 15, No. 1, March 1996, pp. 23–32.

Akbarzadeh, Shahram, 'The Political Shape of Central Asia', *Central Asian Survey*, Vol. 16, No. 4, December 1997, pp. 517–42.

Akiner, Shirin, *Central Asia: Conflict or Stability and Development?* (London: Minority Rights Group, 1997).

Akiner, Shirin, Tideman, Sander and Hay, Jon (eds.), *Sustainable Development in Central Asia* (London: Curzon Press, 1998).

Anderson, John, *The International Politics of Central Asia* (Manchester: Manchester University Press 1997).

Anderson, John, 'Constitutional Development in Central Asia', *Central Asian Survey*, Vol. 16, No. 3, September 1997, pp. 301–320.

Bezanis, Lowell and Elizabeth Fuller, 'There Is Only One Way Out – by Getting Rid of This Leader and This Government', *Transition*, 17 May 1996, pp. 34–38.

Bezanis, Lowell, 'More Echoes of the Past in Turkmenistan', *Transition*, 7 February 1997, pp. 92–93.

Bremmer Ian and Taras, Ray (eds.), *New States, New Politics: Building the Post-Soviet Nations* (2nd Edition, Cambridge: Cambridge University Press, 1997).

Brown, Bess, 'Central Asia: The First Year of Unexpected Statehood', *RFE/RL Resarch Report*, Vol. 2, No. 1 January 1993, pp. 25–40.

Brown, Bess, 'Central Asia', *RFE/RL Research Report*, Vol. 3, No. 13, 1 April 1994, pp. 14–16.

Büyükakinci, Erhan, 'Le processus constitutionnel et la restructuration institutionnelle dans les républiques turcophones de l'ex-URSS: l'Azerbaidjan, le Kazakhstan et L'Ouzbékistan', *Central Asian Survey*, Vol. 18, No. 1, March 1999, pp. 79–98.

Buckley, Mary (ed.), *Post-Soviet Women: From the Baltic to Central Asia* (Cambridge: Cambridge University Press, 1997).

Dawisha, Karen and Parrott, Bruce, *Russia and the New States of Eurasia* (Cambridge: Cambridge University Press, 1994).

Dawisha, Karen and Bruce Parrott (eds.), *Conflict, Cleavage, and Change in Central Asia and the Caucasus* (Cambridge: Cambridge University Press, 1997).

Gleason, Gregory, *The Central Asian States: Discovering Independence* (Boulder: Westview Press, 1997).

Haghayeghi, Mehrdad, *Islam and Politics in Central Asia* (New York: St Martin's Press, 1996).

Hanks, Reuel, 'The Islamic Factor in Nationalism and Nation-Building in Uzbekistan: Causative Agent or Inhibitor', *Nationalities Papers*, 22:2, Fall 1994, pp. 309–324.

Hunter, Shireen, *Central Asia since Independence* (New York: Praeger Publishers, 1996).

Hyman, Anthony, 'Post-Soviet Central Asia', in Roy Allison (ed.) *Challenges for the Former Soviet South* (London: RIIA, 1996).

Kappeler, Andreas, Simon, Gerhard and Brunner, Georg (eds.), *Muslim Communities Reemerge: Historical Perspectives on Nationality, Politics, and Opposition in the Former Soviet Union and Yugoslavia* (Durham, NC: Duke University Press, 1994).

Kirimli, Meryem, 'Uzbekistan in the New World Order', *Central Asian Survey*, Vol. 16, No. 1, March 1997, pp. 53–64.

Kulchik, Yuriy, Andrey Fadin & Viktor Sergeev, *Central Asia after the Empire* (London: Pluto Press, 1996).

Naumkin, Vitaly V. (ed.) *State, Religion and Society in Central Asia: A Post-Soviet Critique* (London: Ithaca Press, 1993).

Olcott, Martha Brill, *Central Asia's New States: Independence, Foreign Policy, and Regional Security* (Washington, DC: United States Institute of Peace Press, 1996).

Paksoy, H.B. (ed.), *Central Asian Reader* (Armonk, NY: M.E. Sharpe, 1994).

Panico, Christopher J., 'Turkmenistan: Unaffected by Winds of Democratic Change', *RFE/RL Research Report*, Vol. 2, No. 4, 22 January 1993, p. 6–10.

Pannier, Bruce, 'In the Land of Manas', *Transition*, Vol. 2, No. 26, 27 December 1996, pp. 32–38.

Pannier, Bruce, 'Central Asia's Closely Watched Media', *Transition*, Vol. 2, No. 21, 18 October 1996, pp. 70–2.

Pannier, Bruce, 'President Acquries More Power in Kyrgyzstan', *Transition*, Vol. 3, No. 2, 7 February 1997), pp. 94–5.

Poliakov, Sergei P. and Olcott, Martha Brill (eds.), *Everyday Islam: Religion and Tradition In Rural Central Asia* (Armonk, NY: ME Sharpe, 1995).

Polonskaya, Ludmila and Malashenko, Alexei, *Islam in Central Asia* (Ithaca Press, 1994).

Pryde, Ian, 'Kyrgyzstan's Slow Progress to Reform', *The World Today*, Vol. 51, No. 6, June 1995, pp. 115–18.

Rieff, David, 'From Khan to Tsar to Comrade to Khan', *Transitions*, Vol. 4, No. 1, June 1997, pp. 14–19.

Rumer, Boris and Zhukov, Stanislav, *Central Asia: The Challenges of Independence* (Armonk, NY and London: M.E. Sharpe, 1998).

Saltmarshe, Douglas 'Civil Society and Sustainable Development in Central Asia', *Central Asian Survey*, Vol. 15, No. 3/4, December 1996, pp. 387–398.

Shugart, Matthew Soberg, 'Executive-Legislative Relations in Post-Communist Europe', *Transition*, Vol. 2, No. 25, 13 December 1996.

Smith, Graham, Law, Vivien, Wilson, Andrew, Bohr, Annette, and Allworth, Edward *Nation-building in the Post-Soviet Borderlands: The Politics of National Identities* (Cambridge: Cambridge University Press, 1998).

Solomon, Peter, 'Against Premature Closure', *Post-Soviet Affairs*, Vol. 9, July–September 1993, pp. 278–290.

Treacher, Adrian, 'Political Evolution in Post-Soviet Central Asia', *Democratization*, Vol. 3, No. 3, Autumn 1996, pp. 306–327.

White, Stephen, Alex Pravda, and Gitelman, Zvi (eds.), *Developments in Russian and Post-Soviet Politics* (Durham, NC: Duke University Press, 1994).

White, Stephen, Gill, Graeme, and Slider, Darrell, *The Politics of Transition: Shaping a Post-Soviet Future* (Cambridge: Cambridge University Press, 1993).

## General Literature on Kazakhstan

Abazov, Rafis, *The Formation of Post-Soviet International Politics in Kazakhstan, Kyrgyzstan, and Uzbekistan* (The Henry M. Jackson School of International Studies, The University of Washington, No. 21, June 1999).

Asfendiarov, S.D., *Istoriia Kazakhstana (s drevneishikh vremen)* (Alma-Ata: Kazakhstanskoe Kraevoe Izd-vo, 1935).

Argynbaev, Kh. A., *Etnograficheskie Ocherki po Skotovodstvu Kazakhov* (Alma-Ata, Nauka, 1973).

Auezov, Mukhtar, *Abai*, 2 Vols (Alma-Ata, 1980).

Buckley, Cynthia, 'Suicide in Post-Soviet Kazakhstan: Role Stress, Age and Gender', *Central Asian Survey*, Vol. 16, No. 1, March 1997, pp. 45–52. I

Erofeeva, Irina V., 'Palaeolitskie Khany XVIII – Serediny XIXv', *Vostok*, No.3, 1997, pp. 5–32.

Erofeeva, Irina, 'Titul i Vlast: K Probleme Tipologii Instituta Khanskoi Vlasti v Kazakhstane V XVII Nachale XIX VV', *Saiasat* (Alamty, 1997), pp. 37–46.

Erofeeva, Irina, 'Kharakter, Sostav i Struktura Pravyashchei Elity Kochevogo Kazakhskogo Obshchestva' (unpublished manuscript, 1999).

Hudson, Alfred E., *Kazakh Social Structure* (New Haven, CT: Yale University Publications in Anthropology, Number 20, Yale University Press, 1938).

Ismagambetov, Talgat, 'Razvitie Kazakhskogo Isteblishmenta V Kontse XIX – Seredine XX Vekov', *Tsentral'naya Aziya*, No. 5, 11, 1997, pp. 7–22.

Januzakova, F., *Kazakhskie Narodnye Skazki* (Alma-Ata: Zazushy, 1982).

Kazymzhanov, Agyn Khairullovich and Tribble, Keith Owen, 'The Political Tradition of the Steppe', *Nationalities Papers*, Vol. 26, No. 3, September 1998, pp. 453–72.

Krivtsov, S.S. (ed.), *Kazakhstan i Kirgiziia* (Moscow: Moskovskoi Oblastnoe Otdelenie Gosizdat RSFSR, 1930).

*Kto Est' Kto v Respublike Kazakhstan* (Almaty: Evraziya-Polis, 1995).

Kunaev, Dinmukhamed, *O Moem Vremeni* (Alma-Ata: Deyir, 1992).

Kunaev, Dinmukhamed A., *Izbrannye Rechi i Stat'i* (Moscow: Politizdat, 1978).

Levshin, Alexis, *Description des hordes et des steppes des Kirghiz-Kazaks ou Kirghiz-Kaisaks*, trans. Ferry de Pigny (Paris: Imprimerie Royale, 1840).

Markov, G.E., *Kochevnichestvo: Istoricheskaia Entsiklopediia* (Sovetskaya Entsiklopedyia, 1965).

Masanov, Nurbulat, *Kochevaya Tsivilizatsiya Kazakhov* (Moscow: Gorizont, 1995).

Olcott, Martha Brill, *The Kazakhs*. 2nd edn (Stanford, CA: Hoover Institution Press, 1995).

Otarbaeva, Bakhytnur, 'A Brief History of the Kazak People', *Nationalities Papers*, Vol. 26, No. 3, September 1998, pp. 421–32.

Suleimenov, Olzhas, *Az-i-ya* (Alma-Ata: Zhalyn, 1990).

Winner, Thomas G., *The Oral Art and Literature of the Kazakhs of Russian Central Asia* (Durham, NC: Duke University Press, 1958).

## Post-Independence Kazakhstan Politics

Abdil'din, Serikbolsyn, *Parlament Kazakhstana: Ot Soiuza k Gosudarstvennosti* (Almaty: Kazakhstan, 1993).

Altoma, Reef, *Deputies Elected to the Supreme Soviet of the Republic of Kazakhstan on 7 March 1994*, American Legal Consortium under USAID's Rule of Law Program, Chemonics International (Almaty, 31 March 1994) and *The 13ᵗʰ Convention of the Supreme Soviet of the Republic Kazakhstan: Spring Session Results*, American Legal Consortium under USAID's Rule of Law Program, Chemonics International (Almaty, 1 August 1994).

Amrekulov, Nurlan and Masanov, Nurbulat, *Kazakhstan: Mezhdu Proshlym i Budushchim* (Almaty: 1994).

Bremmer, Ian and Welt, Cory, 'The Trouble with Democracy in Kazakhstan', *Central Asian Survey*, Vol. 15, No. 2, June 1996, pp. 179–200.

Cummings, Sally N. (ed.), *Oil, Transition and Security in Central Asia* (London and New York: RoutledgeCurzon, 2003), pp. 143–160.

Cummings, Sally N. (ed.), *Power and Change in Central Asia* (London and New York: Routledge, 2002).

Cummings, Sally N., *Kazakhstan: Centre-Periphery Relations* (London and New York: Royal Institue of International Affairs and Brookings Institution, 2000).

Cummings, Sally N., 'Kazakhstan's Parliamentary Elections and After', Former Soviet South Briefing Paper No. 5 (London: Royal Institute of International Affairs, February 1996).

Cummings, Sally N., 'Politics in Kazakhstan: The Constitutional Crisis of March 1995', Former Soviet South Briefing Paper No. 3 (London: Royal Institute of International Affairs, August 1995).

Dave, Bhavna, 'Opposition finds a Voice in Kazakhstan', *Transition*, Vol. 3, No. 2, 7 February 1997, pp. 88–89.

De Cordier, Bruno 'Conflits ethniques et degradation ecologique en Asie centrale, La vallee de Ferghana et le nord du Kazakhstan', *Central Asian Survey*, Vol. 15, No. 4, December 1996, pp. 399–412.

Dzhunusova, Zh. Kh., *Respublika Kazakhstan: Prezident Instituty Demokratii* (Almaty: Jěty Jargy, 1996).

Gati, Charles, 'The Mirage of Democracy', *Transition*, 2:6, 22 March 1996, pp. 6–12.

Gleason, Gregory, 'Kazakhstan's Post-Transition Government', *Analysis of Current Events*, Vol. 9, No. 11, November 1997, pp. 5 and 9.

Jones Luong, Pauline, *Institutional Change and Political Continuity in Post-Soviet Central Asia: Power, Perceptions, and Pacts* (Cambridge: Cambridge University Press, 2002).

Karishap Asan Ata, *Prizrak Nezavisimosti* (Moscow: Academia, 1995).

Khliupin, V.N., *Bol'shaia sem'ia Nursultan Nazarbaeva* (Moscow: Institute of Contemporary Political Research, 1998).

Michnik, Adam, 'Sparring With the Kazak President', *Transition*, Vol. 4, No. 1, June 1997, pp. 26–30.

Nazarbaev, Nursultan, *Without Right & Left* (London: Class Publishing, 1993).

Nourzhanov, Kirill and Amin Saikal, 'The New Kazakhstan: Has Something Gone Wrong?', *The World Today*, Vol. 50, No. 12, December 1994, pp. 225–228.

Nurkadilov, Zamanbek, *Ne Tol'ko O Sebe* (Almaty: Shartarap, 1996).

Olcott, Martha Brill, 'Democratization and the Growth of Political Participation in Kazakstan', in Karen Dawisha and Bruce Parrott (eds.), *Conflict, Cleavage and Change in Central Asia and the Caucasus* (Cambridge: Cambridge University Press, 1997).

*Qazaqstan Respublikasynyn konstitutsiiasy* (Almaty: Edilet, 1993).

Satpaev, D. A., *Lobbizm: Tainye Rygachi Vlasti* (Almaty: 1999).

Tokaev, Kasymzhomart, *Pod Stiagom Nezavisimosti: Ocherki o Vneshnei Politike Kazakhstana* (Almaty: Bilim, 1997).

Warner, Tom, 'Kazakstan's Curious Choice for a Capital', *Transition*, Vol. 2, No. 24, 29 November 1996, pp. 60–1.

Zhigalov K.B. and Sultanov, B.K., *Pervyi Prezident Respubliki Kazakhstan: Nursultan Nazarbaev: Khronika Deiatel'nosti (1.12.1991–31.5.1993)* (Almaty, Kazakhstan XXI Vek, 1993).

# Ethnicity, Language and Tribalism

Aitkhozhin, N.A., 'Problemy vnedreniia Latinitsy v kazakhskii alfabit', *Saiasat*, Vol. 9, October 1997, pp. 24–29.

Akiner, Shirin, *The Formation of Kazakh Identity: From Tribe to Nation-State* (London: The Royal Institute of International Affairs, 1995).

Arynova, R.S., 'Kulturno-Lingvisticheskaia Situatsiia V Respublike Kazakhstan: Tendentsii Razvitiya', *Saiasat*, September 1997, pp. 32–41.

Cummings, Sally N. 'The Kazakhs: Demographics, Diasporas, and 'Return', in Charles King and Neil J. Melvin (eds.), *Nations Abroad: Diaspora Politics and International Relations in the Former Soviet Union* (Boulder: Westview Press, 1998), pp. 133–52.

Dave, Bhavna, 'Kazaks Struggle to Revive their "Language of Folklore"', *Transition*, Vol. 2, No. 24, 29 November 1996, pp. 23–25.

Dave, Bhavna, 'National Revival in Kazakhstan: Language Shift and Identity Change', *Post-Soviet Affairs*, Vol. 12, No. 1, 1996, pp. 51–72.

Edmunds, Timothy, 'Power and Powerlessness in Kazakhstani Society: Ethnic Problems in Perspective', *Central Asian Survey*, Vol. 17, No. 3, September 1998, pp. 463–470.

Esenova, Saulesh, 'The Outflow of Minorities from the Post-Soviet State: The Case of Kazakhstan', *Nationalities Papers*, Vol. 24, No. 4, December 1996, pp. 691–708.

Esenova, Saulesh, '"Tribalism" and Identity in Contemporary Circumstances: The Case of Kazakhstan', *Central Asian Survey*, Vol. 17, No. 3, September 1998, pp. 443–462.

Fierman, William, 'Problems of Language Law Implementation in Uzbekistan', *Nationalities Papers*, Vol. 23, No. 3, September 1995, pp. 573–596.

Fierman, William, 'Language and Identity in Kazakhstan: Formulations in policy documents 1987–1997, *Communist and Post-Communist Studies*, Vol. 31, No. 2, June 1998, pp. 171–86.

Gross, Jo-Ann (ed.), *Muslims in Central Asia: Expressions of Identity and Change* (Durham, NC: Duke University Press, 1992).

Huskey, Eugene, 'The Politics of Language in Kyrgyzstan', *Nationalities Papers*, Vol. 23, No. 3, September 1995, pp. 549–572.

Institute of Development of Kazakhstan, *Kazakh Tribalism today, its characteristics and possible solutions* (Almaty: IDK, 1996).

Ismagambetov, Talgat, 'Geneaologicheskoe Rodtsvo i Etnicheskaia Konsolidatsiia: Opyt Proshlogo,' *Megapolis*, No. 8, 2002.

Jiger, Janabel, 'When National Ambition Conflicts with Reality: Studies on Kazakhstan's Ethnic Relations', *Central Asian Survey*, Vol. 15, No. 1, March 1996, pp. 5–22.

Kendirbaeva, Gulnar, 'Migrations in Kazakhstan: Past and Present', *Nationalities Papers*, Vol. 25, No. 4, December 1997, pp. 741–52.

Kendirbaeva, Gulnar, '"We are children of Alash…" The Kazakh Intelligentsia at the Beginning of the 20th Century in Search of National Identity and Prospects of Cultural Survival of the Kazakh People', *Central Asian Survey*, Vol. 18, No. 1, March 1999), pp. 5–36.

Kolsto, Paul, 'Is Kazakhstan being Kazakhified?', *Analysis of Current Events*, Vol. 9, No. 11, November 1997, pp. 1, 3–4.

Kolsto, Paul, 'Anticipating Demographic Superiority: Kazakh Thinking on Integration and Nation Building', *Europe-Asia Studies*, Vol. 50, No. 1, 1998, pp. 51–69.

Lane, David, 'Ethnic and Class Stratification in Soviet Kazakhstan 1917–39', *Comparative Studies in Society and History*, Vol. 17, No. 2, 1975, pp. 165–189.

Masanov, Nurbulat, Erlan Karin, Andrei Chebotarev and Natsuko Oka, *The Nationalities Question in Post-Soviet Kazakhstan* (Tokyo: Institute of Developing Economies, Jetro, 2002).

Mashanov, M.S. and Arynova, R.S., 'Kul'turno-lingvisticheskaia situatsiia v Respublike Kazakhstan', *Saiasat*, Vol. 8, September 1997, pp. 32–4.

Mukanov, M.S., *Etnicheskaia Territoriia Kazakhov v XVIII – Nachale XX Vekov* (Alma-Ata: Kazakhstan, 1991).

Nazpary, Joma, *Post-Soviet Chaos: Violence and Dispossession in Kazakhstan* (London: Pluto Press, 2001).

Schatz, Edward, 'Framing Strategies and Non-Conflict in Multi-Ethnic Kazakhstan', *Nationalism and Ethnic Politics*, Vol. 6, No. 2, Summer 2000, pp. 70–92.

Schatz, Edward, 'The politics of multiple identities: Lineage and ethnicity in Kazakhstan', *Europe-Asia Studies*, Vol. 52, No. 3, 2000, pp. 489–506.

Schöpflin, George 'Aspects of Language and Ethnicity in Central and Eastern Europe', *Transition*, 29 November 1996, pp. 6–9.

Tankieva, N. Sh., 'Ob izmeneniiakh v obshchestvenno-politicheskoi terminologii kazakhskogo iazyka i nekotorykh printsipakh terminoobrazovaniia', *Saiasat*, Vol. 8, September 1997, pp. 43–51.

Tsentr monitoringa mezhetnicheskikh otnoshenii v Kazakhstane, *Etnopoliticheskii monitoring v Kazakhstane* (Three Volumes) (Almaty: Arkor, 1996).

Tynyshpaev, M., *Materialy k Istorii Kirgiz-Kazakhskogo Naroda* (Tashkent, 1925).

'Zakon Respubliki Kazakhstan. O iazykakh v Respublike Kazakhstan,' *Mysl'*, Vol. 9, 1997, pp. 2–7.

# Economic Reform

Andor, Laszlo and Summers, Martin, *Market Failure: A Guide to the East European 'Economic Miracle'* (London: Pluto Press, 1998).

Brown, Bess, 'Central Asia: The Economic Crisis Deepens', *RFE/RL Research Report* Vol. 3, No. 1, 7 January 1994, pp. 59–69.

Carver, Jeremy P. and Greg Englefield, 'Oil and Gas Pipelines from Central Asia: A New Approach', *The World Today*, June 1994.

Dienes, Leslie and Shabad, Theodore, *The Soviet Energy System: Resource Use and Policies* (London: Wiley, 1979).

Dönmez-Colin, Gönül, 'Kazakh "New Wave": Post-perestroika, Post-Soviet Union', *Central Asian Survey*, Vol. 16, No. 1, March 1997, pp. 115–118.

Dorian, James P., Ian Sheffield Rosi and S. Hartono Indriyanto, *Central Asia's Oil and Gas Pipeline Network: Current and Future Flows* (Honolulu, USA: East West Center, 1994).

Dosmukhamedov, E.K., *Foreign Direct Investment in Kazakhstan: Politico-Legal Aspects of Post-Communist Transition* (Basingstoke: Palgrave Macmillan, 2002).

Ebel, Robert E., 'Central Asian Oil and Natural Gas', paper presented at the Business Council for International Understanding, Washington D.C., May 2–3, 1994.

Economist Intelligence Unit, *Country Report: Kazakhstan* (various years).

Forsythe, Rosemarie, *The Politics of Oil and The Caucasus and Central Asia* (London: International Institute for Strategic Studies, Adelphi Paper 300, 1996).

Grabher, Gernot and Stark, David (eds.), *Restructuring Networks in Post-socialism: Legacies Linkages, and Localities* (Oxford: Oxford University Press, 1997).

Haghayeghi, Mehrdad, 'Politics of Privatization in Kazakstan', *Central Asian Survey*, Vol. 16, No. 3, September 1997, pp. 321–338.

Howell, Jude, 'Poverty and Transition in Kyrgyzstan: How Some Households Cope', *Central Asian Survey*, Vol. 15, No. 1, March 1996, pp. 59–74.

Jeffries, Ian, *Socialist Economies and the Transition to the Market: A Guide* (London and New York: Routledge, 1993).

Jones Luong, Pauline, 'Energy and International Relations in Central Asia', *Analysis of Current Events*, Vol. 9, No. 11, November 1997, pp. 6–8.

Kaser, Michael, 'Economic Transition in Six Central Asian Economies', *Central Asian Survey*, Vol. 16, No. 1, March 1997, pp. 5–26.

Khan, Azizur Rahman and Ghai, Dharam, *Collective Agriculture and Rural Development in Soviet Central Asia* (London: Macmillan, 1979).

Lavigne, Marie, *The Economics of Transition: From Socialist Economy to Market Economy* (Basingstoke: Macmillan, 1995).

Lubin, Nancy, *Labour and Nationality in Soviet Central Asia: An Uneasy Compromise* (Basingstoke: Macmillan in association with St. Antony's College Oxford, 1984).

Maillet, Linda, 'New States Initiate New Currencies', *Transition*, 9 June 1995, pp. 44–49 & 56.

Mearns, Robin, *Commons and Collectives: The Lack of Social Capital in Central Asia's Land Reforms* (Brighton: Institute of Development Studies, 1996).

Mitrieva, Oksana Genrikhovna, *Regional Development: The USSR and After* (London: UCL Press, 1996).

Nove, Alec and Newth, J. A., *The Soviet Middle East: A Model for Development?* (London: Allen & Unwin, 1967).

Nove, Alec, *An Economic History of the U.S.S.R* (London: Penguin, 1972).

McDonell, John, 'The Euro-Asian Corridor: Freight and Energy Transport for Central Asia and the Caspian Region', paper presented to the Post-Soviet Business Forum, Royal Institute of International Affairs, London, 1995.

OECD, *Mass Privatisation: An Initial Assessment* (Paris: OECD, 1995).

Pannier, Bruce, 'Same Game, Second Round', *Transition*, Vol. 4, No. 1, June 1997, pp. 20–25.

Riches, Peter, 'Global Oil Demand and the Development of Kazakhstan's Oilfields and Transportation Routes', paprer presented at *Kazakhstan Oil and Gas Conference*, London, 29–30 April, 1998.

Roberts, John, *Caspian Pipelines* (London: The Royal Institute of International Affairs, 1996).

Rumer, Boris Z., *Central Asia in Transition: Dilemmas of Political and Economic Development* (Armonk, NY: M.E. Sharpe, 1996).

Rutland, Peter, 'Russia's Energy Empire Under Strain', *Transition*, Vol. 2, No. 9, 3 May 1996, pp. 6–11.

*The Oil and Gas Guide to the Former Soviet Union and Baltic States* (London: CIC Publishing, London, Winter 1995/6).

Turnock, David, *The East European Economy in Context Communism and Transition* (London and New York: Routledge, 1997).

Uibopuu, Henn-Juri, 'The Caspian Sea: A Tangle of Legal Problems', *The World Today*, Vol. 51, No. 6, June 1995, pp. 119–123.

White, Stephen, Alex Pravda, and Zvi Gitelman (eds.), *Developments in Russian and Post-Soviet Politics* (Durham, NC: Duke University Press, 1994).

Woo, Wing Thye, Parker, Stephen and Sachs, Jeffrey D., *Economies in Transition: Comparing Asia and Europe* (Cambridge, MA: MIT Press, 1997).

Wyzan, Michael, 'Increased Inequality, Poverty Accompany Economic Transition', *Transition*, Vol. 2, No. 20, 4 October 1996, pp. 24–27.

Wyzan, Michael, 'The Making of the Middle Classes', *Transition*, Vol. 3, No. 5, 21 March 1997, pp. 20–1.

## Central Asian Regional Relations

Ahrari, M.E. *The New Great Game in Muslim Central Asia*, Institute for National Strategic Studies, McNair Paper 47, January 1996.

Alici, Didem Mersin, 'The Role of Culture, History and Language in Turkish National Identity: An Overemphasis on Central Asian Roots', *Central Asian Survey*, Vol. 15, No. 2, June 1996, pp. 217–232.

Aydin, Mustafa, 'Turkey and Central Asia: Challenges of Change', *Central Asian Survey*, Vol. 15, No. 2, June 1996, pp. 157–178.

Allison, Roy and Bluth, Christoph (eds.), *Security dilemmas in Russia and Eurasia* (London: Royal Institute of International Affairs, 1998).

Banuazizi, Ali and Weiner, Myron (eds.), *The New Geopolitics of Central Asia and its Borderlands* (Boulder: Westview Press, 1994).

Bezanis, Lowell, 'China Strikes at Uighur "Splittists"', *Transition*, Vol. 2, No. 17, 23 August, 1996, pp. 34–5.

Crow, Suzanne 'Russia Promotes the CIS as an International Organization', *RFE/RL Research Report*, Vol. 3, No. 11, 18 March 1994, pp. 33–8.

Dannreuther, Roland, *Creating New States in Central Asia: The Strategic Implications of the Collapse of Soviet Power in Central Asia* (Adelphi Papers 288: 1994).

De Cordier, Bruno, 'The Economic Cooperation Organization: Towards a New Silk Road on the Ruins of the Cold War', *Central Asian Survey*, Vol. 15, No. 1, March 1996, pp. 47–58.

Dieter, Heribert, 'Regional Integration in Central Asia: Current Economic Position and Prospects', *Central Asian Survey*, Vol. 15, nos 3/4, December 1996, pp. 369–386

Dorian, James P., Brett Wigdortz & Dru Gladney, 'Central Asia and Xinjiang, China: Emerging Energy, Economic and Ethnic Relations', *Central Asian Survey*, Vol. 16, No. 4, December 1997, pp. 461–86.

Ehteshami, Anoushiravan, *From the Gulf to Central Asia: Players in the New Great Game* (Exeter: University of Exeter Press, 1994).

Ferdinand, Peter (ed.), *The New Central Asia and its Neighbours* (London: RIIA, 1994).

Fuller, Graham E., 'The Emergence of Central Asia', *Foreign Policy* (No. 78, Spring 1992), pp. 49–67.

Fuller, Elizabeth, 'The Tussle for Influence in Central Asia and the Transcaucasus', *Transition*, 14 June 1996, pp. 11–15.

Foltz, Richard, 'The Tajiks of Uzbekistan', *Central Asian Survey*, Vol. 15, No. 2, June 1996, pp. 213–216.

Gross, Jo-ann, *Muslims in Central Asia: Expressions of Identity and Change* (Duke University Press: 1992).

Hyman, Anthony, 'Moving out of Moscow's Orbit: The Outlook for Central Asia', *International Affairs*, Vol. 69, No. 2 1993, pp. 289–304.

Hyman, Anthony, 'Turkestan and pan-Turkism Revisted', *Central Asian Survey*, Vol. 16, No. 3, September 1997, pp. 339–352.

Kangas, Roger D., 'Taking the Lead in Central Asian Security', *Transition*, Vol. 2, No. 9, 3 May 1996, pp. 52–55.

Malik, Hafeez (ed.), *Central Asia: Its Strategic Importance and Future Prospects* (New York: St Martin's Press, 1994).

Martin, Keith, 'China and Central Asia: Between Seduction and Suspicion', *RFE/RL Research Report*, Vol. 3, No. 25, 24 June 1994.

Melet, Yasmin, 'China's Political and Economic Relations with Kazakhstan and Kyrgyzstan', *Central Asian Survey*, Vol. 17, No. 2, June 1998.

Menashri, David (ed.), *Central Asia Meets the Middle East* (London: Frank Cass, 1998).

Mesbahi, Mohiaddin, 'Tajikistan, Iran, and the International Politics of the "Islamic Factor"', *Central Asian Survey*, Vol. 16, No. 2, June 1997, pp. 141–158.

Naumkin, Vitaly V. (ed.), *State, Religion and Society in Central Asia: A Post-Soviet Critique* (London: Ithaca Press, 1993).

Olcott, Martha Brill, 'The Myth of "Tsentral'naia Aziia"', *Orbis*, Vol. 38, No. 4, Fall 1994), pp. 545–565.

Olcott, Martha Brill, 'Central Asia's Post–Empire Politics', *Orbis*, Vol. 36, No. 2, Spring 1992, pp. 253–268.

Pannier, Bruce, 'A Year of Violence in Tajikistan', *Transition*, Vol. 3, No. 2, 7 February 1997, pp. 96–7.

Pannier, Bruce, 'Bordering on Friendship', *Transition*, Vol. 4, No. 6, November 1997, pp. 66–69.

Puri, M.M., 'Central Asian Geopolitics: The Indian View', *Central Asian Survey*, Vol. 16, No. 2, June 1997, pp. 237–68.

Raczka, Witt, 'Xinjiang and its Central Asian Borderlands', *Central Asian Survey*, Vol. 17, No. 3, September 1998.

Rawlinson, Sir Henry Creswicke, *England and Russia in the East: A Series of Papers on the Political and Geographical Condition of Central Asia* (J. Murray, 1875).

Ro'i, Yaacov (ed.), *Muslim Eurasia: Conflicting Legacies* (London: Frank Cass, 1995).

Rossabi, Morris, *China and Inner Asia: From 1368 to the Present Day* (London: Thames and Hudson, 1975).

Rubin, Barnett R. and Snyder, Jack (eds.), *Post-Soviet Political Order: Conflict and State-Building* (London: Routledge, 1998).

Rubinstein, Alvin Z., 'The Geopolitical Pull on Russia', *Orbis*, Vol. 38, No. 4, Fall 1994, pp. 567–83.

Rudelson, 'The Uigurs in the Future of Central Asia', *Nationalities Papers*, Vol. 22, No. 2, Fall 1994, pp. 291–308.

Sadri, Houman A., 'Integration in Central Asia: From Theory to Policy', *Central Asian Survey*, Vol. 16, No. 4, December 1997, pp. 573–86.

Sagdeev, Roald and William E. Sanford, 'War, Peace, and Peacekeeping in Tajikistan', *Analysis of Current Events*, Vol. 10, nos 3–4, March/April 1998, pp. 6–7.

Shashenkov, Maxim, *Security Issues of the ex-Soviet Central Asian Republics* (London: Brassey's for the Centre for Defence Studies, No. 14, 1992).

Shirazi, H.A., 'Political Forces and their Structures in Tajikistan', *Central Asian Survey*, Vol. 16, No. 4, December 1997, pp. 611–22.

Tarock, Adam, 'Iran's Policy in Central Asia', *Central Asian Survey*, Vol. 16, No. 2, June 1997, pp. 185–200.

Wacker, Gudrun, 'China Builds Ties, Trade Across Its Western Border', *Transition*, Vol. 2, No. 17, 23 August 1996, pp. 30–33.

Winrow, Gareth, *Turkey in Post-Soviet Central Asia* (London: RIIA, 1995).

Whitlock, Erik, 'The CIS Economies: Divergent and Troubled', *RFE/RL Research Report*, Vol. 3, No. 1, 7 January 1994, pp. 1–12.

Whitlock, Erik, 'Obstacles to CIS Economic Integration', *RFE/RL Research Report*, Vol. 2, No. 27, 2 July 1993, pp. 34–38.

Wyzan, Michael, 'On the Move: Migration in the CIS', *Transition*, Vol. 5, No. 3, March 1998, pp. 14–15.

# Political Leadership in Communist Systems

Barton Allen H. *et al.*, *Opinion-Making Elites in Yugoslavia* (New York: Praeger, 1973).

Beck, Carl, Fleron, Frederic J., Jr., Lodge, Milton, Waller, Derek J., Welsh, William A. and Zaninovich, M. George, *Comparative Communist Political Leadership* (New York: David McKay Company, 1973).

Bialer, Seweryn, *Stalin's Successors: Leadership, Stability, and Change in the Soviet Union* (Cambridge: Cambridge University Press, 1980).

Brown, Archie (ed.), *Political Leadership in the Soviet Union* (Bloomington: Indian University Press, 1989).

Brown, Archie and Kaser, Michael (eds.), *Soviet Policy for the 1980s* (Basingstoke: Macmillan, 1982).

Fleron, Frederick, 'Notes on the Explication of the Concept "Elite" in Soviet Studies,' *Canadian Review of Slavic Studies*, Vol. II, No. 1, Spring, 1968.

Hahn, Jeffrey W., 'Local Politics and Local Power in Russia: The Case of Yaroslavl', *Soviet Economy*, Vol. 7, No. 4, October–December 1991.

Harasymiw, Bohdan, *Political Elite Recruitment in the Soviet Union* (Basingstoke: Macmillan).

Huskey, Eugene (ed.), *Executive Power and Soviet Politics: The Rise and Decline of the Soviet State* (Armonk, NY: M.E. Sharpe, 1992).

Klugman, Jeffrey, *The New Soviet Elite: How They Think and What They Want* (New York: Praeger, 1989).

Lane, David (ed.), *Elites and Political Power in the USSR* (Aldershot: Elgar, 1988).

Lane, David, 'Gorbachev's Political Elite in the Terminal Stage of the USSR: A Reputational Analysis', *Journal of Communist Studies and Transition Politics*, Vol. 10, No. 1, March 1994, pp. 104–16.

Lane, David, 'The Gorbachev Revolution: The Role of the Political Elite in Regime Disintegration', *Political Studies*, Vol. XLIV, No.1, March 1996, pp. 4–23.

Mawdsley, Evan, 'Portrait of a Changing Elite: CPSU Central Committee Full Members, 1939–1990', in Stephen White (ed.), *New Directions in Soviet History* (Cambridge: Cambridge University Press, 1991), pp. 191–206.

Matthews, Mervyn, *Privilege in the Soviet Union* (London: Allen & Unwin, 1978).

Mitchell, R. Judson, *Getting to the Top in the USSR: Cyclical Patterns in the Leadership Succession Process* Stanford: Hoover Institution Press, 1990).

Rigby, T.H., *Political Elites in the USSR: Central Leaders and Local Cadres form Lenin to Gorbachev* (Aldershot and Vermont: Edward Elgar, 1990).

Rigby, T.H., Brown, Archie, Brown, and Reddaway, Peter (eds.), *Authority, Power and Policy in the USSR* (London: Macmillan, 1980).

Voslensky, Michael, *Nomenklatura: Anatomy of the Soviet ruling class* (London: Bodley Head, 1984).

## Post-Communist Political Leadership

Baylis, Thomas A., 'Plus ça Change? Transformation and Continuity Amongst East European Elites', *Communist and Post-Communist Studies*, Vol. 27, No. 3, September 1994, pp. 315–328.

Beck, Carl and Malloy, James M., *Political Elites: A Mode of Analysis* (University Center for International Studies, University of Pittsburgh, October 1971).

Best, Heinrich and Becker, Ulricke (eds.), *Elites in Transition: Elite Research in Central and Eastern Europe* (Opladen: Leske + Budrich, 1997).

Bunce, Valerie and Echols, John, 'From Soviet Studies to Comparative Studies: The Unfinished Revolution', *Soviet Studies*, Vol. XXXI, No. 1, January 1979.

Colton, Timothy J. and Tucker, Robert C. (eds.), *Patterns in Post-Soviet Leadership* (Boulder: Westview Press, 1995).

Fleron, Frederic J. and Hoffman, Erik (eds.), *Post-Communist States and Political Science: Methodology and Empirical Theory in Sovietology* (Boulder: Westview Press, 1993).

Garton Ash, Timothy, *We the People: The Revolution of 89* (London: Granta, 1990).

Geddes, Barbara, *Politician's Dilemma: Building State Capacity in Latin America* (Berkeley CA: University of California, 1994).

Geddes, Barbara, 'A Comparative Perspective on the Leninist Legacy in Eastern Europe', *Comparative Political Studies*, No. 28, July 1995.

Gill, Graeme (ed.), *Elites and Leadership in Russian Politics* (Basingstoke: Macmillan, 1998).

Hanson, Stephen, 'Analyzing Post-communist Economic Change: A Review Essay,' *East European Politics and Societies*, Vol. 12, Winter 1998, pp. 145–70.

Higley, John and Burton, Michael G., 'The Elite Variable in Democratic Transitions and Breakdowns', *American Sociological Review*, Vol. 54, No. 1, 1989, pp. 17–32.

Higley, John and Pakulski, Jan, 'Revolution and Elite Transformation in Eastern Europe', *Australian Journal of Political Science*, Vol. 27, No.1, March 1992, pp. 104–119.

Higley, John, Kullbert, Judith and Pakulski, Jan, 'The Persistence of Postcommunist Elites', *Journal of Democracy*, Vol. 7, No. 2, April 1996, pp. 133–147.

Higley, John, Jan Pakulski and Wesolowski, Wlodzimierz (eds.), *Postcommunist Elites and Democracy in Eastern Europe* (Basingstoke: Macmillan Press, 1998).

Hughes, James, 'Sub-national Elites and Post-communist Transformation in Russia: A Reply to Kryshtanovskaya & White', *Europe-Asia Studies*, Vol. 49, No.6, 1997, pp. 1017–1036.

Jensen, Donald N., 'Patrimonalism in Post-Soviet Russia', *RFE/RL Newsline*, Vol. 1, No. 1, Part 1, 17 July 1997.

Kryshtanovskaya, Olga and White, Stephen, 'From Soviet Nomenklatura to Russian Elite', *Europe-Asia Studies*, Vol. 48, No. 5, July 1996, pp. 711–734.

Lane David, 'The Transformation of Russia: The Role of the Political Elite', *Europe-Asia Studies*, Vol. 48, No. 4, June 1996, pp. 535–550.

Lane, David, 'Transition under Eltsin: The Nomenklatura and Political Elite Circulation', *Political Studies*, Vol. 45, No.5, December 1997, pp. 855–874.

Lane David, 'The Role of Elite and Class in the Transition in Russia', paper presented to the Political Studies Association Communist and Post-Communist Studies Conference, South Bank University, London, 6 February 1999.

Lane, David, 'What Kind of Capitalism for Russia? A Comparative Analysis', *Communist and Post-Communist Studies*, Vol.33, No.4, December 2000, pp. 485–504.

Lane, David and Ross, Cameron, 'The Changing Composition of the Political Elites', in David Lane (ed.), *Russia in Transition* (London: Longman, 1995), pp. 52–75.

Lane, David and Ross, Cameron, 'Russian Political Elites, 1991–1995: Recruitment and Renewal', *International Politics*, Vol.34, No.2, June 1997, pp. 169–192.

Lane, David (ed.), *The Legacy of State Socialism and the Future of Transformation* (Lanham MD, Oxford: Rowman & Littlefield, 2002).

Linden, Ronald H. and Bert A. Rockman (eds.), *Elite Studies and Communist Politics: Essays in Memory of Carl Beck* (University Center for International Studies, University of Pittsburgh, 1984).

Morrison, John, *Boris Yeltsin: From Bolshevik to Democrat* (London: Penguin, 1991).

Paige Glenn D., *The Scientific Study of Political Leadership* (London and New York: The Free Press, 1973).

Pridham, Geoffrey (ed.), *Transitions to Democracy: Comparative Perspectives from Southern Europe, Latin America and Eastern Europe* (Aldershot: Dartmouth, 1995).

Przeworski, Adam, *et al.*, *Sustainable Democracy* (Cambridge: Cambridge University Press, 1995).

Steen, Anton, *Between Past and Future: Elites, Democracy and the State in Post-Communist Countries: A Comparison of Estonia, Latvia and Lithuania* (Aldershot: Ashgate, 1997).

Taras, Ray (ed.), *Postcommunist Presidents* (Cambridge: Cambridge University Press, 1997).

*Theory and Society*, special issue on 'Circulation vs Reproduction of Elites during the Postcommunist Transformation of Eastern Europe', Vol. 24, No. 5, October 1995.

Whitefield, Stephen (ed.), *The New Institutional Architecture of Eastern Europe* (New York: St. Martin's Press, 1993).

Wollmann, Hellmut, 'Change and Continuity of Political and Administrative Elites in Post-Communist Russia', *Governance*, Vol. 6, No. 3, July 1993, pp. 325–340.

## General Literature on Political Elites and Political Power

Andrews, W.G., *Constitutions and Constitutionalism* (Princeton: Van Nostrand, 1961).

Andorka, Rudolf, 'Regime Transitions in Hungary in the 20th Century: The Role of National Counter-Elites', *Governance*, Vol. 6, No. 3, July 1993, pp. 358–71.

Apter, David E., 'A Comparative Method for the Study of Politics,' *American Journal of Sociology*, Vol. 64, November 1958, pp. 221–37.

Aristotle, *Politics* (trans. by T.A. Sinclair, London: Penguin, 1962).

Aron, Raymond, 'Social Structure and the Ruling Class', *British Journal of Sociology*, Vol. 1, 1950, pp. 1–16.

Bacchi, Carol Lee, *The Politics of Affirmative Action: 'Women', Equality and Category Politics* (London: SAGE, 1996).

Bachrach, Peter, *The Theory of Democratic Elitism* (London: University of London Press, 1967).

Bachrach Peter, and Baratz, Morton S., *Power and Poverty: Theory and Practice* (New York: Oxford University Press, 1970).

Banting K. and Simeon, R. (eds.), *The Politics of Constitutional Change in Industrial Nations: Redesigning the State* (London: Macmillan, 1985).

Barber, J.D., *The Lawmakers* (New Haven: Yale University Press, 1965).

Barrow, Clyde W., *Critical Theories of the State: Marxist, Neo-Marxist, Post-Marxist* (Madison, WI: University of Wisconsin Press, 1993).

Beck, Carl, *A Survey of Elite Studies* (Washington, DC: American University, 1965).

Bendix, Reinhard, 'Social Stratification and Political Power', *American Political Science Review*, Vol. 46, June 1953.

von Beyme, Klaus, *Die Politische Elite in der Bundesrepublik Deutschland* (Munich: R.Piper, 1971).

Bilton, Tony *et al.*, *Introductory Sociology*. 2nd edn (London: Macmillan, 1986).

Blau, Peter M. (ed.), *Approaches to the Study of Social Structure* (London: Open Books, 1976).

Bottomore, T.B., *Elites and Society* (London: Penguin, 1974).

Brzezinski, Zbigniew and Huntington, Samuel P., *Political Power: USA/USSR* (New York: Viking Press, 1964).

Burling, Robbins, *The Passage of Power: Studies in Political Succession* (New York and London: The Academic Press, 1974).

Dahl, Robert, 'A Critique of the Ruling Elite Model', reprinted in Edward Laumann, Paul Siegel and Robert Hodge (eds.), *The Logic of Social Hierarchies* (Chicago: Markham, 1970).

Dennis, J., 'Major Problems of Political Socialisation Research,' *Midwest Journal of Political Science*, Vol. 12, February 1968, pp. 85–144.

Deutsch, Karl, 'Social Mobilization and Political Development', *American Political Science Review*, Vol. 55, No. 3, September 1961, pp. 493–514.

Dogan, Mattei and Higley, John (eds.), *Elites, Crises, and the Origins of Regimes* (Lanham, Boulder, New York and Oxford: Rowman & Littlefield Publishers Inc., 1998).

Duchacek, Ivo D., *Constitutions and Politics* (Boston: Little, Brown, 1970).

Duchacek, Ivo D., *Power Maps: Comparative Politics of Constitutions* (Santa Barbara: ABC Clio, 1973).

Durkheim, Emile, *The Division of Labour in Society*, trans. G. Simpson (Glencoe, IL, 1951).

Dye, Thomas R. and Zeigler, L. Harmon, *The Irony of Democracy*, 2nd edn (Belmont, CA: Wadsworth, 1972).

Dyrberg, Torben Bech, *The Circular Structure of Power: Politics, Identity, Community* (London: Verso, 1997).

Easton, David, 'An Approach to the Analysis of Political Systems,' *World Politics*, Vol. 9, No.3, April 1957, pp. 383–400.

Edgell, Stephen, *Class* (London and New York: Routledge, 1993).

Edinger, Lewis J., 'Political Science and Political Biography II', *Journal of Politics*, Vol. 26, August 1964, pp. 648–676.

Edinger Lewis and Searing, Donald, 'Social Background in Elite Analysis: A Methodological Inquiry', *American Political Science Review*, Vol. 61, June 1967, pp. 428–45.

Elderveld, Samuel J., *Political Elites in Modern Societies: Empirical Research and Democratic Theory* (Ann Arbor, MI: The University of Michigan Press, 1989).

Elderveld, Samuel J., Kooiman, Jan and van der Tak, Theo, *Elite Images of Dutch Politics: Accommodation and Conflict* (Ann Arbor, MI: The University of Michigan Press, 1983).

Eulau, Heinz, and Sprague, John D., *Lawyers in Politics* (Indianapolis: Bobbs-Merrill, 1964).

Finer, S.E., *et al.*, *Backbench Opinion in the House of Commons* (London: Penguin, 1961).

Frey, F.W., *The Turkish Political Elite* (Cambridge: MA: MIT Press, 1965).

Friedrich, C.J., *Constitutional Government and Democracy* (New York: Ginn and Company, 1950).

Gellner, Ernest, *Thought and Change* (London: Weidenfeld and Nicholson, 1964).

Gellner, Ernest and Waterbury, John (eds.), *Patrons and Clients in Mediterranean Societies* (London: Duckworth, 1977).

Giddens, Anthony, 'Elites in the British Class Structure,' in Philip Standath and Anthony Giddens (eds.), *Elites and Power in British Society* (Cambridge: Cambridge University Press, 1974).

Giddens, Anthony, *The Constitution of Society: Outline of the Theory of Structuration* (Cambridge: Polity Press, 1984).

Giddens, Anthony, *A Contemporary Critique of Historical Materialism: The Nation-state and Violence* (London: Polity, 1985).

Goodin, Robert E., *The Theory of Institutional Design* (Cambridge: Cambridge University Press, 1996).

Greenstein, Fred I., *Personality and Politics* (Chicago: Markham, 1969).

Greenstein, Fred I. and Lerner, Michael (eds.), *A Source Book for the Study of Peronality and Politics* (Chicago: Markham, 1971).

Hall, Peter A. and Rosemary C. R. Taylor, 'Political Science and the Three New Institutionalisms', *Political Studies*, Vol. XLIV, 1996, 936–957.

Harris, C.C., *Kinship* (Buckingham: Open University Press, 1990).

Hay, Colin, *Political Analysis: A Critical Introduction* (Basingstoke, Hampshire: Palgrave, 2002).

Hay, Colin, 'Marxism and the State', in A. Gamble, D. Marsh and T. Tant (eds.), *Marxism and Social Science* (London: Macmillan 1999), pp. 164–71.

Hay, Colin, 'Crisis and the Structural Transformation of the State: Interrogating the Process of Change', *British Journal of Politics and International Relations*, Vol. 1, No. 3, October 1999, pp. 317–44.

Hay, Colin, 'The 'Crisis' of Keynesianism and the Rise of Neo-Liberalism in Britain: An Ideational

Institutionalist Approach', in J.L. Campbell and O.K. Pedersen (eds.), *The Second Movement in Institutional Analysis* (Princeton, NJ: Princeton University Press, 2001).

Hempel, Carl, *Aspects of Scientific Explanation and Other Essays in the Philosophy of Science* (New York: Free Press, 1965).

Hunter, Floyd, *Community Power Structure: A Study of Decision Makers* (Chapel Hill, NC: University of North Carolina Press, 1953).

Janowitz, Morris, *The Professional Soldier* (New York: Free Press, 1960).

Jessop, Bob, *State Theory: Putting Capitalist States in their Place* (Cambridge: Polity, 1990).

Kamenka Eugene and Krygier, Martin (eds.), *Bureaucracy: The Career of a Concept* (London: Edward Arnold, 1979).

Kaplan, Abraham, *The Conduct of Inquiry* (Scranton: Chandler, 1964).

Keller, Suzanne, *Beyond The Ruling Class: Strategic Elites in Modern Society* (New York: Random House, 1963).

Kopstein, Jeffrey and Lichbach, Mark (eds.), *Comparative Politics: Interests, Identities and Institutions in a Changing Global Order* (Cambridge: Cambridge University Press, 2000).

L'Etang, Hugh, *Fit to Lead?* (London: William Heineman Medical Books Ltd, 1980).

Lasswell, Harold D., 'Agenda for the Study of Political Elites' in Dwaine Marvick (ed.), *Political Decision-Makers* (Glencoe, IL: The Free Press, 1961).

Lasswell, Harold D., Lerner Daniel, and Rothwell, C. Easton, *The Comparative Study of Elites: An Introduction and Bibliography* (Stanford, CA: Stanford University Press, 1952).

Lasswell, Harold D. and Lerner, Daniel, *World Revolutionary Elites. Studies in Coercive Ideological Movements* (Cambridge, MA: M.I.T. Press, 1965).

Lemarchand, R., 'Political Clientelism and Ethnicity in Tropical Africa: Competing Solidarities in Nation-Building', *American Political Science Review*, Vol. LXVI, March 1972, pp. 68–90.

Lipset, S.M., *Political Man* (London: William Heineman, 1960).

Lipset, Seymour Martin and Solari, Aldo (eds.), *Elites in Latin America* (New York: Oxford University Press, 1967).

Lukes, Steven, *Power: A Radical View* (London: Macmillan, reprinted 1990).

Lukes, Steven, *Essay in Social Theory* (London: Macmillan, 1977).

McIntyre, Angus (ed.), *Aging and Political Leadership* (Melbourne: Oxford University Press, 1988).

Mann, Michael, *The Sources of Social Power: History of Power from the Beginning to A.D. 1760. Volume 1* (Cambridge: Cambridge University Press, 1986).

Mannheim, Karl, *Man and Society in an Age of Reconstruction* (London: Routledge and Kegan Paul, 1946).

Matthews, Donald R., *The Social Background of Political Decision-Makers* (New York: Random House, 1962).

Mazlish, Bruce, *The Leader, the Led, and the Psyche: Essays in Psychohistory* (Hanover, NH and London: Weslyan University Press/University Press of New England, 1990).

Meisel, James, *The Myth of the Ruling Class: Gaetano Mosca and the Elite* (Ann Arbor, MI: University of Michigan Press, 1962).

Michels, Robert, *Political Parties: A Sociological Study of the Oligarchical Tendencies of Modern Democracy* (New York: Dover, 1959).

Mills, C. Wright, *The New Men of Power: America's Labor Leaders* (New York: Harcourt Brace and Company, 1948).

Mills. C. Wright, *The Power Elite* (New York: Oxford University Press, 1959).

Mills C. Wright and Dahl, Robert, *Who Governs?* (New Haven: Yale University Press, 1961).

Mircev, Dimitar, 'Ethnocentrism and Strife among Political Elites: The End of Yugoslavia', *Governance*, Vol. 6, No. 3, July 1993, pp. 372–85.

Moore, Barrington, Jr, *Politiical Power and Social Theory* New York: Harper & Row, 1958).

Moore, Gwen, 'The Structure of a National Elite Network' in Marvin E. Olsen and Martin N. Marger (eds.), *Power in Modern Societies* (Boulder: Westview Press, 1993), pp. 183–95.

Mosca, Gaetano, *The Ruling Class* (ed by Arthur Livingston, London: McGraw-Hill, 1939).

Needham, R., *Rethinking Kinship and Marriage* (London: Tavistock, 1971).

Olsen, Dennis, *The State Elite* (Toronto: McClelland and Stewart, 1980).

Olsen, Marvin E. and Marger, Martin N. (eds.), *Power in Modern Societies* (Boulder: Westview Press, 1993).

Parry, Gerraint, *Political Elites* (New York: Praeger, 1969).

Porter, John, *The Vertical Mosaic: An Analysis of Social Class and Power in Canada* (Toronto: University of Toronto Press, 1965).

Putnam, Robert, *The Comparative Study of Political Elites* (Englewood Cliffs, N.J.: Prentice-Hall, 1976).

Quandt, William B., *The Comparative Study of Political Elites* (Berkeley, CA: Sage, 1969).

Robins, R.S., 'Elite Career Patterns as a Differential: A Use of Correlation Techniques and the Construction of Uniform Strata', *Behavioral Science*, Vol. 14, May 1969, pp. 232–238.

Rustow, Dankwart, 'Transitions to Democracy: Toward a Dynamic Model', *Comparative Politics*, Vol. 2, No. 3, 1970, pp. 337–63.

Rustow, Dankwart, 'The Study of Elites: Who's Who, When and How', *World Politics*, Vol. 18, No. 3, July 1966, pp. 690–717.

Sartori, Giovanni, 'Concept Misformation in Comparative Politics', *American Political Science Review*, Vol. LXIV, No. 4, December 1970, pp. 1033–53.

Sazblowski, George J., 'Governing and Competing Elites in Poland', *Governance*, Vol. 6, No. 3, July 1993, pp. 341–57.

Schlesinger, J.A., *Ambition and Politics: Political Careers in the United States* (Chicago: Rand McNally, 1966).

Searing, D.D., 'The Comparative Study of Elite Socialization', *Comparative Political Studies*, Vol. 1, January 1969, pp. 471–500.

Spiro, Herbert. J., *Government by Constitution* (New York: Random House, 1959).

Spiro, Herbert. J., 'Comparative Politics: A Comprehensive Approach,' *American Political Science Review*, Vol. 56, No. 3, September 1962, pp. 577–95.

Szablowski, George J. and Derlien, Hans-Ulrich, 'East European Transitions, Elites, Bureaucracies, and the European Community', *Governance*, Vol. 6, No. 3, July 1993), pp. 304–324.

Thelen, Kathleen, 'Historical Institutionalism in Comparative Politics', *Annual Review of Political Science*, Vol. 2, June 1999, pp. 369–404.

Thelen, Kathleen and Steinmo, Sven, 'Historical Institutionalism in Comparative Analysis', in Sven Steinmo, Kathleen Thelen and Frank Longstreth (eds.), *Structuring Politics: Historical Institutionalism in Comparative Analysis* (Cambridge: Cambridge University Press, 1992).

Turner, Bryan S., *Status* (Milton Keynes: Open University Press, 1988).

Vile, M.J.C., *Constitutionalism and the Separation of Powers* (Oxford: Oxford University Press, 1967).

Wahlke, John C. *et al.*, *The Legislative System: Explorations in Legislative Behavior* (New York: John Wiley, 1967).

Wilkinson, Paul, *Social Movements* (London and Basingstoke: Macmillan, 1971).

Wriggins, W.H., *The Ruler's Imperative: Strategies for Political Survival in Asia and Africa* (New York: Columbia University Press, 1969).

Wrong, Denis H., *Power: Its Form, Bases and Uses* (Oxford: Blackwell, 1979).

Zuckerman, Alan, 'The Concept "Political Elite": Lessons from Mosca and Pareto', *The Journal of Politics*, Vol. 39, No. 2, May 1977, pp. 324–44.

Zurcher, A.J. (ed.), *Constitutions and Constitutional Trends since World War II* (New York: New York University Press, 1955).

# Nationalism

Anderson, Benedict, *Imagined Communites: Reflections on the Origin and Spread of Nationalism.* 2nd edn (London: Routledge, 1991).

Barth, Fredrik (ed.), *Ethnic Groups and Boundaries* (Boston: Little, Brown and Co., 1969).

Beissinger, Mark, 'Elites and Ethnic Identities in Soviet and Post-Soviet Politics', in Alexander J. Motyl (ed.), *The Post-Soviet Nations: Perspectives on the Demise of the USSR* (New York: Columbia University Press, 1992), pp. 141–69.

Billig, Michael, *Banal Nationalism* (London: Sage, 1995).

Brass, Paul R.., 'Elite Groups, Symbol Manipulation, and Ethnic identity among the Muslims of South Asia', in D. Taylor and M. Yapp (eds.), *Political Identity in South Asia* (London: Curzon Press, 1979).

Brubaker, Rogers, *Nationalism Reframed: Nationhood and the National Question in the New Europe* (Cambridge: Cambridge University Press, 1996).

Carrere d'Encausse, Helene, *The End of the Soviet Empire: The Triumph of the Nations* (New York: Basic Books, 1993).

Cohen, Abner, *Two-Dimensional Man: An Essay on the Anthropology of Power and Symbolism in Complex Society* (Berkeley: University of California Press, 1974).

Dahl, Robert, *Modern Political Analysis* (Englewood Cliffs, N.J.: Prentice-Hall, 1984).

Dahl, Robert, *Who Governs? Democracy and Power in an American City* (New Haven, CT: Yale University Press, 1961).

Deutsch, Karl W., *Nationalism and Social Communication*. 2nd edn (Cambridge, MA: MIT Press, 1966).

Dunleavy, Patrick and O'Leary, Brendan, *Theories of the State: The Politics of Liberal Democracy* (Basingstoke: Macmillan, 1987).

Epstein, A.L., *Ethos and Identity: Three Studies in Ethnicity* (London: Tavistock, 1978).

Geertz, Clifford (ed.), *Old Societies and New States: The Quest for Modernity in Asia and Africa* (New York, 1967).

Gellner, Ernest, *Nations and Nationalism* (Oxford: Basil Blackwell, 1983).

Giddens, Anthony, *Modernity and Self-Identity. Self and Society in the Late Modern Age* (Cambridge: Polity Press, 1991).

Glazer, Natthan and Moynihan, Daniel P. (eds.), *Ethnicity: Theory and Experience* (Cambridge, MA: Harvard University Press, 1975).

Hall, Stuart, 'Cultural Identity and Diaspora', in John Rutherford (ed.), *Identity: Community, Culture and Difference* (London: Lawrence and Wishart, 1990).

Hobsbawm, Eric and Ranger, Terence (eds.), *The Invention of Tradition* (Cambridge: Cambridge University Press, 1983).

Hutchinson, John, *Modern Nationalism* (London: Fontana Press, 1994).

Hutchinson, John and Anthony D. Smith (eds.), *Nationalism* (Oxford: Oxford University Press, 1994).

Khoury, Philip S. and Kostiner, Joseph (eds.), *Tribes and State Formation in the Middle East* (Berkeley: University of California Press, 1990).

McCrone, David, *The Sociology of Nationalism* (London and New York: Routledge, 1998).

Pile Stephen and Thrift, Nigel, *Mapping the Subject: Geographies of Cultural Transformation* (Routledge: London and New York, 1995).

Renan, Ernest, *Qu'est-ce qu'une nation*, trans. Ida Mae Snyder (Paris: Calmann-Levy, 1882).

Simons, Anna, 'Democratisation and Ethnic Conflict: The Kin Connection', *Nations and Nationalism*, Vol. 3, No. 2, 1997, pp. 273–289.

Smith, Graham (ed.), *The Nationalities Question in the Post-Soviet States*. 2nd edn (Harlow: Essex: Longman, 1996).

Smith, Graham (ed.), *The Nationalities Question in the Soviet Union* (Harlow: Essex: Longman, 1990).

Suny, Ronald Grigor, *The Making of the Georgian Nation*. 2nd edn (Bloomington and Indianapolis: Indiana University Press, 1994).

Welsh, William A., *Leaders and Elites* (New York: Holt, Rinehart and Winston, 1979).

Wendt, Alexander E., 'The Agent-Structure Problem in International Relations Theory', *International Organization*, Vol. 41, No. 3, Summer 1987, pp. 335–370.

Zhusupov, S., Zhusupov, B., and Ezhenova, K., *Dinamika Obshchestvennykh Protsessov v Kazakhstane (Dinamika 1)* (Almaty: Kazakhstan Institute of Strategic Research under the President of Kazakhstan, Newspaper 'Panorama', Republican Centre of Public Opinion, 1997).

Zhusupov, S., Zhusupov, B., and Ezhenova, K., *Dinamika Obshchestvennykh Protsessov v Kazakhstane (Dinamika 2)* (Almaty: Panorama and Gruppa VIProblem, 2002).

## Newspapers, institution reports and serials

*Ana tili*

*Delovaia nedelia*

*Delovoi Mir*

*European Bank for Reconstruction and Development, The Economics of Transition (Oxford: Oxford University Press for the EBRD, annually)*

*The Economist*

*Economist Intelligence Unit, Country Report: Kazakhstan (quarterly; various years).*

*Egemen Qazaqstan*

*Express-K*

*The Financial Times*

*Focus Central Asia*

*The Jamestown Monitor*

*Jaz Alash*

*Interfax*

*ITAR-TASS News Agency*

*Karavan*

*Kazakhstanskaia Pravda*

*Obshaia Gazeta*

*OMRI Daily Digest*

*Panorama*

*Panorama Shimkenta*

*RFE/RL Research Report*

*RFE/RL Newsline*

*Rossiiskaia Gazeta*

*Slovo Kyrgyzstana*

*Statististicheskoe Obozrenie Kazakhstana (Almaty: National Statistics Agency).*

*Sovety Kazakhstana*

*Trud*

*Turkestan*

*UNDP Human Development Report: Kazakhstan (United Nations Development Program, various years).*

*Vremia po grinvichy*

*Zaman Qazaqstan*

# INDEX